I read a lot of books on preaching – some geared for rookies, some for veterans. Once in while a book is written that speaks to both, to rookies and veterans alike. And Mark Meynell has done this with much skill. I especially appreciate that Mark does not move to the "how to" stage of preaching the different genres of the New Testament until he takes us through the "what are they?" investigation, which he does in engagingly fresh ways. His sample sermons are amazing: exposition that immediately connects with culture. What a joy to be called to proclaim with Mark wh

GW00503647

Darrell Johnson
Teaching Fellow, Regent College
Professor of Preaching, Carey College
Vancouver, Canada
Author of *The Glory of Preaching*

After reading Mark Meynell's book, one truly understands "what angels long to read" as he, in a pedagogical, passionate and pastoral way, helps preachers to see God as the master storyteller whose central figure, the incomparable Jesus, is unveiled for all through literary treasures crafted by the Holy Spirit. Mark makes these figures accessible so that we and the world are captivated by the Father's story.

Jorge Atiencia
Langham Preaching, Colombia
Missionary, Latin America Mission (Canada)

What Angels Long to Read is designed for preachers, but will be of real benefit to all who read it as it explores different approaches to reading, teaching and preaching the Bible. With a readable and accessible style, Mark Meynell combines theological knowledge, powerful illustrations and practical wisdom to help equip ordinary Christians to prepare teaching materials and interpret the Scriptures. His biblical insights give a renewed understanding of the Scriptures that is both refreshing and challenging.

Rev Elnur Jabiyev
Founder and CEO, Turkic Belt Ministries

I have known the Rev Mark Meynell as a man who loves God and is devoted to the preaching of the gospel. Memories of him as a deep theologian and biblical preacher are still fresh in my mind and in the minds of many who studied under him at Kampala Evangelical School of Theology (KEST) in Uganda, and those who heard him preach during the years he was a missionary in Uganda.

The title of this book, *What Angels Long to Read,* is based on 1 Peter 1:12 which says that "Even angels long to look into these things." This is an interesting, mind captivating, and spirit-inspiring piece of work. The book helps readers to appreciate the entire Bible and to see a beautiful and relevant coherence between the two Testaments – the Old and the New. Meynell emphasizes that in all of our preaching, Jesus must remain the central and only point of reference because he is the basis of our testimony as Christians. *What Angels Long to Read* is a relevant book that is a must-read by all serious thinkers and preachers. I highly commend it to all who base their preaching on the Word of God – the Bible.

Rt Rev Edward Muhima, PhD
Retired Bishop of North Kigezi, Uganda

Mark Meynell offers contemporary preachers a wonderfully readable guide for sermons on the New Testament that does justice to a biblical book, its genre, the geographical and historical context, as well as the individual angle of each writer. He has succeeded in bringing years of academic scholarship on the Scriptures into a condensed, connected and relevant whole for the benefit of sermon preparation. This is an essential manual for every preacher's library.

Myrto Theocharous, PhD
Professor of Hebrew and Old Testament,
Greek Bible College, Athens, Greece

Mark Meynell does a favour for preachers at every level by making simple the macroscopic view of the Bible without sacrificing the microscopic details. The book serves to make simple many complex theological, hermeneutical and textual questions the conscientious preacher encounters. Its lack of academic jargon doesn't negate its intellectual credibility. Every preacher can learn something from reading this useful book.

Sam Tsang, PhD
Faculty Member,
Hong Kong Baptist Theological Seminary, Hong Kong
Ambrose University, Calgary, Alberta, Canada

Mark writes like a skilled friend and seasoned mentor. He knows the work ahead of you. He cares deeply about both you and the work. This book is practical, biblical, global, wise and helpful. As Mark teaches us to communicate Jesus from the Scriptures, our love for Jesus and the Bible that reveals him, deepens.

Zack Eswine, PhD
Director of Homiletics,
Covenant Theological Seminary, St Louis, Missouri, USA
Author of *Preaching to a Post-Everything World*

Soon

What Angels Long to Read

Reading and Preaching the New Testament

Mark Meynell

Wishing you every blessing

June '17

Langham

PREACHING RESOURCES

© 2017 by Mark Meynell

Published 2017 by Langham Preaching Resources
An imprint of Langham Creative Projects

Langham Partnership
PO Box 296, Carlisle, Cumbria CA3 9WZ, UK
www.langham.org

ISBNs:
978-1-78368-266-9 Print
978-1-78368-268-3 Mobi
978-1-78368-267-6 ePub
978-1-78368-269-0 PDF

British Library Cataloguing in Publication Data
A catalogue record for this book is available from the British Library

ISBN: 978-1-78368-266-9

Cover & Book Design: projectluz.com

Dedicated to
David Jackman
Preacher and Teacher,
Mentor and Friend

Contents

Foreword

O f course, neither Jesus nor Paul ever did what this book aims to help its readers do. They never preached from the New Testament. They never read it either (though we assume Paul read over his own dictated letters before posting them, and sometimes we might wish he had proofread them more thoroughly in a few places). It's an unusual thought, but worth pondering for a moment.

When we read, preach, and teach from the Scriptures of the Old Testament, we are handling what Jesus and Paul (and all the apostles) knew in great depth. We have their assurance that those Scriptures speak with authority, breathed-out by God, written for our learning, profitable for instruction, correction and training in righteousness, and so on. We follow Jesus's resurrection hermeneutics lectures in Luke 24, or at least the outline of them, in all the Law, the Prophets and the Writings. We do our best to unravel Paul's scriptural exegesis and love the way he sees the whole story of God and Israel in the Old Testament recapitulated and fulfilled in Christ and now being transplanted among the nations, where it had always been headed. Given the scale of the exposition of the Old Testament in the New, you'd think we should have every motivation and some very good models for preaching it ourselves. The fact that many preachers do not, or struggle to know how to, is the justification for the companion book to this one, my own, *Sweeter than Honey: Preaching the Old Testament*.[1]

However, while we don't see Jesus or Paul preaching from what we now call the New Testament, we certainly see in them some wonderful models of communication to varied audiences. As this book makes beautifully clear, Jesus was a superb preacher, teacher, storyteller – a communicator of enormous skill and power. And Luke has made sure that we get to see and hear some classic examples of Paul in preaching mode, whether expounding the Scriptures to Jews, or preaching the message and truth of the Scriptures, without quoting them, to Gentiles.

But they not only provide us with models. Even though they did not (because they could not) preach from the New Testament, both Jesus and

---

1. (Carlisle: Langham Preaching Resources, 2015). Published in the USA as *How to Preach and Teach the Old Testament For All It's Worth* (Grand Rapids: Zondervan, 2016).

Paul mandated their disciples to preach and teach what would eventually be contained in our New Testament. Jesus's Great Commission specifies that the task of making disciples must include "teaching them to obey all that I have commanded you." And the legacy of all that Jesus did and taught and commanded is now, of course, entrusted to us in the four Gospels. Sheer missional obedience must drive us to preach the Gospels.

And Paul instructs Timothy to take what he had learned from Paul (which would include the content of what we now have in his letters) and entrust it to those who would faithfully pass it on to others – so the task of preaching the Epistles is, at least in principle, mandated by Paul himself. So, by their example and their instruction, Jesus and Paul summon us to do what they never did themselves – to preach and teach that collection of inspired writings we are now privileged to call the New Testament.

But why should we do so at all? Perhaps the most succinct answer to that, appropriate for a book in the series of Langham Preaching Resources, is to recall the "Langham Logic" bequeathed to us by the founder of Langham Partnership, John Stott. We have three biblical convictions and one inescapable conclusion, he would say:

- *First, God wants his church to grow up* – not just to grow bigger. That is, God wants his people to grow to maturity in Christ.
- *Second, the church grows through the word of God.* When a church is fed by the word of God, it will grow in depth and maturity. When it is not, it may easily fall into error or die out.
- *Third, the word of God comes to the people of God mainly through preaching.* Even though there are other ways Christians may study the Bible for themselves, for very many believers the only way they will be fed by God's word is when someone opens it up and preaches from it.

If these three things are true, John Stott would say, then the logical question to ask is, *What can we do to raise the standards of biblical preaching?*

That is the goal to which all three programmes of the Langham Partnership aspire, and Mark Meynell's book will undoubtedly play a very significant part in raising the standards of preaching the New Testament.

It is a great joy to welcome this book with gratitude as a faithful, clear and relevant guide, and a happy companion to my own.

Chris Wright
International Ministries Director
Langham Partnership

Preface

Istanbul. Constantinople. Byzantium.

Three different names for the same ancient, extraordinary city. This city is a bridge between West and East, between the two continents of Europe and Asia. It is no longer the capital of Turkey, but it remains the country's cultural heart. My first visit in 2008 fulfilled a lifelong dream. The city's unique history seems to glow from every street corner, with leftovers everywhere of the ancient Greeks, the late Roman Empire, Byzantine Christianity and Ottoman Islam.

Then to be involved in training Turkish preachers? It felt like a dream come true. What a privilege, not least because over the last decade it has enabled me to make good friends in the tiny Turkish-speaking church in that Muslim majority country. They are a tiny minority – perhaps a few thousand – in a population of nearly 80 million.

One short series that I preached there will always stick in my mind, not so much because of its impact on its listeners but because of its impact on the preacher. I was working through the first two chapters of 1 Peter during a weekend workshop on preaching the epistles. Only ten of us were in the room. Despite the heat, the reverberations of the afternoon calls to prayer had forced us to close the windows. Then I read Peter's opening line:

> Peter, an apostle of Jesus Christ, to God's elect, exiles, scattered throughout the provinces of Pontus, Galatia, Cappadocia, Asia and Bithynia . . .

It suddenly hit me right between the eyes. Peter was writing to brothers and sisters who lived two millennia ago in the *very place* I was standing. In his day, the region was known as the Roman province of Bithynia. Then, as now, believers formed a tiny minority, surrounded by a majority culture that neither understood nor respected their beliefs. From time to time this disrespect swelled into persecution and even martyrdom.

Peter wrote to pastor, to encourage, and to embolden those isolated and often vulnerable believers. His timeless words have consoled and challenged ever since. His tactic is to show how the eternal gospel is true even in the toughest circumstances – and that is because God really is in control through it all (1 Pet 1:2–9). One of his arguments is truly startling.

> Concerning this salvation, the prophets, who spoke of the grace that was to come to you, searched intently and with the greatest care, trying to find out the time and circumstances to which the Spirit of Christ in them was pointing when he predicted the sufferings of the Messiah and the glories that would follow. It was revealed to them that they were not serving themselves but you, when they spoke of the things that have now been told you by those who have preached the gospel to you by the Holy Spirit sent from heaven. **Even angels long to look into these things.** (1 Pet 1:10–12)

Dwell on that last sentence for a moment.

It means that being able to study the Scriptures is nothing less than a heavenly privilege. Each time we open up the Scriptures, we are drawn into an experience that God's celestial servants do not have! That's presumably because those who constantly live and serve in God's presence don't actually need these things to be revealed. However, not needing a Bible is clearly insufficient to quieten angelic curiosity about the gospel. They would apparently *love* to have what we have and do what we do!

What an encouragement that was as we opened the Scriptures that day! Despite being surrounded by millions who considered what we were doing irrelevant or worse, the ten of us in that stifling Istanbul room found that deeply inspiring. It gave us all a new boldness to preach beyond those four walls, whenever and wherever we had the opportunity.

We must never forget this as we consider how to proclaim what was revealed to Peter and his friends and gospel partners. Our sense of privilege should never fade. Intriguingly, the more I study and preach the Bible, the more that sense deepens. I grow in astonishment at its message, at its coherence and consistency, at its beauty and surprises. This spurs me on to proclaim it.

I hope you will have a similar experience as your read this book. It is certainly what we long for in the Langham Preaching movements around the world. This is because learning and growing as preachers is not simply a matter of refining our skills, or memorizing information, or even improving as communicators (although those things all have their place – and this book will have a clear focus on skill development). It is certainly *not* about gaining enough assets to climb ministry career ladders. It is simply, and wonderfully, becoming aware of the privilege we have in serving our gracious God as his ambassadors and proclaimers.

Acknowledgements

There are many people to thank for this project.

First. I must thank my Langham colleagues – It's a privilege to be part of such a diverse but united and encouraging team.

- India: Paul Windsor, Programme Director, based in Bangalore
- Canada: Jennifer Cuthbertson, Training Coordinator, Vancouver
- France: Mike McGowan, Francophone Africa consultant, Dinard
- Bosnia & Herzegovina: Slavko Hadzic, Pastor, Balkans Regional Coordinator, Sarajevo
- Colombia: Jorge Atiencia, Latin America team, Medellin

I am grateful too to Benji Stephen who works with Paul in Bangalore. He has been very patient in dealing with my incessant questions about his cultural context.

In writing this book, I have tried to make it as cross-cultural and translatable as possible. In this effort, I have been greatly helped by the following friends who have read and commented on the manuscript.

- Hong Kong: Heewoo Han, Minister, Shatin Anglican Church
- Uganda: Robert Atwongyeire, Pastor, Kampala
- Spain: Andres Reid, Director of Escuela Evangélica de Teología of FIEIDE, Barcelona
- Turkey: Bayram Erdem, Istanbul
- Hungary: Tamas Schauermann, IT specialist and preacher, Pécs, Hungary
- Austria: Sharon McClaughlin, former church worker, now in Vienna
- UK: Jonathan Lewis, and Dan Wells, London

I am very grateful to my Langham Literature editor, Isobel Stevenson for her incredibly hard work in making this transferable and relevant to as many different cultures as possible. I'm also very thankful for Pieter Kwant, Programme Director of Langham Literature, for all his support and encouragement for this project.

The book is dedicated to David Jackman, the founding director of the Cornhill Training Course in London. It is no exaggeration to say that my year at Cornhill (1994–1995) gave me not only my wife but also my ministry in Sheffield and London, as a seminary teacher in Kampala, Uganda, and as an itinerant member of the Langham Preaching global leadership team. Each has been an immense privilege. But more than that, David has been an inspiring model of winsome, generous and faithful service. I regularly thank God for him!

Finally, my family has endured far more than they deserve to, and so deserves far more of me than they get! But I am, as ever, eternally grateful for the love and support of Joshua and Zanna, and ultimately, of course, of Rachel who is without question one of the kindest and most selfless people I know.

August 2016
Bergh Apton, Norfolk
SDG

1

Understanding the Bible's Big Picture

Whenever I visit a new place, I want to look at a map of it. Without one, I feel quite disoriented. That was especially true when I first visited Istanbul – but it happens even in parts of my home city of London. Even though I was born here, and it has been my home on and off for many years, there are still huge parts of it that I haven't even heard of, let alone explored. I could easily get lost in them!

This is where the usefulness of maps comes in. Maps help put everything in context, globally, nationally, and locally. They are therefore crucial for planning any journey. But we need different types of map to help us with different stages in planning a journey.

- **Continent maps**: These are the big picture maps, the ones that enable us to see a whole continent at a glance. They show the major landmarks like mountains, oceans and rivers, and the boundaries between countries. If I know that Istanbul is in Turkey, a continent-wide map shows where Turkey lies in relation to other countries.
- **Country maps**: These maps cover a whole country, like Turkey, and are intended to help travellers get from place to place. They keep us on the right roads between cities and towns by showing only the most significant buildings or roads. They omit details that would be confusing and distracting. Using a national map, I can easily find my way to Istanbul.
- **Local maps**: Once I arrive in Istanbul, however, a continental map and a national map are useless if I am trying to get around the city on foot. What I need now is a local map, that shows tiny details and landmarks like mosques, shops and hidden alleyways.

But what has all this to do with the Bible?

The answer is that you may find it helpful to think of the Bible as a vast territory that you need to explore. There are, of course, parts of it that we know well and naturally turn to given the choice. But even if we have been studying and preaching the Bible for years, there are still parts that confuse us or seem to raise more questions than we might like. That is inevitable with a book as diverse and profound as the Bible. There is easily enough in it to occupy us for a lifetime. That is why the sixth century theologian known as Gregory the Great described the Bible as a river that is shallow enough for lambs to wade in and deep enough for elephants to swim in. It has surprises and treasures in store for the toddler and the scholar, the new convert and the longest church member.

There is always more to learn, and we would be wise to make the most of all the help we can get. The aim of this book, and its companion, Chris Wright's *Sweeter than Honey*,[1] is to provide some help as you explore the Bible by providing different levels of maps that will enable you to be better equipped to help others understand the Scriptures.

1. Mapping Bible Journeys

As you read this book, you will encounter certain symbols that indicate what type of "map" of the Bible you are currently looking at in that.

 Bible Continents: We can think of the Old Testament and New Testament as two continents, joined together, like Africa and Asia linked through the Middle East. This is a global view of the Bible, which explains the importance of grasping what is sometimes called *biblical theology* (the themes and storyline that hold the whole book together). Because the whole Bible is actually a story, this is sometimes called its *story* or *narrative arc*. I use a map of Africa to indicate places where we are taking this "continental" view.

 New Testament Countries: Because it is a place that means a great deal to our family (and was where my wife was born), I'm going to use a map of Uganda as a symbol to indicate that we are focusing on key elements of the New Testament. We could do this in two different

---

1. Christopher J. H. Wright, *Sweeter than Honey: Preaching the Old Testament* (Carlisle: Langham Preaching Resources, 2015).

but equally valid ways: giving an overview of each individual book,[2] or mapping out the different types of terrain we will encounter. In this book, we will take the second approach and will consider the four key types of terrain in the New Testament:
- narratives (as in the Gospels and Acts)
- parables (the stories Jesus told)
- letters (to individuals and groups)
- apocalyptic (the vivid visions and dreams that we find especially in Revelation)

 New Testament Localities: Even when we have a good grasp of the terrain of the New Testament, we may still find ourselves lost in strings of words that we can't find a path through. So the book also includes local maps will help us find our way around individual paragraphs and chapters.

As we go along, we will be shifting between all three levels of map. So you need to think of yourself as sitting at a desk with three different maps spread out in front of you.

Let us start by seeing what a continental map might look like. I have just said that we can think of the Old Testament and New Testament as two continents, joined together. To get an idea of what I mean by this, look at those important words from Peter's first letter that I quoted in the Preface:

> Concerning this salvation, the prophets, who spoke of the grace that was to come to you, searched intently and with the greatest care, trying to find out the time and circumstances to which the Spirit of Christ in them was pointing when he predicted the sufferings of the Messiah and the glories that would follow. It was revealed to them that they were not serving themselves but you, when they spoke of the things that have now been told you by those who have preached the gospel to you by the Holy Spirit sent from heaven. (1 Pet 1:10–12)

When Peter speaks about "the prophets," he is referring to the writers of the Old Testament as a whole. These prophets were "not serving themselves but you" because when they wrote, they served the New Testament generation who would first witness the fulfilment of the prophets' preaching.

---

2. A great example of this is *How to Read the Bible Book by Book: A Guided Tour* by Gordon Fee and Douglas Stuart (Grand Rapids: Zondervan, 2014).

The news of "this salvation" in Christ might have been new for Peter's first-century readers. But it was hardly something only recently concocted. God had spent centuries laying the groundwork for Israel's Messiah to be revealed as Jesus of Nazareth. And it had all been enshrined for us to read in the Jewish Scriptures. Including the suffering that Jesus would have to endure for following God's path.

This means it is essential for all New Testament readers and preachers to have a grasp of what the Old Testament teaches and points forward to. After all, it covers more than half the Bible's story! It also provides all the key images and ideas, precedents and expectations that get developed in the New Testament. Reading the New Testament without the Old would be like starting a movie two-thirds of the way through it and expecting to be able to understand everything. We would never know who all the characters were and why they were enduring their particular battles.

2. Following the Bible's Story

At this stage, I am going to change my metaphor from "a map" to "a story" as we start off our exploration of the "continent" by looking at the story line or narrative arc of the Bible. Yes, it will come as a surprise to many that the entire Bible does actually form a story. It is a complex, and long story. But it is a story nonetheless. What does that mean for our understanding and preaching of it?[3]

Let's begin by asking what ingredients make for a good story. What would you need to include if you were asked to tell a story, perhaps for children or a group of friends?

- **Interesting context:** Where and when does this story take place? What are the challenges and opportunities it presents? Let us suppose that we decide to tell an adventure story set in Antarctica. The challenge would then be obvious: it's cold all year round!
- **Engaging characters**: The characters are the people who are the centre of the story, and the more lifelike they are the better. That probably means that no one is wholly bad or wholly good. So we could focus our story on two very different sailors and explorers: an Englishman Robert Falcon Scott, and a Norwegian, Roald

---

3. In his book *Sweeter than Honey: Preaching the Old Testament*, Christopher J. H. Wright also stresses the importance of seeing the Bible as one whole story. His outline of the drama of Scripture in six stages is slightly different from the one proposed here, but the overall outline and shape of the story are the same.

Amundsen. They were very different in culture, background, and temperament.

- **Powerful themes**: Similar themes can be found in stories from all cultures. For example, there is the battle between good and evil/injustice; the pilgrimage or journey of discovery; the individual who overcomes great obstacles on the way to triumph; the tragedy that befalls someone because of a fatal character flaw or decision. There are, of course, many variations on these themes, and the same events can be described from different angles and according to different themes. So Amundsen's story could be told as one of overcoming hostile conditions in order to achieve a heroic goal. Scott's might be the story of arrogance and lack of preparation leading to tragedy.
- **Gripping plot**: Something actually needs to happen in the story! So our story involves the 1910 race to be the first to reach the South Pole. The plot will involve the challenges faced by both teams. In the end, Amundsen beat Scott by five weeks, and Scott's team all died on their return journey.

Now let's look at how the Bible compares to this list of the features of a story:

- **Interesting context**: The context of the Bible is God's universe, and in particular our planet. That is automatically interesting to us, because it's home!
- **Engaging characters**: The characters in the Bible's story are credible and intriguing (even when they only appear for a page or two). They're just like us, which certainly helps us relate to them. But there is one exception: God himself. He is the only character who holds the whole story together, and is in fact the central character. When he reveals himself as Jesus of Nazareth, we encounter the most astonishing person who has ever walked the earth. He was sinless but magnetic, powerful but merciful, was in control but suffered terribly. There has never been anyone like him!
- **Powerful themes**: The themes of the Bible's story echo all the great stories of the world. Or perhaps it is more accurate to say that the world's great stories all echo the Bible's story! So when a story tells of an individual who stands up for truth despite what everyone around them is saying, or someone is brought low by their pride or experiences the life-changing power of forgiveness, their stories reflect the heart of the big themes of God's ultimate story.

- **Gripping plot**: The Bible certainly has a gripping plot, but it is such a huge plot that I think we need to look at it separately from the other elements of a story.

The plot of the Bible

We need to be aware of the Bible's plot as we set out on the New Testament part of our journey. This is because the New Testament does not stand alone – it is the conclusion of a far bigger plot. Neither testament makes sense without the other – precisely because the Bible *is* a grand story.

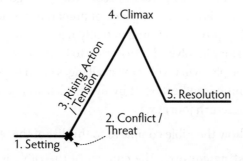

This diagram above sets out the key features of a good plot:[4]

- **Setting**: the characters are introduced against the background to the tension to come.
- **Conflict**: caused by a change in circumstances or the plans and actions of one or more characters.
- **Tension**: the conflict deepens as tension rises – in some of the great stories, it is not always possible to guess what will happen next.
- **Climax**: whatever caused the conflict or threat in the first place is removed or conquered.
- **Resolution**: the results of the plot, especially in terms of how they leave the original setting changed or unchanged.

The whole of the Bible fits very neatly into this pattern, as you can see in the matching diagram below.

- **Setting = Creation.** It is precisely because God created everything that he is concerned for it and has rights to rule it.

---

4. Adapted from Jeffrey D. Arthurs, *Preaching with Variety* (Grand Rapids : Kregel, 2007), p. 70.

- **Conflict = the Fall.** The tragedy of Genesis 3 is that God's creatures reject the blessing their Creator's rule, with devastating consequences for the whole of Creation.

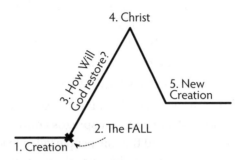

- **Tension = How will God restore creation?** From Genesis 4 onwards, the Bible faces the question of what God will do about those consequences. The story's tension derives entirely from the fear that human rebellion might thwart God's promises.
- **Climax = Christ.** As we have seen from 1 Peter 1, everything in the Old Testament anticipated the ultimate expression of God's promise-keeping. Jesus of Nazareth perfectly reveals God the Father, provides through his Spirit all that his people need to live for him, and perfectly fulfils God's creation-restoration plan. Of course, it doesn't all happen at once. We will see why, when we start looking at the Gospels in more depth. But this much is clear: *he* is the Saviour.
- **Resolution = The New Creation:** Because of Jesus's triumph in his incarnation, death, resurrection and ascension, there is now a sure hope of restoration. But as we will see when we come to the book of Revelation, the new creation will somehow be even more perfect than the perfection of the original creation (although it's impossible to get our heads around that!).

As you can see from these diagrams, the Bible's story is gradually unfolding, with each stage adding to what has gone before. King David knew things that Abraham didn't. Jeremiah knew things that David didn't. And we know things that Jeremiah didn't – because we live after God's ultimate revelation of himself in Christ (see Heb 1:1–4).

Why is it important to grasp this point? Well, think about the following statement, that I have heard from people on four continents:

> God wanted to restore people to himself, and so he created a nation to follow him. That is "Plan A." He showed them how they should follow him by revealing his law, as summarized in the Ten Commandments. But they failed miserably. The Old Testament is their story. So God had to come up with an alternative – that is why he sent Jesus. Jesus is God's "Plan B." Where law failed, grace triumphs.

If you can see the plot of the whole Bible, you will recognize that what is being said there is an unhelpful distortion that spreads confusion. It is certainly true that God revealed his law, and that the people failed to keep it. But if that came as a surprise to God, or caused him problems, it suggests that human sinfulness outsmarted God. It turns Jesus's coming to a desperate mission of last resort. But once we see the Bible as one coherent story, it becomes clear that God and his consistent character is what holds it all together. It means that God has no "Plan B."

The first hint of this comes right at the start, in God's judgment on the snake.

> And I will put enmity between you and the woman, and between your offspring and hers; he will crush your head, and you will strike his heel. (Gen 3:15)

We have no idea who this is yet. But it's a clear promise of a "serpent-crusher"! It will take someone who is human to do this, and he will get wounded in the process – but his victory will be complete. He will rid the world of the Fall's root cause by crushing the snake's head.

Then turn to the other end of the Bible. Don't worry too much about the imagery for now – we'll come to that! John speaks of the cosmic battle being waged in our world. Notice how he describes Jesus:

> All inhabitants of the earth will worship the beast – all whose names have not been written in the Lamb's book of life, the Lamb who was slain from the creation of the world. (Rev 13:8)

In other words, it was *always* God's plan for Jesus to die as the Lamb on the cross. That is breathtaking. It is impossible to understand it fully. But we can trust God's goodness and grace – after all, as we have suggested, his character is *the* thread that holds the whole story together. There is no "Plan B" – it is all "Plan A." God is the hero of His-story.

Different angles on the story

Great storytellers keep their audiences or readers gripped even with old and familiar stories by approaching them from a fresh angle. Even though many of the details remain unchanged, we see them from a different perspective. This is what happens repeatedly in the Bible. The outline I've just offered only scrapes the surface of all the twists and turns in its plot, and doesn't even mention the wide variety of themes that flow through it.

We can think of these themes as different routes to our destination. For example, on my continental map, I can see that to get to Istanbul I can fly west across Europe or east across Asia. My journey would start and finish in the same place, but because I was flying different routes, I would see different things as I looked out the window. I would become aware of things I had not noticed before. The same is true of the Bible story. We can start and end at the same destination, but take different routes to get there as we look at the story from different angles.

So let's look at three different routes through the Bible story. Each presents the story from a different angle. Obviously, each also deserves much more thought and study than there is space for here, but you can follow them up for yourself later. For now, let us focus on just a few landmarks along the way. The more we understand how the Bible develops these themes, the better our preaching will be.

(i) The covenant angle

A covenant is an agreement between two individuals or groups in which each side shows its commitment to the other by making promises to be faithful to specific terms and conditions. Some covenants are agreed to in the context of public rituals, which adds to the seriousness of the commitment, as does the common addition of a public sign to remind everyone of what has taken place. Some covenants are between equals (as in the biblical ideal of marriage). Others are not (as when a conqueror imposes his rule on an occupied nation). It would be impossible for creatures to initiate a covenant with their Creator – we are not his equals. So if there is to be any agreement between God and us, it must begin with him.

The most significant aspect of covenants, though, is that they establish, and even deepen, relationships. Our Creator wants to have a relationship with his creatures. That is a remarkable truth. And it is a truth that gives the whole Bible its heartbeat.

In the course of history, God has made a number of covenants with his creation, but all of them are part of the same unfolding story.

The journey goes from the general to the specific:

- God's commitment not to destroy humanity with a flood (revealed to Noah).
- God's promises for and about a nation (Abraham is promised a family, and his descendants shown through Moses how to live).
- God promises that this nation will be ruled by a unique king (one of David's descendants will reign forever).
- God's covenant inaugurated by Jesus Christ.

Keeping the covenant theme in view helps us to remember that God's purposes have always been for the whole world. That is obvious in the case of the promise to Noah – but it is also the case with the promises he made to Abraham, Moses, and David. Even if the nation in focus is Israel, God's purpose has always been global. Here is God's first revelation to Abraham:

> I will make you into a great nation, and I will bless you;
> I will make your name great, and you will be a blessing.
> I will bless those who bless you, and whoever curses you I will curse;
> and all peoples on earth will be blessed through you. (Gen 12:2–3)

The ultimate blessing then will come through Jesus, who establishes the new covenant through his blood by dying on the cross and offering his followers a memorial of his death at the Last Supper. The wonder is that this is for people of all nations (Matt 26:27–29; 28:16–20).

The following table summarizes these covenants and shows where to find them in the Bible.[5]

---

5. Note that direct quotations from the Bible are in italic.

Covenant	Promise	Sign?	Conditions?
Noah	**Protection through Judgment** *But I will establish my covenant with you, and you will enter the ark.* (Gen 6:18) *I establish my covenant with you: never again will all life be destroyed by the waters of a flood.* (Gen 9:11)	**The Rainbow** (Gen 9:13)	
Abram/ Abraham	**A Promised People in a Promised Home** A people as "countless as the stars" who will live in a land God gives them. All peoples on earth will be blessed through this people. (Gen 12:1–3; 15:1–21; 17:1–14)	**Male Circumcision** (Gen 15:10–12)	**Trusting God** *Abram believed the* LORD *and it was credited to him as righteousness.* (Gen 15:8)
Moses	**A People Rescued from Egyptian Slavery** *The Israelites groaned in their slavery and cried out, and their cry for help because of their slavery went up to God. God heard their groaning and he remembered his covenant with Abraham, with Isaac and with Jacob.* (Exod 2:23–24)	**Rest on Sabbath** *[The Sabbath] will be a sign between me and the Israelites forever, for in six days the* LORD *made the heavens and the earth, and on the seventh day he rested and was refreshed.* (Exod 31:16–17)	**Obedience** *You yourselves have seen what I did to Egypt, and how I carried you on eagles' wings and brought you to myself. Now if you obey me fully and keep my covenant, then out of all nations you will be my treasured possession. Although the whole earth is mine, you will be for me a kingdom of priests and a holy nation.* (Exod 19:4–6)

Covenant	Promise	Sign?	Conditions?
David	**A Royal Dynasty for God's People** *The LORD declares to you that the LORD himself will establish a house for you . . . Your house and your kingdom shall endure forever before me; your throne shall be established for ever.* (2 Sam 7:11–16)		
Prophets	**A Promised New Covenant** *"The days are coming,"* declares the LORD, *"when I will make a new covenant with the people of Israel and with the people of Judah."* (Jer 31:31–34)		
Jesus	**An Inaugurated New Covenant** *This is my blood of the covenant, which is poured out for many for the forgiveness of sins.* (Matt 26:28; see also 1 Cor 11:25) *But in fact the ministry Jesus has received is as superior to theirs as the covenant of which he is mediator is superior to the old one, since the new covenant is established on better promises.* (Heb 8:6)	**The Lord's Supper** Bread and wine	**Repent and Believe**

This table shows how each successive covenant fits into the same unfolding story. Perhaps we can see this more clearly if we look at Jeremiah's prophecy of a new covenant in a little more detail. (This prophecy was what Jesus referred to when he instituted the Lord's Supper.) If it is correct to say that the new covenant is an upgrade or extension of the old, we would expect to find the same elements as we find in the previous versions. But as with any upgrade, there are new developments. So let's look at what remains unchanged from what had been revealed before Jeremiah's time, and what was new and innovative in the revelation to Jeremiah about God's new covenant that would be inaugurated by Jesus Christ.

- **Unchanged**: the same God who made promises to Abraham and revealed his name to Moses continues to make promises to his people in Jeremiah's time

  The time is coming, declares the LORD, when I will make a new covenant with the house of Israel and with the house of Judah. (Jer 31:31)

- **Unchanged**: the same aim

  I will be their God and they will be my people. (Jer 31:33)

- **Changed**: a new method

  It will not be like the covenant I made with their forefathers . . . because they broke my covenant though I was a husband to them. This time I will put my law in their minds and write it on their hearts. (Jer 31:32–33)

- **Changed**: a new universality. All will have access to knowing God, not just the elite.

  No longer will a man teach his neighbour or a man his brother saying "Know the LORD" because they will all know me from the least of them to the greatest. (Jer 31:34a)

- **Changed**: a new confidence

  For I will forgive their wickedness and will remember their sins no more. (Jer 31:34b)

While the core elements remain the same, other elements are extended or deepened. That is entirely what we might expect in an unfolding story. It reinforces our point that the New Testament should never be understood as a major change in direction – it is the revealed conclusion to God's eternal purposes.

(ii) The kingdom angle

 Another angle from which we can approach the big story of the Bible is the kingdom angle.[6] This angle is useful because it helps us to put the covenant theme into an even wider perspective. It is as if we are looking at an even bigger map than we were before.

Some assume that the idea of the kingdom of God is a New Testament invention because Jesus was the one who taught about it the most. Yet as soon as we take a continental look at the Bible, remembering the relationship between the two Testaments, it is clear why that cannot be the case.

Do you remember the terms in which Samuel rebuked the people for requesting a king so that they could become "like other nations" (1 Sam 8:20)?

> But when you saw that Nahash king of the Ammonites was moving against you, you said to me, "No, we want a king to rule over us" – even though the LORD your God was your king. (1 Sam 12:12)

Ultimately, Samuel did anoint a king over Israel. But throughout the reign of Saul and David and all kings who followed them, the idea was that the king was subject to God, the even greater king. The writers of the books of Kings and Chronicles judged the kings by the extent to which they obeyed God.

But the idea of the kingdom of God goes even further back than the kingdom of Israel. That kingdom was merely a stage in a bigger process. We can say that the idea of the kingdom of God began in the garden of Eden. How can we say this? Well, think about the requirements for any kingdom. There must be a king who rules over people in a specific place. Now let's see how those ideas apply to God's kingdom in Eden:

- **A king.** God clearly fulfils that role in Genesis 1–2.
- **God's people.** The first man and woman were created in God's image, which set them apart from all other creatures (Gen 1:27). They were uniquely able to serve God's purposes and reflect God's character.

---

6. An Australian teacher Graeme Goldsworthy has written a number of books about this approach, including *According to Plan* (Leicester: IVP/Grand Rapids: Eerdmans 1991, and *Preaching the Whole Bible as Christian Scripture* (Leicester: IVP/Grand Rapids: Eerdmans, 2000). Vaughan Roberts has popularized it in his short but helpful book, *God's Big Picture* (Leicester: IVP, 2009).

- **God's place**: God is the creator of the cosmos, but he marked out a garden bursting with life as the perfect habitat for the man and woman. This was where he would come to visit them in "the cool of the day" (Gen 3:8).
- **God's blessing and rule**: The garden had physical boundaries, but it's unlikely the man and woman would have been too concerned about them. For with immense generosity, God had provided for their every need within it (including access to the tree of life – see Genesis 3:22). More significant was the spiritual boundary God put in place when he commanded them not to eat from the tree of the knowledge of good and evil, or face terrible consequences (Gen 2:16–17). This was a test of their loyalty and devotion to their Creator. It was a test of whether or not they would live under their rightful king.

There is an additional element too, that we often overlook. Genesis 1–2 implies it, and it is developed in the next few chapters, but it only becomes explicit in Genesis 12. This is the fact that Yahweh is the King of ALL. He is the creator of everything, and therefore has concern for everyone. So from the start, it should be clear that the Old Testament is not exclusively concerned with one Middle Eastern people group. Israel is just the focus for God's plans, but it is not the totality of God's plans. Look again at what God promises Abraham if he travels to the new land.

> I will make you into a great nation, and I will bless you; I will make your name great, and you will be a blessing. I will bless those who bless you, and whoever curses you I will curse; and all peoples on earth will be blessed through you. (Gen 12:2–3)

Just as God's provision and care is a blessing to his people, so Israel is to be a blessing to all peoples. God's promise to Abraham launches God's global restoration plan. That plan will take centuries to be fulfilled. In fact, we are still waiting for the final pieces of the jigsaw puzzle to be in place by the one greater than Abraham: Jesus himself (see John 8:53–59).

But we are getting ahead of ourselves! If we trace the kingdom thread through the whole Bible, the kingdom theme plays out like this.[7]

KINGDOM OF GOD	God's People	God's Place	God's Rule
Creation	Adam & Eve	Garden of Eden	God's Word
God's Judgment	**THE FALL**		
Promised	Abraham & Family	The Promised Land	The Covenant with Abraham
After Egypt	Moses & Israel	The Tabernacle	The Covenant at Sinai
In the Land	David, Solomon Judah & Israel	The Land & Temple	The Covenant at Sinai
God's Judgment	**THE EXILE**		
Prophets' Hope	A Remnant of Judah & Israel	The Land & Temple restored	A New Covenant Promised
The GOSPEL AGE	JESUS	JESUS	JESUS
The Last Days	The Body of Christ	The Church as Temple of the Spirit	A New Covenant of Word & Spirit
The Last Day:	**HELL**		
Hell or Heaven?	The Bride of Christ	Heaven (no Temple)	Around God's Throne

Much more could be said. But this table should make it clear why the kingdom angle helps us to see how the entire Bible story fits together.

(iii) The in-and-out angle

Christopher Ash is a British preacher who likens Bible overviews to photographs of the same scene taken from different angles. How on earth can you capture the grandeur of a majestic mountain range with just one two-dimensional image? It's impossible. But by looking at different photographs of those mountains, you can get at least some idea of

---

7. Adapted from both Goldsworthy's and Roberts' books mentioned above.

what they are like. In the same way, Ash suggests that we need to look at the Bible from different angles to get a sense of its majesty.[8]

Ash noticed that the Bible is a sequence of human scatterings and gatherings, with sin the root cause of division, and divine reconciliation the only means of gathering. This is a theme that is very relevant to our contemporary world. Wherever we live, our newspapers are full of conflict, within homes, between races and ethnic groups, and across borders.

While studying Ash's ideas, it occurred to me that geography is frequently significant in the Bible as well. When God gathers his people, it is often to a particular place (promised ahead of time). When things go wrong, they are expelled from that place. This makes the story feel a bit like the tides of the sea, coming in, going out, coming in again. Just as the earth's tidal fluctuations are entirely caused by the gravitational pull of the moon, so the movements of gospel people are dependent on the sovereign God.

Laying out the Bible's storyline as illustrated in the chart on the following page brings a number of details to the fore.

- It focuses attention on the theme of being in God's place (the left-hand column). Each stage is in some ways an expansion on the previous one, and each is also a prefiguring of the next stage. But the story is never complete until we reach the final stage, in the new Jerusalem. This fits precisely with what the writer to the Hebrews said about Abraham and the other old covenant believers not mistaking the territorial dimensions of the land with what God was ultimately promising.

  > They were longing for a better country – a heavenly one.
  > Therefore, God is not ashamed to be called their God, for
  > he has prepared a city for them. (Heb 11:16)

- It also points to God's work beyond the borders of his promised places (the right-hand column). Adam and Eve still experience his grace after their exclusion (Gen 3:15 and 3:21) as do others in exile. Some of the greatest Old Testament heroes of the faith were used by God at precisely these difficult times when the people were in the wrong place (think of Moses, Daniel, Queen Esther). Most significantly, the final box on the right (number 8) reminds the modern Christian believer how we are to see ourselves. While we

---

8. Christopher Ash, *Remaking A Broken World* (Milton Keynes: Authentic, 2010).

> do have many kingdom blessings, there are many ways in which we
> do not quite belong in this world, or, as Peter puts it, we are "exiles"
> who are "scattered."

Each of these angles on the story of the Bible is compatible with the others. Where the covenant angle focuses on God's rule, the kingdom angle focuses on God's people and the in-and-out angle highlights God's place.

Seeing the Bible story in this light counteracts the individualistic mindset that is seeping into many churches, a way of thinking that reduces being a Christian to simply a matter of me on my own with God. But that is absurd, as well as self-centred. I am *not* the centre of the universe – it is only my sin that deludes me into believing that. God's saving work is about a cosmos being restored. It is only by his grace that we find a place in that.

3. Engaging in a Lifelong Conversation

Looking at all these different angles on the Bible may have left you with mixed feelings. You may have found them helpful and convincing, but at the same time you may be a bit depressed. You may wonder how on earth you will ever be able to see some of the other possible camera angles on your own, without others' help. This underlines the earlier point that we never stop learning in the Christian life, and especially in Christian ministry. There is always more!

Nobody is expecting you to come up with radically new angles on the Bible. But what we do all need to do is to evaluate any themes that do occur to us as we do our own Bible reading. We might not necessarily be looking for them, but the more familiar we are with the whole Bible, the more often we see connections, or what appear to be connections, between the passages we are studying and other parts of the Bible.

One way to think about this is to assume that when we study the Scriptures, we are involved in what needs to be seen as a lifelong conversation. None of us is able to know everything. Certainly not in this life, anyway. This is *especially* true in the things of God and his revelation.

To encourage you, let me tell you about an incident that taught me a lot about lifelong conversations with Scripture. It happened one day in London. I was walking along the street when I suddenly saw John Stott, the founder of Langham Partnership coming towards me. We stopped to chat, and he asked, "Do you have Malcolm Muggeridge's 1969 book *Jesus Rediscovered*? I'm currently doing some thinking about the incarnation."

1: IN – EDEN
God's people live and work in his garden – he provides everything they need to flourish under his generous hand. *(Gen 2)*

2: OUT – EAST OF EDEN
God's people cast out of the garden for their rebellion. *(Gen 3:22–24)*
But God is at work . . .
(Gen 3:15, 21)

3: IN – PROMISED LAND
God promises to give Abraham's nomadic family a land to settle in. *(Gen 12:1–3)*

4: OUT – EGYPT SLAVERY
Egypt is initially a place of protection from famine, but having settled in Egypt, later generations are enslaved there. *(Exod 1:8–10)*
But God is at work . . .
(Exod 2:23–25)

5: IN – THE LAND
God rescues his enslaved people under Moses, to form a new nation under his good rule. They then enter the promised land 40 years later under Joshua. *(Exod 12:40–42; Josh 11:23)*

6: OUT – BABYLON EXILE
After centuries of rebellion, God exiles his people by using the Babylonian empire. *(2 Kgs 24:15–17)*
But God is at work . . .
(Jer 29:10–14)

7: IN – JESUS IN JUDEA
Jesus fulfils all that God promised his people and ushers in God's kingdom on earth by coming as the servant who gives his life as a ransom. *(Mark 1:14–15; 10:45)*

8: OUT – STRANGERS IN THE WORLD
There is no longer a land or a temple, but God's people are spread across all nations, to reach all nations.
But God is at work . . .
(Matt 28:18–20; 1 Pet 2:8–9)

9: IN – NEW JERUSALEM
God will gather all his redeemed people around him in the city that has come down to earth. *(Rev 21:1–8)*

Several things struck me about that. For a start, John Stott had known Muggeridge quite well and would certainly have read the book at least once before. Second, Stott had written often about Christ and his incarnation, particularly in his wonderful book *The Incomparable Christ*.[9] Third, he was by then in his mid-80s, and could so easily put his feet up in retirement. Yet he was determined to continue deepening his understanding and love for Christ! That short encounter made a huge impact on me. I resolved, and I hope you will too, that I should be a lifelong learner. This is particularly important for Bible preachers and teachers, for the Bible is such a vast book.

As we conduct our ongoing conversation with the Bible, we will find that it splits into two conversations.

Conversation between a particular text and the big picture

Sometimes you find yourself reading a passage that doesn't seem to fit with the rest of the Bible. Perhaps it appears to contradict a general truth about God, or it challenges widespread views about the Bible's story. If we work on the basic assumption that the Bible is God's book and therefore consistent, we then have two options: Either we have made a mistake in interpreting the specific text we are reading, or we have got the Bible's big uniting themes a bit wrong. This type of conversation requires humility. We need to accept that we have gone wrong somewhere.

The next step is to work out where we are wrong. This can take time. And it is not something we can easily do on our own. We need to invite other people to join us in the conversation: fellow disciples, teachers and pastors, interpreters past and present. The conversation will go on as we listen to other preachers, read books, talk to trusted friends. One good place to conduct this type of conversation is in a Langham preaching club. These take different forms in different parts of the world, but they all involve Bible teachers coming together to learn more about the Bible and how to preach it.

The book of Proverbs sums it up beautifully: "As iron sharpens iron, so one person sharpens another" (Prov 27:17). There is always more to learn, and we learn it from one another. This is because we are all engaged in a lifelong conversation in which we allow our grasp of the whole Bible to shape and be shaped by our engagement with specific parts of it. It is a process that is never complete in this life.

---

9. John R. W. Stott, *The Incomparable Christ* (Leicester: IVP, 2015).

Conversation between my framework and God's framework

While we are engaged in our conversation between different parts of the Bible, we may come to realize that there is another participant in the conversation. That participant is the culture to which you belong. We don't always recognize it, but our culture (our national culture, our church culture, and our home culture) will affect the way we interpret the Bible. Here are a few examples of this.

- **Upbringing and family life:** Our experiences with our human families, which are shaped by our national cultures, also shape how we read the Bible. It will affect how we understand relationships between men and women. It will also affect how we understand concepts like the family of God. For example, the quality of the relationship we have with our human fathers (good or bad) has a profound impact on how we relate to God as our Father, and to how we interpret the Bible's teaching about him. If you had a very strict father, you may find yourself focusing on God's commands and God's wrath; if you had a very loving father, you may focus on God's love and desire for us to communicate with him.

- **Conversion and church experience:** If you grew up in a different faith, or came to Christ late in life, you will have a very different perspective from someone who grew up in the church and has been surrounded by Christians since they were a child. Your different perspectives will affect how you see the world and understand your faith.

- **Denominational and national background:** Your interpretation of Scripture will be affected by the beliefs of your church. For example, does your church baptise babies or consider involvement in national politics inappropriate for believers?

Many other things also influence us: our age, our education and qualifications, how often we have crossed cultures, the amount of suffering we have endured. All shape our outlooks, the framework in our minds that help to make sense of God's world and God's word.

The problem is that many Christians presume too quickly that *their own* understanding of the world automatically became identical to God's at their conversion, or when they got a theology degree, or became a pastor! Or they assume that *their* denomination is correct, while all others are dangerously flawed. Or that their own national culture is superior to that of others in regard to, say, its attitude to senior citizens.

These background elements combine to form what we might call our framework for interpreting the world and the Bible. If we are not careful, when we preach, we simply preach our frameworks, not what the Bible actually teaches. So it is a journey of a lifetime to allow God to transform our frameworks so that they increasingly resemble his (as the diagram indicates).

This is what Paul meant when he told the Roman Christians:

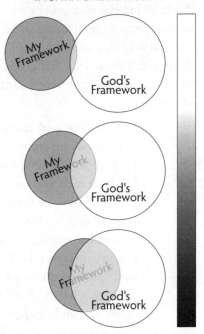

A LIFETIME'S GROWTH IN SPIRITUAL MATURITY

> Do not conform to the pattern of this world, but be transformed by the renewing of your mind. Then you will be able to test and

approve what God's will is – his good, pleasing and perfect will. (Rom 12:2)

The conversation between our personal framework and God's framework will take place as we study the Scriptures and try to live by them. As we grow in our knowledge and our experience of discipleship, we will also grow in Christian maturity. Slowly, our frameworks will start to become more like God's revealed framework.

Section 1

Preaching the Gospels and Acts

For many, the thought of sitting under the stars, around a crackling fire, listening to a thrilling storyteller is the stuff of dreams. As populations shift to cramped and crowded cities, what once was the normal, if not only, evening entertainment has become a once-in-a-lifetime experience for the lucky few.

But stories still matter! Why else do we sit glued to televisions? Why else would bookshops sell so many paperback novels? Good storytellers are still respected and followed the world over.

That must be the most basic reason for the gospels' enduring popularity. They are superb, gripping stories! Unfortunately, many preachers (perhaps especially in Western churches) seem to have forgotten this. They seem content to treat them as no different from a dense paragraph from Romans, from which they'll draw (usually three!) points of systematic theology. Such sermons may well communicate gospel truth and the truth will always be helpful; and God is gracious enough to use any sermon, however poor. But that is no excuse for forgetting that the gospels are stories!

God communicates his truth not just through words but also through the form (or genre) that those words come in. This means that a failure to do justice to a passage's form may well result in a failure to be faithful to a passage's meaning.

For any Christian preacher, Jesus will be the focus of our faith, the heart of our message and the foundation for our ministry. Without him, we would have no faith, no message, and no ministry. No wonder we love to talk about him – to tell stories about him. And that is what the gospels do. Our task is to make Jesus "walk off the pages" of these books and into people's lives. Can there be a greater joy than to introduce people to him and to see faces brighten and hearts burn as the scales fall from their eyes?

2

The Challenges of Preaching the Gospels

If we love and follow Christ, it is natural to love the gospels. Yet many of us find them difficult to preach well. There are several reasons why we might struggle.

1. They Are Too Familiar

Have you ever gone into the kitchen or bedroom to look for something – maybe it was tea or clean socks? You open cupboards or drawers and look inside, but you can't see what you are looking for anywhere. So you call your wife, and she walks in and finds it immediately, in the place you were looking. You just hadn't seen it. Perhaps it was in a different package or you had forgotten the colour and so weren't look carefully enough. Because you are so familiar with the setting, you don't look at the details carefully.

The same thing happens when it comes to the gospels. We feel more than familiar with them already. For example, we *know* the story of Jesus's temptations in the desert or the parable of the Good Samaritan – in fact, we can probably plan the sermon outline without even opening the Bible! But that is dangerous and can lead to all kinds of strange interpretations and inaccuracies. Perhaps we half-remembered Matthew's temptation account, without realizing that his is subtly different from Luke's. The result is that we completely miss *Luke's* point when we preach on his gospel. Much of the power of his story gets lost. The same thing happens in reverse when we preach on Matthew.

In the next two chapters of this book, my aim is to puncture your assumption that you know the gospels and to prove that the gospels are often stranger and more surprising than we realize.

The danger of over-familiarity: **Our sermons miss the point.**

2. We Treat Them as Morality Tales

Every culture has folktales and children's stories that are handed down from generation to generation. They tell of great heroes in the past, or of ordinary people overcoming terrible situations, or of animals that talk and act in surprising ways – which makes them perfect for children's bedtimes. The key thing about them, though, is that they illustrate important life lessons. Take the classic story by the ancient Greek storyteller, Aesop, of the race between the tortoise and the hare. Because hares are fast and tortoises are slow, the hare assumes he can easily win the race. So he stops to take a nap half-way through the race. Unfortunately, he wakes up too late and sees the tortoise cross the finishing line ahead of him. The lesson is clear: never underestimate your opponents or be complacent about your own apparent superiority. It's just the kind of lesson we expect from a morality tale.

Now, as responsible preachers we all long for our sisters and brothers to grow to maturity and make wise decisions. So in our sermons and group studies we want to address specific problems they are facing. Sometimes, this motivates us to identify appropriate passages to study and preach on. But it can also lead to what we could call *preacher's impatience*. We are often in a hurry to get to the application, and so we cut corners in studying the Bible's text. The result is similar to what happens when we are over-familiar with the gospels. The gospel writer's purpose for telling a story gets overshadowed by our own agendas in preaching, even if that isn't what we intended to happen.

Of course, Bible stories do present a greater challenge. How should we apply them in the first place? Are we primarily told these stories to give us examples to follow or avoid? Are they divine morality tales, designed to show us how to be good little boys and girls?

Take this example:

> Very early in the morning, while it was still dark, Jesus got up,
> left the house and went off to a solitary place, where he prayed.
> (Mark 1:35)

Why does Mark give us this detail? Is he trying to tell us that we should always have our devotional time before dawn? But what happens if you, like me, are an evening person, not a morning person? Was that Mark's main reason for describing Jesus's schedule?

The context will help here. In the very next section, Mark gives us a brief insight into the demands on Jesus's time. Might this early prayer time have had something to do with the difficult prioritizing that was necessary for accomplishing his mission? (Mark 1:36–39). Wouldn't it be more likely that Mark's point is that it is always wise to pray before big or difficult decisions? But does that mean we have to get up early in the morning to pray? Surely we are on safer ground when answering that question if we start by asking why Jesus got up so early.

This point is even clearer when we look at Jesus's desert temptations. Matthew tells us that the devil tried to lure him with three specific challenges:

- Turn stones into bread (4:3)
- Throw yourself off the temple roof to be caught by angels (4:6)
- Worship the devil in exchange for global power (4:9)

Each time, Jesus responded with a quotation from Deuteronomy 6 or 8. But again, why are we told this? Is it primarily a model for how we are to deal with temptation?

Nobody denies that quoting Scripture when being tempted is wise. But isn't there something unique about Jesus's temptation here? I've never met anyone who has battled with those specific challenges. Would it help us if we remembered that here the devil is attempting to divert Jesus from his God-given mission to go to the cross, and in the short-term, to sabotage his faithfulness to the Father? That was the sort of the thing the devil had done successfully when he tempted the people of Israel as they wandered in the desert at the time of the exodus. That is why Jesus fights back by quoting Moses's sermon in Deuteronomy. There is so much more going on here than just a model for our behaviour!

Reducing the Bible's stories to morality tales will have two unfortunate results: First, we will be sending people to sleep. This is because our sermons will be so predictable. Our congregation will be able to see the application coming a mile off. In fact, some members of the congregation will probably be able to anticipate exactly what will be said as soon as the reading is announced! And as we will see, few gospel stories are written primarily to give us things to do. Their goal is far more often to have our eyes opened wide by Jesus.

A far more serious result of reducing the gospel to morality tales is that we undermine the gospel. None of us wants to do that, but it can easily happen. What do people take away from our sermons week by week? Is it good news? Or is it a list of rules?

If we treat the gospel narratives as morality tales, then a sermon series on Matthew will be just a list of rules. We may assume that the *only* thing God wants for us is to be perfect and holy and devout and religious. We will think that the measure of the Christian is how much money we give, how many prayers we offer, how righteous we have become. These are all good things, as Jesus's Sermon on the Mount makes clear. But to reduce the gospel to them completely misses its wonder, and in fact, Matthew's point. The Bible is a message of grace from cover to cover. The gospel concerns Jesus's rescuing us from our failures, not a command to do better. Whenever the Bible calls on us to be holy, it is always in response to that rescue. A message that suggests anything different is not Christianity, but a religion based on works.

The danger of moralizing narratives: **our sermons are dull and legalistic.**

3. We Treat Them as Coded Messages

If we should not moralize the gospel stories, what should we do with them instead? Unless we are careful, we will go to the opposite extreme and forage for a story's hidden meanings. We will treat it as an allegory.

Do you remember the 2006 film *The Da Vinci Code?* It suggested that Leonardo da Vinci's beautiful painting of the Last Supper was a coded message about the life of Jesus rather than a depiction of an important event in the gospels. Both the film and the book it was based on were controversial because of their absurd claims. It is easy to pour scorn on the movie, but the allegorical way some pastors handle the gospels suggests that they, too, think of themselves as expert code-breakers.

Allegories are essentially stories written in some sort of code. The purpose may be to intrigue readers or to communicate a message while protecting those under threat. Whatever the reason, the true meaning of the story lies deep below the surface. Each detail is a symbol of something else.

Consequently, the interpreter's job is to explain the symbols, to unlock their hidden meanings. This is more common perhaps with Old Testament stories. The story of David and Goliath is interpreted primarily as an encouragement to fight "the giants in your life" with David's smooth stones (as if they perhaps represented different Christian virtues and gifts). The same sort of thing can happen with New Testament stories like the feeding of the 5,000, so that the number of fish and loaves is interpreted as symbolic in some way.

Of course, that makes the preacher look clever and impressive (which is probably why some like to do it like this). But all too often, there is nothing to rein in an interpreter's creative imagination. As a result, the interpretation has precious little to do with the original passage. Another side effect is that those listening to an allegorical sermon then assume that understanding the

Bible is the exclusive preserve of the truly spiritual or professional Christian. That is disastrous.

The Bible undoubtedly does contain allegories (we will consider some examples in future chapters). But before treating the gospel narratives as allegorical, we must first establish whether their authors *intended* them to be allegorical. If not – and there is no evidence that they did – then we must not treat them as such.

The danger of allegorizing: **our sermons lose their biblical moorings altogether.**

Rather than spending our time hunting down concealed meanings, we should give all our attention to the surface meanings, *as the gospel writers communicate them*. I guarantee this will provide more than enough material to preach on. For help with doing that, read on!

3

The Nature of the Gospels

One of the fascinations of the four gospels is not their similarity but their differences. Each has a subtly contrasting, though always compatible, purpose. But it is still useful to ask what all four books have in common. That is our concern now as we consider what types of books these are. It might seem obvious. After all, we all know that they are what we call "gospels."

Yet that statement is less helpful than it might appear. For no one had ever written a "gospel" before Mark first put pen to paper. In fact, he probably didn't even think he was writing "a gospel" at all. That's why he introduced his work by simply stating it was "the beginning of the good news (or the 'gospel') about Jesus the Messiah, the Son of God" (1:1). Such was the influence of these four New Testament writers, however, that a whole new type of literature was created. But what we need to do is to figure out what *they* thought they were writing.

1. Are They Biographies?

I love reading the biographies of impressive or influential people. One of my favourite biographies is about someone that few outside Britain have ever heard of: William Pitt the Younger. He became our youngest-ever Prime Minister at only 24 in 1783 (a record that is unlikely to be beaten). You may well have heard of one of his closest friends though – William Wilberforce, the great anti-slavery campaigner. Pitt held the highest office for almost twenty years, before dying in 1806 at only 46. So he easily merits a biography of 600 pages. His was a remarkable life at a turbulent time that included the French Revolution, the wars against the Emperor Napoleon, and the battles over the slave trade.

Because the gospels narrate Jesus's own remarkable life, it is no surprise that these books are called his ancient biographies. Those who have studied ancient writers detect parallels with their accounts of the lives of Greek orators or Roman emperors.

Yet the gospels are hardly typical biographies, by either ancient or modern standards. Consider these curiosities. How would you explain them?

- Mark tells us nothing about Jesus's birth or upbringing – in fact, he seems to ignore most of the details of his life.
- Matthew and Luke do offer brief accounts of Jesus's birth. Then with just one exception (Jesus aged twelve in Luke 2:41–52), they skip forward to his baptism (which is where Mark starts).
- Matthew arranges his book around major sections of Jesus's preaching – but John takes this to extremes. Almost half his book is focused on teaching that reveals more of Jesus's identity.

These are strange decisions. Modern biographers obsess over a person's formative years, trying to discover clues to their adult fame. Not so the gospel writers. Then at the other end of life, the Pitt biography describes his final days, his death, and its causes, in only four pages out of 600. That's only 0.6 per cent of the book.

Contrast that with Mark's book. Roughly 42 per cent of it deals with Jesus's final days, death and its causes! That comes as no surprise for believers, but it does if you think he's writing biography. But he's not. What Mark has written is something else altogether.

2. Do They Follow Strict Timelines?

If a modern biography was found to have made factual errors, or confused the dates of significant events, there might be concerns about its reliability in other matters. No wonder people are surprised to discover oddities like these:

- Return to Jesus's temptation in the desert. We have already seen Matthew's version. But Luke reverses the order of the second and third temptation. He ends with the temptation to throw himself off the temple (Luke 4:9–12).
- Luke and Mark describe Jesus healing a blind man on the way into Jericho (Mark 10:46–52; Luke 18:35–43). But Matthew has two blind men and Jesus is leaving Jericho (Matt 20:29–34). What is going on here? Are they conflicting accounts of the same miracle, or separate miracles? It is not immediately clear, but at the very

least we must assume that if God inspired both writers, it is not a significant problem.

- Jesus's stormy visit to the temple comes at a climactic moment after his triumphal entry into Jerusalem in Matthew 21, Mark 11, and Luke 19. These three are often called the "Synoptic" Gospels (a Greek word meaning "seeing together"). However, John presents things rather differently. He has the adult Jesus visit the temple several times, but describes him expelling the money changers right at the start of his ministry (John 2:13–25).

So, should we give up on these books altogether? Sceptics say we should.

However, this is to confuse genres. The gospel writers should not be judged by twenty-first-century standards. Whatever they were doing, they were clearly not troubled by changing the order of events (which is why Matthew often edited or adapted Mark's material, for example).

This does *not* make these books unreliable. It simply means we must adjust to their way of writing, not the other way around. Their purpose is clearly not to provide detailed timelines but convey their message. We can still be sure Jesus's miracles did happen, and Jesus did teach the things he taught.

But what *were* these writers up to?

3. Are They Biographical Sermons?

Think back to Mark's introduction: "The beginning of the good news." He is stating that he has good news for any who wants to read it. It concerns Jesus the Messiah, the Son of God.

It is not a big step to assume that everything he writes subsequently is part of this good news. This does not make this news easy to hear. For example, Jesus's teaching about the sinfulness of the human heart in Mark 7:20–23 is difficult to accept (at least initially).

The message about Jesus is precisely what makes this news good. He both reveals to us and secures God's grace for us. The correct response is surely to trust Jesus for that grace – or in the words of his first sermon in Mark: to "repent and believe the good news!" (Mark 1:15)

So there is a sense in which Mark is preaching to us, his readers. And God by his Spirit is using this ancient book to speak to modern people today. The same can be said for Matthew, Luke, and John.

This explains the curiosities we have already noted:

- Their selectivity over which stories and details to include.
- Their lack of concern about changing the order of events.
- The surprising emphasis given to Jesus's final days and hours in contrast to the almost complete silence about his family life and early adulthood.

Each oddity can be explained as simply the author's desire to communicate the gospel message as well as possible. Each author brought unique talents to the task; each had a subtly different purpose or angle; each assembled his material to serve that purpose.

But in the end, all four shared a longing for their readers to believe the good news and follow them in following Christ. This means that whenever we preach from any part of the gospels, we must be mindful of one crucial question. Is my interpretation *good* news? If not, then I have certainly gone off course.

4

Following the Gospels' Clues

Treasure Hunt is a game my parents used to play with us as children, and which they now play with my children. It is a very simple idea, though it requires a great deal of preparation on their part. This involves writing a list of clues and then leaving them at various points around the house or village. 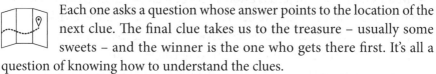 Each one asks a question whose answer points to the location of the next clue. The final clue takes us to the treasure – usually some sweets – and the winner is the one who gets there first. It's all a question of knowing how to understand the clues.

There is a sense in which we are doing something similar when we open the gospels. Because the writers are telling a story, they tend not to communicate their message by making bald theological statements. They let the truths come through the stories and scenes themselves. It is as if each story is a clue that they plant, and as we follow these clues, we are guaranteed to find great treasure.

So for the rest of this chapter, we are going to go on a gospel treasure hunt, a search for the various types of clues that the gospel writers planted in the text centuries ago. While this is a difficult task, it is not an impossible one because they did leave us some tips on what to look for, where to look, and how to interpret the clues they have planted.

This gospel treasure hunt is far more thrilling than any children's game because the treasure is far more valuable. We will find that our vision of the Lord Jesus Christ deepens and grows as we learn how to read the clues well.

Clue 1: Discern the Writer's Purpose

The first clue/tip each writer of the gospels gives us is his own statement about why he has written this book. But strangely enough, we often ignore this information when we read the gospels. That is a bit like picking up a modern book and never checking the descriptions of its contents on the cover before you buy it. You may be in for a surprise when you start reading the book if that is how you choose them!

So let's look at what each gospel writer has to say about the purpose for which he is writing:

Matthew: the disciple-maker

Matthew's clue as to why he is writing is well hidden. Unlike the other three gospel writers, he does not offer a neat statement of the kind that could be put on the cover of a book. He leaves us to figure it out as we go along. A technique that works very well here (and is useful for studying many Bible books) is to look at the opening and closing verses of the book.

Matthew opens with Jesus's astonishing genealogy (Matt 1:1–17). We may find it boring, but it would have been thrilling for first-century Jewish readers. It proclaims loud and clear that Jesus is *Jewish* (he is descended from Abraham – 1:2) and *Royal* (he is descended from King David – 1:6).

But when we turn to the book's conclusion, we find a statement by Jesus that is found only in Matthew's gospel.

> Then Jesus came to them and said, "All authority in heaven and on earth has been given to me. Therefore go and make disciples of all nations, baptizing them in the name of the Father and of the Son and of the Holy Spirit, and teaching them to obey everything I have commanded you. And surely I am with you always, to the very end of the age." (Matt 28:18–20)

This passage is often referred to as the Great Commission because in it Jesus inaugurates God's global mission. He has the authority to do this, because he wields heaven's authority (28:18). He is the divine Son, who rules alongside the Father and Spirit, and in whose name and power the apostles are sent.

But many of us misinterpret this clue because we miss the full picture of what this mission seeks to achieve. Jesus's goal is not just to make converts all over the world, but to make *disciples* all over the world. The word "disciple" literally means "learners" – not just of facts, but of how to live. What Jesus is looking for are not just people who learn some facts about him, but people who obey everything he has taught. Maybe this is a clue to why Matthew has arranged his book around major blocks of teaching about discipleship, like the Sermon on the Mount (Matt 5–7).

So perhaps, as we preach from Matthew's gospel we should ask how the passage in question helps us in the lifelong learning that Jesus has called us to. Jesus seeks disciples not converts! We will flesh this out more in the next chapter.

How might these passages fit with Matthew's theme of lifelong discipleship?

- A paralysed man is healed (Matt 9:1–8)
- A mother's request (Matt 20:20–28)
- Do not imitate the Pharisees (Matt 23:1–12)

Mark: the bringer of good news

Mark's clue to the purpose of his book is hidden in the very first sentence of his gospel:

> The beginning of the good news about Jesus the Messiah, the Son of God. (Mark 1:1)

Presumably, therefore, any interpretation of his book must also offer good news, as I said in the section where we were discussing whether the gospels were morality tales. But there is more to this clue than just that point.

Mark clearly states that what makes his message "good news" is its focus on Jesus's identity and mission. So he says that the good news is "about Jesus the Messiah," or "Jesus the Christ" ("Christ" is the Greek version of the Hebrew word "Messiah"). Literally, the word "Messiah" means "the Anointed One." Whenever a new king of Israel was installed, he was anointed with oil, as happened when Samuel anointed the shepherd boy David (1 Sam 16:13). This action declared that he was God's anointed king, replacing King Saul. In announcing that Jesus is the Messiah, Mark is announcing that Jesus of Nazareth is the ultimate Messiah at the head of a long line of kings.

But Mark's next statement about Jesus is often misunderstood. It is perhaps natural to assume that the reference to "the Son of God" is a statement about Jesus's divinity and his identity as a member of the Trinity. But that's not quite correct. If you had been talking to Mark and spoke of "the Trinity," he would probably have looked at you blankly (even though he would certainly have believed in the Trinity once the meaning of the expression was explained to him). But the expression itself was invented long after he died.

To find out what Mark meant, we must look to what *he* knew, rather than what *we* know. We will be talking more about that in Clue 4.

Luke: the reassuring researcher

Luke is the gospel writer who gives us the clearest clue about his purpose in writing:

> Many have undertaken to draw up an account of the things that have been fulfilled among us, just as they were handed down to us by those who from the first were eyewitnesses and servants of the word. With this in mind, since I myself have carefully investigated everything from the beginning, I too decided to write an orderly account for you, most excellent Theophilus, so that you may know the certainty of the things you have been taught. (Luke 1:1–4)

We have no idea who Theophilus was. It may have been someone's actual name, or it may be a code name to protect his identity (it literally means "lover of God"). Some people suggest that Luke is using it as a code for "anyone who loves God," but that doesn't seem likely because Luke does seem to have someone specific in mind. It doesn't really matter who exactly he was writing to.

But I like to imagine conversations between Luke and Theophilus, perhaps late into the night, about what they understood of Jesus. Luke was never an eyewitness of these momentous events, and so had to rely on the descriptions of those who were. It seems that Theophilus was in the same boat. But somewhere along the way, his confidence seems to have been shaken. This motivates Luke to write his account, primarily to shore his friend up in his faith. He is quite open about borrowing from other writers (almost certainly including Mark and perhaps also Matthew's source) – but he has a subtly different aim, as his introduction explains.

Luke's reassurance has four ingredients.

(i) "The things that have been fulfilled"
Jesus's life and ministry was anticipated, and often explicitly predicted, in the Old Testament. For someone who struggles with the claims made about Jesus's

identity, it is no small matter to see how often he fulfils these ancient Jewish Scriptures. The accumulative effect is a great encouragement. Jesus was no sudden phenomenon who appeared from nowhere. He was the climax of an ancient, even eternal, plan.

(ii) Investigations and Eyewitnesses

Perhaps Theophilus felt insecure after missing out on the events Luke talked about. So, notice how Luke reassures him. Because he had not been a witness either, Luke made sure he talked with those who were. Like a good modern historian, he probably visited all the places he refers to in the book – which would certainly fit with his fascination with geography (see the next chapter) and dates. Being reliable clearly matters to him.

(iii) Orderly account

Luke then assembles all his material – from his research trips, interviews, and collection of other writers' accounts (the many who "have undertaken to draw up an account"). This does not imply that everything is in chronological order; more likely he means that everything is arranged to fit with his overall purpose.

(iv) "To know the certainty of what you have been taught"

The heart of Christian faith is trusting in Christ for all he promises to his followers. This brings blessings that are quite literally endless. So, it matters both that the accounts about him are trustworthy (he actually made these promises) and that he is trustworthy (he can keep those promises). Luke wrote his book to ensure that Theophilus has this double confidence.

What is said above is not guesswork – it is simply taking Luke at his word. So when we preach from Luke, we should always bear this reassurance agenda in mind. Each passage and section will of course have its own purpose and application. But we should never lose sight of Luke's overall purpose.

 Consider how these passages might fit with Luke's overall purpose:
- The centurion's faith (Luke 7:1–10)
- The crippled woman healed on the Sabbath (Luke 13:10–17)
- The rich ruler (Luke 18:18–30)

John: the Jesus-believer

John's style is very different from that of the first three gospels. He seems to be less interested in action-packed storytelling and more concerned with deep ideas and eternal truths. So, in contrast to the other gospels, he begins his book far away from the Roman province of Judea. Instead, he writes about the mind and purpose of God. His intriguing and mysterious introduction deliberately echoes the opening verses of Genesis.

He holds back the clue to why he is writing right until the very end of his gospel. But once we reach it, his point is easy to grasp. Because, despite our first impressions, John's aim is simple:

> Then Jesus told him, "Because you have seen me, you have believed; blessed are those who have not seen and yet have believed." Jesus did many other miraculous signs in the presence of his disciples, which are not recorded in this book. But these are written that you may believe that Jesus is the Christ, the Son of God, and that by believing you may have life in his name. (John 20:29–31)

Jesus says these words after Thomas's unique opportunity to verify his faith, by touching Jesus's all too real crucifixion wounds. None of the other disciples were invited to do that. They didn't need to because they had seen enough to believe.

Like Theophilus and Luke, and even Mark, none of us were present when these events took place. But John was, and he writes for our sakes. He is far more selective about which of Jesus's deeds he reports than the other writers (as he implies in v. 30) – but what he does include serves his aim of drumming home a series of points that make up a simple logical sequence.

(i) Signs to Jesus

John selects only a handful of miracles from Jesus's ministry, culminating in the greatest one, his resurrection. But he has done so with care, because they all point beyond what happens to far bigger truths. That is why he calls them *signs*.

Think of it this way. When you are driving to your capital city, you naturally look for road signs to make sure that you are heading in the right direction. It would be ludicrous to stop at one of these signs for a picnic and believe that you had reached your destination. A sign only works if you go where it points. So in his gospel John is simply saying, "Don't get so focused on the miracles that you miss what they reveal."

(ii) Identity of Jesus

Did you notice anything familiar about the identity to which these signs point? John uses precisely the same words as Mark 1:1: "the Christ, the Son of God." That fact suggests that John is not as different from the other gospels as some think he is. So each time we read a sign in John, we must be alert to how John connects it to a particular aspect of Jesus's identity.

(iii) Trust in Jesus

John is not interested in simply offering his readers information or facts, let alone claims. He expects what he writes to make a difference. He expects a response, albeit a simple one. It is precisely because we now understand who Jesus is that we are to put our trust in him. To put it another way, Christian faith is about believing truths about Jesus and relying on promises made by Jesus. In John's thinking, that leaves one more vital piece –

(iv) Life from Jesus

Life is God's ultimate gift – but it might seem like a strange thing to mention here. After all, the ability to read these words suggests you are alive already. Of course, John explains what he means in his book – and Jesus offers something far greater than biological life (even though this is what Lazarus received from him in John 11). "Life in his name" has eternal implications, as we will see.

So here is the logic behind the response John hopes for from his readers.

Having looked at each gospel's overarching purpose, we need now to work out what to do when studying an individual passage. How do we use the clues we have to find treasure there and thus preach its truths faithfully? The focus for the rest of the chapter will be on how Mark lays out clues in his storytelling, although we could equally have chosen one of the others to make precisely the same points.

Clue 2: Expect Surprises

A treasure hunt would be a lot less fun if the person setting it up used the same clues each year and hid them in the same places each time. Unpredictability is what makes the search exciting. You never know what the next clue will look like or where exactly it will send you.

The same is true of storytelling (and of preaching, for that matter). Audiences and readers stop listening attentively if they know what is going to happen next. Who would bother to watch a crime drama on TV if the first scene told us everything about *who* the criminal and the victim are, *how* the crime was committed, and *why*? It is the uncertainty about those questions that keeps us watching. But if we already know the answers, we turn off the TV or change to another programme.

The problem with the gospels for many of us is that we don't come to them with any sense of expectation. We know them too well, or at least we *think* we do. After all, we all know that Jesus dies on the cross, and that he also rises again. We know that the Pharisees are the bad guys, and that the disciples get things wrong a lot (most?) of the time. We can already see the yawns in church as we stand up to preach about Jesus tackling the Pharisees' hostility and the disciples' blindness.

The only way we can keep our listeners gripped by sermons on gospel stories is if we preachers are gripped by them too. So how can we make sure that happens? The short answer is that it all depends on the questions we ask of the story. Without exception, the most important question we can ask is this: *What is surprising?*

When you ask this question, a passage that seemed very familiar suddenly begins to feel different. It is like climbing a tall tree in your neighbourhood for the first time and having a good look around. You may have lived in that neighbourhood for years, but from that angle, everything suddenly looks different.

There are different ways of putting the question, but it comes down to the same thing: *What is surprising?*

- What might the characters in the story have expected to happen? How did it turn out differently?
- What would have seemed odd or shocking for someone who knew the Old Testament in Jesus's day?
- If I was writing this account, how might I have done it differently?
- What difference does it make if we pretend not to know what will happen next, or at the end of Jesus's life?

Take the famous account of the healing of the paralysed man in Mark 2:1–12. This is an old favourite for children's Sunday school classes. It has everything! For the really enterprising communicator with a knack for visual aids that people will never forget, you can even try to re-enact digging through the ceiling. (Not recommended unless you know exactly how to reassemble it!)

A few days later, when Jesus again entered Capernaum, the people heard that he had come home. They gathered in such large numbers that there was no room left, not even outside the door, and he preached the word to them. Some men came, bringing to him a paralysed man, carried by four of them. Since they could not get him to Jesus because of the crowd, they made an opening in the roof above Jesus by digging through it and then lowered the mat the man was lying on. When Jesus saw their faith, he said to the paralysed man, "Son, your sins are forgiven."

Now some teachers of the law were sitting there, thinking to themselves, "Why does this fellow talk like that? He's blaspheming! Who can forgive sins but God alone?"

Immediately Jesus knew in his spirit that this was what they were thinking in their hearts, and he said to them, "Why are you thinking these things? Which is easier: to say to this paralysed man, 'Your sins are forgiven,' or to say, 'Get up, take your mat and walk'? But I want you to know that the Son of Man has authority on earth to forgive sins." So he said to the man, "I tell you, get up, take your mat and go home." He got up, took his mat and walked out in full view of them all. This amazed everyone and they praised God, saying, "We have never seen anything like this!" (Mark 2:1–12)

What is odd here?

A number of things strike us once we ask what people were expecting. The man's friends had come to Jesus for one thing only: healing. That was what drew the crowds (see Mark 1:45). It would not be surprising if they were a little bit disappointed by what Jesus actually gave him in verse 5.

But then it gets even stranger. For starters, the man's feelings do not even seem to be a factor in what happens next. What is it that causes Jesus to heal the man's legs? It is not the man's faith, but the law-teachers' shock and hostility (2:6–7). He heals him to prove that he has the authority to forgive sins (2:10). Of course, the man was still granted the greatest gift of all, which is divine forgiveness. But it is an unsettling thought to realise that the man's healing was not for its own sake.

Anybody can *say* "your sins are forgiven" because it is impossible to verify whether that has happened. There is nothing to see. It takes genuine power to say "get up and walk." Failure is immediate and obvious. So Jesus achieves what is *harder to say* (physical healing) in order to prove that he can achieve what is *harder to do* (bringing forgiveness). It would take the events of the rest of Mark's gospel to explain that. For now, Mark just wants us to read on.

By asking what is strange, we begin to rediscover how radical, subversive, and even disturbing, Jesus was. We must be sure to bring that out in our preaching. Jesus is *always* full of surprises.

What are the oddities or surprises about these passages?
- Jesus at home (Mark 6:1–6)
- The blind beggar (Luke 18:35–43)

Clue 3: Look at the Details

In a treasure hunt, a good clue always includes some significant details. It won't just say "Look in a book," but "Look inside a red book" or "Find a book that is in the wrong place." The details help you to get the specific information you needed to make use of the clue.

In our Bible treasure hunt, here are some of the details you need to look for in the Bible's stories:

- How is the scene set? Does it impact how we understand the drama taking place?
- Who are the main characters? How does *this* passage describe them?
- If there is dialogue, who says what, to whom, and who is listening?
- Are there any repeated words or images? Do they link with other moments in the book?

Of course, this does not mean every detail carries the same importance. But you won't know which details are important until you have studied the whole passage.

I discovered the importance of focusing on details early in my ministry when I worked for a church in which we preached through the whole Gospel of Mark over eighteen months. I discovered that I was to preach on the feeding of the 5,000 in Mark 6, and then two weeks later, on the feeding of the 4,000 in Mark 8! Now, that was stressful! There was no way I could preach the same sermon twice – people would have noticed (I hope!).

In preparing for those sermons I learned some very important lessons about Bible study, as well as about Mark. That crisis forced me back to the text to pay attention to the details, however small and seemingly irrelevant they seemed. It quickly dawned on me that there was no need to preach the same sermon twice – Mark knew what he was doing when he included *both* stories!

The feeding of the 5,000 is in fact the only one of Jesus's miracles found in all four gospels (apart from the resurrection, that is). Interestingly, Mark is the only writer to mention that the grass is green (6:39). That detail cannot be that important if all the others omit it. If there is any significance to it at all, it is probably because it suggests an eyewitness source. In a hot and dry climate like Judea's, the grass's colour was unusual enough to merit a mention.

The feeding of the 4,000 is not mentioned in either Luke's or John's account. So it is surprising (that word again!) that Mark thinks it necessary to include it as well as the feeding of the 5,000. After all, his is the shortest of the gospels. We would have expected him to include a very different miracle or a brief section of teaching. So let us look at it more closely. What details in the two miracles overlap, and what details differ?

	Feeding of 5,000 (Mark 6:30–44)	Feeding of 4,000 (Mark 8:1–13)
Location	Home area around Galilee (see 6:4) A remote place (6:32)	The region of the Decapolis (7:31) A remote place (8:4)
Jesus sees the crowd	Compassion on them, sheep without a shepherd (6:34 – see Num 27:17 & Ezek 34:5)	Compassion on them, hungry with nothing to eat (8:2 – see Num 27:17 & Ezek 34:5)
Disciples' response	Confusion: would cost over half a year's wages to feed them (6:37)	Confusion: where will we find food here? (8:4)
Jesus's response	He feeds the people by "teaching them many things" (6:34)	He feeds the people by giving them bread (8:6f)
Available food	Five loaves and two fish (6:38)	Seven loaves and a few small fish (8:6–7)
Leftovers	Twelve basketfuls, from 5,000 men (plus unnumbered women and children?) (6:43–44)	Seven basketfuls, from 4,000 present (8:9)

Both miracles remind us of the miracles performed by Yahweh to feed Israel after the exodus in the desert (e.g. Exod 16). So we might call these exodus miracles – now performed by Jesus. He has compassion on both crowds, he feeds them both with bread and fish, there are huge amounts left over.

But the differences are significant, even if at first they seem incidental. They stand out when we contrast the locations and the numbers. The first is in Jesus's home area, presumably largely populated by Jewish people. Twelve baskets of leftovers remind us of the twelve tribes of Israel. In other words, there is plenty more food where this came from – enough for the whole nation.

The 4,000 are fed in the Decapolis, which was an area east of Jordan, and was inhabited primarily by Gentiles (today that area is part of the country of Jordan). There were seven basketfuls of leftovers. Now, in the Old Testament the number represents completion or fullness, derived from the seven days of the world's creation in Genesis. By mentioning that number, Mark is suggesting that there are leftovers enough for all of God's creatures, the whole of humanity. Yahweh in Jesus has therefore performed an exodus miracle for Gentiles.

It is no accident that just a few verses before in Mark, Jesus was impressed by a daring Syro-Phoenician woman. This ritually unclean Gentile had the courage to ask him for leftover breadcrumbs and beg him to cast the demon out of her daughter (7:24–30).

Professional scriptwriters and novelists are often advised, "Show. Don't Tell." So instead of dialogue or description informing the reader about what they should think or see, it is far better to act it out and let them pick it up themselves. That is what grips an audience or readership.

It is the same with the gospels. Mark could simply have stated, "Jesus offered a formerly Jewish privilege (that of being fed by God in the desert) to Gentiles." But that is much less interesting and inspiring than telling the story of Jesus actually doing it.

Notice that this is not an arbitrary interpretation. We are not trying to explain every single detail (as if this was an allegory); nor are we letting our imaginations run riot. We are simply trying to be sensitive to the details that Mark gives us. In a way, we're just asking, "why does the author say it this way, rather than that way?" "What theological truths is he offering in the story he tells?"

Read Mark's all too brief description of Jesus's final moments. (15:37–39)
- What is strange?
- How does he teach theological truth through narrative detail?

Clue 4: Look for Traces of the Old Testament

As we grew older, we could cope with more complex clues in treasure hunts. Rather than just saying "Look in a red book," the clue might read, "To be or not to be?" – and we would head to my parents' copy of Shakespeare's plays to find the next clue.

New Testament writers do something similar when they quote the Old Testament. Of course, their reason for doing so was much more profound. As we have already seen, the event or truth they are describing fulfils something from the Jewish Scriptures. But there is another, even more basic, reason.

The Old Testament provides the background framework for understanding Jesus's entire world and culture. So trying to understand the wonders of Jesus's gospel is almost impossible without trying to understand the Old Testament. Even the descriptions and titles used of him (such as Son of David, Lamb of God, and King of the Jews) make little sense without going back to it. In fact, there is rarely a lot of point to consulting secular dictionaries to understand the Bible better because as a general rule, *Bible words have Bible meanings.*

Old Testament ideas: Bible words have Bible meanings

So let us return to the title that Mark and John both give to Jesus: *Son of God.* What might that mean to an Old Testament believer? Or, to put it another way, had anyone else been called the "son of God" before?

This is a difficult question to answer by ourselves. But there are several tools that can help us, especially a concordance. This is a reference book (or these days, Bible software) that lists each time an important words or phrases is used in the Bible. Of course, when using a concordance, it is important to remember that just because a word is regularly repeated, it does not necessarily have the same meaning each time.

The concordance shows that Mark was not the first writer to use the phrase "son of God." It had already been used to refer to several different people:

- **Human beings**: Perhaps taking its cue from the reference to the "sons of God" in Genesis 6:2, the term is used to refer to all the descendants of Adam. This idea is picked up in Luke's genealogy, which concludes with a description of Adam as "the son of God" (Luke 3:38).

- **People of Israel**: God gave Moses explicit instructions for what to say to Pharaoh. "This is what the LORD says: Israel is my firstborn son, and I told you, 'Let my son go, so he may worship me.' But you refused to let him go; so I will kill your firstborn son" (Exod 4:22–23). God's people collectively are therefore God's son.

- **King David's successors**: After rejecting David's offer to build him a house, God makes some staggering promises to him. His throne will last forever, God will say to his greatest successor: "I will be his father, and he will be my son" (2 Sam 7:14). As a result, it became common for all occupants of David's throne to be called "son of God." That is why Psalm 2 was used for Israel's coronation ceremonies (notice Ps 2:6–7).

- **Immanuel**: Isaiah announces something genuinely startling for a Jewish mind when he says that the Lord himself will give a sign: "The virgin will conceive and give birth to a son, and will call him Immanuel" (Isa 7:14). The name "Immanuel" means "God with us." This is swiftly followed up by the promise of a "great light" for those "walking in darkness" in Isaiah 9 – a son will be born to reign on David's throne and be called (among other things) "Mighty God, Everlasting Father" (Isa 9:6–7). The implication is clear: God will somehow occupy David's throne himself.

Look at this list carefully, remembering what was said earlier about the continent-wide view of the Bible. Do you see the pattern in the developing use of the title? Over time, it narrowed from a reference to all human beings to just God's people, and then to the king alone, the representative and figurehead of God's people. So we can see that Mark is using the title *Son of God* to emphasize not Jesus's divinity but his royalty.

Now apply this back to Mark and John's purpose statements, in which both announce that their central message concerns "Jesus the Messiah, the Son of

God." Because we have done our Old Testament homework, we can now see that both these two titles mean almost the same thing. Both refer to Jesus's mission to be God's king for God's people.

But there is one difference between the two titles. Thanks to Isaiah's prophesies about a Davidic king who is also divine, we know that this "Son of Man" about whom Mark is going to be telling us in his gospel is not just a human king; he must be something more than an ordinary human being.

 Trace the Old Testament background for the following ideas:
- The Son of Man
- Fig trees and their fruit
- The cup of wrath

Old Testament references: follow the trail!

The New Testament is soaked in the Old Testament. Every single chapter seems to contain at least one Old Testament concept, allusion or quotation. But they are not there just for decoration or to make it sound more impressive. If a gospel writer quotes from the Old Testament, it is almost certain that he wants his readers to look up those verses. And he may also want us to read the verses surrounding the verse he quotes so that we can see that verse in its original context and grasp how it fits his purpose. So part of our discipline in handling any part of the New Testament is to go where the author wants us to go. If we do that, we are often in for some nice surprises. What before seemed over-familiar now gains a far deeper significance.

Some Bible translations helpfully provide the references to Old Testament quotations in the margins. But because not all do, we have added a list of all the significant references in the New Testament in Appendix 4 at the back of this book. There is no excuse now not to follow them up!

But what do we do once we have established where a quotation originates? Let's answer that question by looking at the opening verses of Mark's gospel, which are full of Old Testament clues. Even though Mark launches straight into the action with John the Baptist's preparation for Jesus's ministry, he wants us to grasp its significance in God's plans. The Old Testament background ensures this.

Can you identify all the clues that Mark gives?

> The beginning of the good news about Jesus the Messiah, the Son
> of God, as it is written in Isaiah the prophet:
>
>> "I will send my messenger ahead of you,
>> who will prepare your way" –
>> "a voice of one calling in the wilderness,
>> 'Prepare the way for the Lord,
>> make straight paths for him.'"
>
> And so John the Baptist appeared in the wilderness, preaching
> a baptism of repentance for the forgiveness of sins. The whole
> Judean countryside and all the people of Jerusalem went out to
> him. Confessing their sins, they were baptised by him in the River
> Jordan. John wore clothing made of camel's hair, with a leather
> belt round his waist, and he ate locusts and wild honey. And this
> was his message: "After me comes the one more powerful than I,
> the straps of whose sandals I am not worthy to stoop down and
> untie. I baptise you with water, but he will baptise you with the
> Holy Spirit." (Mark 1:1–8)

How many did you see? How do they help us to understand what Mark
is teaching?

Who is coming next (Mark 1:2)

Mark informs us that he is quoting "Isaiah the prophet" – but, as the chart in
Appendix 4 shows, the opening words of his quotation actually come from
Malachi 3:1. It is only in verse 3 that he quotes Isaiah 40:3. What is going on?

Mark has not made a mistake. "Isaiah" was a common shorthand way
of referring to all the prophets in the Jewish Scriptures. In fact, Mark has
deliberately chosen to combine verses from Isaiah and Malachi because they
represent the first and last books of the Prophets.

Both verses speak of God sending a messenger ahead of someone else.
But the shock comes when we realise just *who* that someone is. Read the two
quotations in their original context:

> In the wilderness prepare the way for the LORD; make straight in
> the desert a highway for our God . . . And the glory of the LORD
> will be revealed, and all people will see it together. (Isa 40:3, 5)

I will send my messenger, who will prepare the way before me. Then suddenly **the Lord you are seeking will come** to his temple . . . But who can endure the day of his coming? Who can stand when he appears? For he will be like a refiner's fire or a launderer's soap. (Mal 3:1–2)

Mark's point leaps out at you when you know the original context of these verses. The one for whom the way is being prepared for is none other than *Yahweh*, the Covenant God of Israel. That is why Isaiah calls him "LORD" (the shorthand form of the Hebrew divine name) instead of "Lord" (from *Adonai*, which simply means "Master" or even "Sir"). Malachi does use the word *Adonai*, but again there is no doubting whom he refers to. Who else can call the temple his own?

So by quoting these two verses, Mark is letting his readers know that the one who is coming is God!

But that isn't all that is hidden in this clue. If we look at the wider contexts of these two prophecies, we can learn even more.

What God is coming to do? (Isaiah 40 & Malachi 3)

Isaiah's prophecy looks forward to a day when his people will be comforted because their hard service has been completed (Isa 40:1–2). It is clear that he is referring to the end of the Babylonian exile (he predicted the start of that exile in the previous chapter). According to Isaiah, the first hint that the agony of exile is ending will be someone speaking from the desert. And the best part of this announcement is that Yahweh is coming IN PERSON to restore his people!

That announcement is very different from the announcement in Malachi's vision. The messenger he is speaking about is not telling the people that God is going to comfort them; rather, he is warning them that God is going to come and judge his people, and in particular the temple. He will refine and purify it, to make the people "acceptable" to Yahweh once again (Mal 3:3–4).

In summary then:

- Isaiah sees God coming to *rescue the people*
- Malachi sees God coming to *judge the people*

It's actually happening! (Mark 1:3–8)

The next thing we know is that John the Baptist has started speaking in the desert about one coming "whose sandals I am not worthy to stoop down and untie" (1:7). But stop to think about that for a moment. What does it imply about the points just made from Isaiah and Malachi?

For starters, it suggests that the exile is only ending now (despite the fact of King Cyrus's liberation of the people from Babylon in 538 BC). Second, it strongly implies that the Jesus, who suddenly appears in verse 9, is none other than Yahweh himself. No wonder John is unworthy to stoop!

But that is not the end of the clues in this paragraph, for there are others buried deep inside it. For these, Mark does not directly quote the Old Testament but just alludes to it. However, readers who knew their Old Testament history would have spotted them immediately. So we see John

- ministering in the desert alongside the River Jordan (1:4–5 ⇒ 2 Kgs 2:6–8).
- making some bizarre lifestyle and dietary choices (1:6–7 ⇒ 2 Kgs 1:8).
- calling on people to repent and prepare (1:4, 7–8 ⇒ 1 Kgs 18:36–39).

Doesn't this sound very like the prophet Elijah?

But before we can move on from Mark's Old Testament trail, there is one more surprise in store for those who read around his quotations. For Isaiah's "voice" and Malachi's "messenger" do actually get named. In Malachi 4, we read more of the day of God's righteous judgment. Then his book concludes:

> See, I will send the prophet Elijah to you before that great and dreadful day of the LORD comes. He will turn the hearts of the parents to their children, and the hearts of the children to their parents; or else I will come and strike the land with total destruction. (Mal 4:5–6)

Bring this all together and what do we have?

God has been planning to judge and rescue for centuries – but now it is finally coming to fruition, as John prepares the way for his cousin Jesus by taking on the prophetic role of Elijah. That must mean that Jesus is Yahweh – in Jesus, God himself gets his feet muddy in the River Jordan!

Now Mark could have written a lengthy explanation of all of that, full of deep theology and complex biblical history and imagery. But many of us would have stopped reading, especially if we're not really into that sort of thing. Instead, he tells a story. And with an incredibly light touch, he squeezes all that into just eight verses! All we had to do was follow the trail of Old Testament clues.

Have a look at Mark 11:1–11 (Jesus's triumphal entry into Jerusalem).
- What is the significance of the colt? (See Zechariah 9:9)
- Why do the crowds sing Psalm 118:25–26?
- In what ways does this passage connect to Mark 1:1–8?

Now that we have worked on the key elements within our passage, we are able to see how they fit together.

Clue 5: Identify Narrative "Episodes"

When participating in a treasure hunt, it's a bad idea to get so excited by the start of a clue that you don't bother to read the whole clue. Unfortunately, some of us do make that mistake when reading the Bible.

But, of course, there is a complication here. A game clue is written down on one small piece of paper. You know where it begins and ends. It's a bit more complicated when the clues are buried inside the text of a book. How do you know where things begin and end?

For help with this, let's return to what constitutes a great story. Identifying those ingredients helps us to see what verses are part of each story, or individual episode. If we don't do this, we may find ourselves preaching on only half a story, from which we may draw all kinds of conclusions that are alien to the author's purpose. To take an obviously ludicrous example, imagine your passage is Joseph's discovery of Mary's pregnancy. It would make nonsense of the story if you decided to preach Matthew 1:18–19 without the rest of that section. The conclusion of your "story" would be Joseph's decision to divorce Mary quietly. Quite apart from the difficulties we might have in finding an application from that, it rather distorts the original point!

Identifiying the key ingredients in a story also helps us to discern which details get us to the heart of that story and which merely set the scene. We are back to the difference between the green grass (which is not that important) and the number of baskets (which genuinely is).

To recap, here are the key story ingredients again:

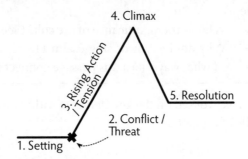

- **Setting**: the background that explains what follows
- **Conflict**: between two or more of the characters
- **Tension**: this is the vital ingredient that keeps us gripped
- **Climax**: the threat or conflict is overcome
- **Resolution**: the resulting situation

How might the feeding of the 5,000 fit into this story structure?

Setting	Crowds have followed Jesus into the desert. (Mark 6:30–34)
Conflict	Jesus faces no opposition here, but there is still a big problem: it is late in the day and the people will be hungry. The obvious thing to do is to tell them to go home. (Mark 6:35–36)
Tension	Weirdly, Jesus tells the disciples to feed them (perhaps knowing that the crowd won't leave). The disciples are confused, especially because there are only five loaves and two fish. (Mark 6:37–38)
Climax	Jesus tells the people to sit down in manageable groups. He then miraculously feeds them. (Mark 6:39–41)
Resolution	Everyone is satisfied, and there are twelve baskets of leftovers. (Mark 6:42–44)

Having identified each of the steps in the story, we can be confident of preaching it as a self-contained episode. We are much less likely to distort or twist its meaning.

Note that I am not saying that a sermon or Bible study must be restricted to only one episode. As we will see, that is sometimes impractical and unnecessary. It is simply that we should avoid preaching *less* than a complete narrative episode.

Before we move on from this clue, there is one other advantage to doing this work: It makes it easier to preach in an interesting way. This is because the story's tension lends itself easily to giving the sermon some tension. The longer that tension can remain unresolved in the sermon, the longer it is possible to grip listeners. That will certainly help the preacher to resist flattening the passage into a series of dull but doctrinally sound theological points.

For example, when preaching on the feeding of the 5,000, you could try to help your listeners feel something of the disciples' stress and bewilderment. Mark's narrative allows us to heighten the tension in preaching it, because the impossibilities seem overwhelming: the vast crowd; in the middle of nowhere; enough food for just a few people; Jesus's infuriating calmness while the disciples are panicking. It can actually be quite funny – and it all serves to demonstrate Jesus's complete mastery over the situation.

 Identify the narrative elements in these passages, and consider how you might use the episode's tensions in a sermon.
- The healing of the paralysed man (Mark 2:1–12)
- The faith of the Syro-Phoenician woman (Mark 7:24–30)
- James and John's request (Mark 10:35–45)

Clue 6: Spot the Wider Connections

When constructing a treasure hunt, you need a plan. You need to know from the outset where it will end up so that you can anticipate how the participants will get from the one clue to the next. In other words, the whole treasure hunt needs to be mapped out, even if the players never get to see the map until after it is finished.

The gospel writers, too, carefully mapped out their books. They had a plan and carefully worked out where each episode or block of teaching would fit in the context of the whole book. Our job is simply to figure out their thinking.

In doing this, it can be very helpful to look for deliberate juxtapositions, to pay attention to what story follows or precedes another. You will soon find that, in the spirit of "don't tell, just show," the gospel writers make theological points by placing one episode next to another.

Here are a few examples of how Mark uses this technique.

Combinations that point to the bigger picture

Why might Mark tell the story of Jesus walking on water (Mark 6:45–56) immediately after the feeding of the 5,000 (Mark 6:30–44)?

The short answer is obvious: it happened like that! That would certainly explain why Matthew, Mark, and John all have these events in the same sequence. In fact, this is the only time (apart from the cross and resurrection, as already mentioned) that John puts two miracles in the same order as the other two. The only gospel writer who chooses to do things differently is Luke (Luke 9:10–17). But might there also be a *theological* reason for the other three to keep the same order?

The Old Testament again provides the clue. Feeding people in the wilderness and walking across the sea are similar to the miracles performed at the time of the exodus from Egypt. Both exhibit God's divine power over the created order. By keeping these two events together, we are reminded yet again that Yahweh truly has come (just as Isaiah promised).

Combinations that explain both elements

We now turn to an event that has puzzled Bible interpreters for centuries.

> They came to Bethsaida, and some people brought a blind man and begged Jesus to touch him. He took the blind man by the hand and led him outside the village. When he had spat on the man's eyes and put his hands on him, Jesus asked, "Do you see anything?"
>
> He looked up and said, "I see people; they look like trees walking around."
>
> Once more Jesus put his hands on the man's eyes. Then his eyes were opened, his sight was restored, and he saw everything clearly. Jesus sent him home, saying, "Don't even go into the village." (Mark 8:22–26)

It is unsettling. What is going on? Did Jesus get it wrong first time round? Was he tired and running out of energy, rather like a pair of old batteries?

There is no need to resort to such explanations if we pay attention to Mark's storytelling. He does not tell us what it means. Instead he moves swiftly on to the next episode, as he always does – even though it must have occurred at least a few hours if not days later (8:27 locates this crucial conversation at an unspecified later time). So there must presumably be a connection between two episodes.

Look at what follows:

- Peter's confession of the Messiah (8:29)
- Peter's rebuke of the Messiah (8:32) – denounced as *satanic* (8:33)

Now think about the juxtaposition. The blind man sees in two stages – after the first he can only see a blurred shape. He can tell that what he is seeing are people, even though they look like trees. Peter also "sees" in two stages. First, he sees that Jesus is Messiah; but he can't see how that fits with the crucifixion. The implication is clear: *both* stages require a miraculous intervention by Jesus. Peter could never have worked it out on his own, with or without the crucifixion.

This reflects a common connection in the gospels – miracles involving physical sight often symbolize Jesus's ability to heal spiritual sight. However, Peter is going to have to wait a while – he will not stop seeing "trees walking around" until after Jesus's death and resurrection. Then he will "get it." Jesus really is the Messiah who must die.[1]

Recognizing this also helps to explain the centurion's confession in Mark 15. There is no logical way for even the most astute observer to identify the *Son of God* from looking at a battered and tortured corpse on a cross – it must have been a sight miracle.

Finally, the combination helps to explain the two-stage physical healing. Jesus had not failed or lacked enough power – he was deliberately pointing to something bigger.

Combinations that work like sandwiches!

Mark is not the only Bible writer to make sandwiches, but he does particularly love them. He seems to enjoy wrapping one episode (the "bread," if you like) around another episode (the "filling"). The purpose is to shine theological light on the "filling" story without the narrative flow being interrupted by a clunky explanation. Recognizing this helps us to explain any oddities in the "bread" story.

The cursing of the fig tree is perhaps the most famous example of this.

BREAD: Fig tree cursed (Mark 11:12–14)
    FILLING: Temple cleansed (Mark 11:15–18)
BREAD: Fig tree withered (Mark 11:19–25)

---

1. As he explains in his letters: 1 Peter 2:21–25 and 3:18–22.

If we read this story without seeing this wider connection, Jesus's anger seems totally irrational (especially because Mark tells us in verse 13 that "it was not the season for figs"). It seems that Jesus is acting like someone who kicks the cat just because he is having a bad day. His behaviour certainly confused the disciples, for they brought the subject up again a few verses later. These two mentions of the same subject are the bread for the sandwich. The filling is the cleansing of the temple.

At this point, it will help to remember some of the tips for interpreting clues that we looked at earlier.

- *Understand the Old Testament background*: Figs, like grapes in a vineyard, are sometimes symbols of being fruitful for God in a spiritual sense (see Hos 9:10).
- *Picking up Old Testament quotations*: We saw in our study of Mark 1:1–8 that Malachi anticipated the arrival of Yahweh himself to judge and refine his temple. This is precisely the focus of Mark 11.

Mark's sandwich now makes perfect sense. The fig tree is being used to illustrate Israel's lack of spiritual faithfulness to God. The temple is "a den of robbers" (quoting Jeremiah 7:11, which sadly refers to precisely this problem). It is no longer fit for its intended purpose of being a "house of prayer for all nations" (Isa 56:7). So Yahweh comes to judge and refine it.

Sandwiches are an elegant storytelling device to avoid lengthy explanations. Mark can simply show without needing to tell. This explains why Matthew and Luke sometimes borrow his sandwiches intact.

 Here are some other examples of Mark's sandwiches. How does their combination help with interpretation?
- Jesus's family reject him (3:20–21)
  - Jewish leaders reject him (3:22–30)
- Jesus's family reject him (3:31–35)

- Request to heal Jairus's daughter (5:21–24)
  - Woman with chronic bleeding (5:25–34)
- Healing of Jairus's daughter (5:35–43)

- Jesus sends out the Twelve (6:6–13)
  - How John the Baptist died (6:14–29)
- Jesus gathers the Twelve (6:30–31)

Clue 7: Follow the Themes

 There was a time when Mark was accused by some scholars of being merely a collector of random stories, who didn't even attempt to construct his book carefully. But all that we have considered so far proves how wrong that is. In Mark, God raised up a brilliant writer and artist – far from giving us a string of random beads, he has shaped a beautiful necklace. Under God, the way he places the stories together builds a remarkable theological message.

The key to finding this structure is to reread the whole book several times so that you can get the big picture and spot ideas and themes that recur or contrast. Look for repeated scenarios, or conversation topic, or even Old Testament references.

It is relatively easy to do this with Mark because his book is short. And the exciting thing is that this does not have to be the preserve of professional Bible commentators; anyone can do it. The more we get to know a Bible book, the more we can see the thematic threads that hold it together.

Let's look at a few of them.

Titles for Jesus. In the opening verse of his gospel, Mark says that his news is good because Jesus is the Messiah and the Son of God (Mark 1:1). So we would naturally expect these titles to crop up in the course of the book. And they do – in Mark 8:27–30 and Mark 15:33–39. In those passages, two very different people acknowledge Jesus: a Jewish fisherman appointed chief disciple and a Gentile soldier appointed Jesus's executioner.

Peter calls him *Messiah*; the soldier calls him *Son of God*; both, as we have seen, are royal titles. They thus correspond to the notice pinned to the cross: *The King of the Jews* (Mark 15:26). Nobody in their right mind would make those connections to the son of God in Isaiah from just looking at Jesus on the cross – so it is remarkable that the centurion does so.

Secrets revealed. Here is another curiosity about Mark. Jesus several times commands the disciples to keep his identity quiet. He reveals nothing about his death until after Peter has openly acknowledged his identity. Then he does so three times in quick succession (8:34; 9:31; 10:33–34). Put the pieces together and we end up with this skeleton outline of the whole gospel.

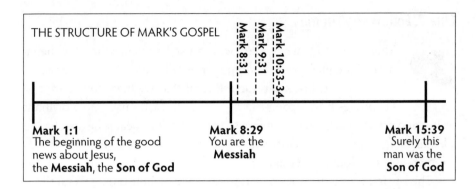

THE STRUCTURE OF MARK'S GOSPEL

Mark 8:31
Mark 9:31
Mark 10:33-34

Mark 1:1
The beginning of the good
news about Jesus,
the **Messiah**, the **Son of God**

Mark 8:29
You are the
Messiah

Mark 15:39
Surely this
man was the
Son of God

So why might Jesus do it like this?[2] Presumably because acknowledging that Jesus is Messiah is only half the battle. People also need to accept him as a crucified Messiah. Which makes no logical sense at all.[3] Kings reign on thrones; kings emphatically do not die on crosses. That is why Peter tried to rebuke Jesus immediately after his astonishing confession, only to receive an even more heart-stopping rebuke (Mark 8:34).

Then where does the second confession take place? Alongside the cross, of course – where Jesus is the ironically crowned and crucified king. Jesus is a king who has come to die.

Elijah. As you read through the whole of Mark's gospel, you may notice that Elijah keeps being mentioned or alluded to. Simply do a concordance or computer search for him in Mark's gospel, and what do you find? (See the table on the opposite page.)

It is clear that Elijah's name was on many lips in Jesus's day. In the grand scheme of Scripture, he is the first and greatest Old Testament prophet in the tradition of Moses. There is a nice symmetry in John the Baptist's being identified with him, because John was effectively the last of these prophets.

But the most significant background link is probably the one we have already considered: the promise that Elijah would return to prepare for Yahweh's arrival (Mal 4:5–6). The sense of anticipation of this great historic moment would have been huge. By repeating Elijah's name several times in his book, Mark is keeping that sense alive. It is as if he is tapping into it – but with one big difference. He is saying, "Yes, this really IS taking place RIGHT NOW!"

---

2. This diagram, together with the others illustrating the basic structure of the gospels, are adapted from those in Craig Blomberg, *Jesus and the Gospels* (Nottingham: Apollos, 1997).

3. This is precisely the point that Paul makes in 1 Corinthians 1:23: "But we preach Christ crucified: a stumbling-block to Jews and foolishness to Gentiles."

1:6	John the Baptist deliberately echoes Elijah's ministry by his location and strange clothing (although this reference will obviously not come up in a concordance search – you just have to know this one!).
6:15	Who is John the Baptist? Some say that he is Elijah.
8:28	Who is Jesus? Some say John the Baptist, some say Elijah; still others, one of the prophets.
9:2–8	At Jesus's transfiguration, he is joined by Moses and Elijah.
9:11–13	Peter, James and John ask: Why do the teachers say Elijah must come first? Jesus: Elijah does come first; Elijah *has* come.
15:35–36	When Jesus cried out *Eloi, Eloi lama sabachthani*, onlookers say "Listen, he's calling Elijah . . . Let's see if Elijah comes to take him down."

It is not just the Gospel of Mark that has themes running through it – so do the other three gospels. They can all be analysed with the same approach. We can then build up the picture from story to story.

On the following page you can see another analysis, this time of three key chapters in Luke covering the run-up to Jesus's final days in Jerusalem. Spend some time following through some of these themes.

The Intricate Tapestry of Luke 18–20

Sections			Jesus on the Journey			
			Jesus & God's Kingdom	Outcasts not In-crowds	Jesus Opposed	Jesus & the Fickle Crowds
18:1–8	Parable	Persistent Widow	a kingdom of justice	a widow		
18:9–14	Parable	Pharisee & The Taxman		a religous outcast		
18:15–17	Journey encounter	Little Children	18:16 belongs to childlike	children	18:15 by disciples!!	
18:18-30	Journey encounter	Rich Ruler	18:29–30	ruler leaves sad. Who can be in?		18:26 who then *can* be saved?
18:31–34	Journey encounter	Jesus's Death Predicted		Jesus will be outcast	18:32–33 want to kill him	
18:35–43	Journey encounter	Blind Beggar Healed	here is King David's son!	a blind beggar	18:39 crowd vs beggar	18:43 they praise God
19:1–10	Journey encounter	Zacchaeus	*Jesus* defines sons of Abraham	a religious outcast	19:7 people grumble	19:3 big crowds round him
19:11–27	Parable	The 10 Minas	19:11 not imminent	servants of the king	citizens hate the king	
19:28–40	Jerusalem	The King in His Capital	19:38 the king is blessed	ordinary people cheer	19:39 Pharisees	
19:40–44	Jerusalem	Weeping for Jerusalem			Jerusalem herself!	
19:45–48	Jerusalem	Cleansing of the Temple			19:47 want to kill him	19:48 hang on every word
20:1–8	Jerusalem	Authority Attacked			by what authority?	they protect him...for now
20:9–20	Parable	The Vineyards & Tenants	Vineyard is God's kingdom	servants vs tenants (leaders)	20:14–15 kill the heir	20:16 may this never be

Jesus's Return	Lessons for the Journey				
Jesus's Return	Praying to God	Nature of Faith	Money & Wealth	Sight & Blindness	The OT Background
18:8 faith when comes?	18:1 keep on praying	Praying 18:8			Deut 10:24
	2 men, 2 prayers	18:14 takes humilty	18:12 boasts re tithing		Deut 14:22
	childlike dependence	18:17 it's childlike			
18:30 rewards in new age	*he fails to ask for the impossible*	18:27 trusts God for the impossible	18:22 sell it all and give to poor!		Exod 20:1–17
		disciples don't get it		18:34 hidden from disciples	Dan 7:13–14
	asks for sight	trusts in God's king		18:41 I want to see *(even tho' he did!)*	
		focused on Jesus	Zacchaeus repays the defrauded	19:3–4 Zach wanted to see Jesus	
19:12 king *will* return		*servant gets the king wrong*	invest *king's* money well		
praise to the king!					Zech 9:9 Ps 118:26
19:43 the days will come . . .		*Jerusalem ignorant re peace*		19:42 source of peace hidden	
cf. Malachi background	19:46 temple a den not prayer house				Mal 3:1–2 Is 56:7 Jer 7:11
20:17–18 rejected rock is capstone		produces fruit for the owner	you owe fruit to landlord		Is 5:1–7 Ps 118:22

5

Four Routes from Jesus to Us

In the previous chapter, we considered some of the features that all four gospels have in common. The clues in the gospel treasure hunt are found in each of them. In this chapter, we are going to focus on the aspects of each gospel that make them unique.

Imagine you need to travel to one of your country's major cities. You probably have a variety of options: you could go by car or bus. In some parts of the world, a boat might be a good option (as in parts of DR Congo, or in the Amazon region). Often the quickest route may actually be longer, simply because it is on better roads. But you may decide to take the more scenic route and travel at a more leisurely pace. When I was growing up, my father would drive us all crazy by insisting on never using the same route twice if he could help it.

Whichever route you choose, you will reach your destination – but there will be different sights to notice on the way! The same is true of the gospels.

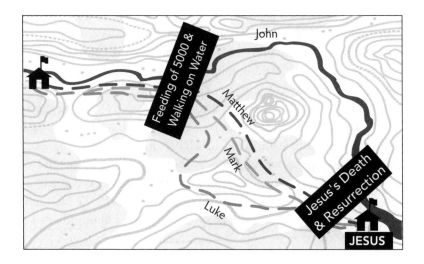

God has given us four gospel accounts to bring us to Jesus. Each has the same destination, each is concerned to proclaim his life and ministry, each longs for us to place our trust in him. Without wanting to stretch the analogy too far, perhaps we can see the Synoptics as offering us three routes we can travel by car, while the route John offers feels so different that it is more like a river journey. There are occasions when the four routes come close to each other, as we have already seen. (Both John and the Synoptics link the feeding of the 5,000 with the walking on water miracle, and of course all include Jesus's death and resurrection.) However, even though the Synoptics often follow similar routes, there are subtle ways in which each offers different elements to surprise and excite us on the journey.

The challenge is to understand what each is doing. A common urge when preaching or studying the gospels is to merge them together. This is often called harmonizing the gospels – and there is a place for that, of course. For example, we might want to identify as accurately as possible Jesus's hour-by-hour movements in the last week of his life. However, the problem with doing that is that we miss out on the great views that each separate journey gives us. God gave us *four* gospels for a reason!

So make every effort to understand how each gospel writer individually tells the story, paying special attention to any differences of perspective, however slight. Resist the temptation to rush to Matthew's account of an event while studying and preaching Luke (even if Matthew's is the better known). I want to hear more about Luke's account (*especially* if it is less familiar).

Before working through the gospels in turn, here is a roadmap or summary of the distinctives of each gospel.

- **Matthew**: Jesus is presented as the fulfilment and personification of Jewish old covenant hope. Just as Moses gave the law on Mount Sinai and is the author of the five books of the Pentateuch, so Jesus proclaims from a mountain the shape of the new covenant lifestyle (the first of five teaching blocks).
- **Mark**: Mark is like a film director, constantly pushing the action forward from miracle to conversation to teaching opportunity. There are unsettling features (such as Jesus's insistence on people keeping his identity secret for a time) – but everything points to two key aspects of the gospel: who Jesus is and what he has come to do.
- **Luke**: We really are taken on a journey by Luke – a fact that only becomes apparent when his gospel is placed alongside its sequel, the book of Acts. Acts makes it clear that while Jesus's life's work

was completed at the cross, that is just the beginning of the global kingdom story. This is a kingdom with a difference though: it welcomes and gives a special place to the world's rejects, outsiders and the vulnerable. This has always been God's plan for his world.

- **John**: John's approach is slower and more reflective than that of the Synoptic Gospels, but John's presentation of Jesus is no less authentic than theirs. It appears repetitive, but only at a superficial level. Jesus's "signs" point to his identity and gift of life for all his followers, as we see him from slightly different angles. The cumulative effect is the Bible's most breathtaking statement of Jesus's divine nature and mission of grace.

1. One by One: Heading Up *and* Down

Rivers flow down from higher ground towards the sea. That is the natural effect of gravity, and it makes travelling downstream fairly effortless. Modern roads, on the other hand, are less dependent on the terrain, and can be constructed to go up hills and over, under, or even through, obstacles in their way.

This image can actually help us distinguish between the two approaches to introducing Jesus's identity and mission (or to use the technical term, Christology).

- The river going *downhill*: John's Gospel – a Christology from above
- The roads going *uphill*: the Synoptic Gospels – a Christology from below

This difference is obvious the moment each of the gospels is opened.

John launches into the highest description of Jesus possible from the very first verse. He is the Word, who "was with God," and "was God" from the beginning (John 1:1). In other words, John does not build a case for believing in Jesus's divinity – he merely proclaims it. The evidence will come as his book goes on. The reader is therefore given a perspective on Jesus that his contemporaries, and even his family, did not have to begin with.

By contrast, the Synoptics start at ground level. They believe the same things as John, of course, but they allow the evidence to build up. This puts us in the shoes of the first believers as they encounter someone who seems to be a man no different from us . . . until he starts doing and saying strange things that point to something more.

This explains the repeated question, "who is this that can . . ." speak with such authority, or command the wind and waves, or cast out demons. It also explains why in Mark, we must wait eight chapters for Peter to say "you are the Messiah" (Mark 8:29), whereas John has Andrew say, "We have found the Messiah" almost immediately (John 1:41). This is not a contradiction – merely an illustration of different writers' purposes.

We have already given some thought to Mark's gospel in the previous chapter. We will now work through the others.

JOHN: Flowing downstream with the one Jesus loved

 John opens his book with a Prologue that contains some of the most breathtaking words ever written (John 1:1–18). The first oddity to strike us as we read it is the initial anonymity of "the Word." Of course, it is not hard to guess that he is Jesus, especially because of how the book continues. It is still strange that the Prologue does not mention him by name, nor is the title "Word" ever repeated after 1:18.

While books have been written about those brief paragraphs, here it is enough to say that all the big themes of the gospel at least get hinted at, and some are explicitly flagged. Here are just a few of them.

- Just as words reveal the mind of the person speaking them, so the Word reveals God. But this Word is more than just a source of revelation – he is the Creator of the universe (1:1–4).
- John the Baptist prepares for the Word by calling people to put their trust in the Word (1:5–8).
- Despite his identity, many people reject the Word. But some trust him and receive life (1:9–13).

Then comes the most staggering paragraph of all. There is only space to focus on its opening and closing lines, verses 14 and 18.

> The Word became flesh and made his dwelling among us. We have seen his glory, the glory of the one and only Son, who came from the Father, full of grace and truth . . .

> No one has ever seen God, but the one and only Son, who is himself God and is in the closest relationship with the Father, has made him known.

As we should expect by now, these verses are soaked in the Old Testament, although it is not perhaps immediately clear where we should turn for help in understanding them. The biggest clue comes from the combined imagery of the invisible God and his glory being made visible.

Those well versed in the Scriptures will recall Moses's request to be shown God's glory only to be told "no one may see my face and live" (Exod 33:18–20). So Moses was given no more than a glimpse of God's "back" from a cleft in the rock. The book of Exodus, in which this event takes place, then closes with the filling of the tabernacle with God's glory. Even Moses was then barred from entering it (Exod 40:34–38).

Now return to John. We are told that the Word "made his dwelling among us" – but John's expression here is a strange one. His phrase could also be translated as "tabernacled among us." Does this help you to see what he is up to?

He is insisting that the Word does more than reveal God. He *is* God – that much is clear from the allusion to Exodus. But this time, far from keeping his glory hidden, he displays it for all to see. As John says in 1:18, "he has made him known." What was invisible is now visible.

So from the start, John's Christology is bold and breathtaking. He really does start as high as he can get. Everything that follows fleshes this out in more detail. What makes it all the more astonishing is that John may have known Jesus better than anyone else (apart from his family, that is). He seems to be pointing to himself when he refers to "the disciple whom Jesus loved" (John 13:23; 19:26; 21:7). He was with Jesus in all the normal experiences of daily life – and yet he could *still* write these statements.

Take a sheet of paper and divide it into two columns.

Read John 1:1–18 and note down key images and ideas in the left-hand column.

Now read through the whole of John's Gospel. In the right-hand column, note down the verses where these images are developed or alluded to.

John's spiral staircase

After reading through the whole gospel, it is clear that John often repeats his big themes. But this does not make him dull. Each time he returns to a theme, he adds a subtly different element to it, so that there is a cumulative effect.

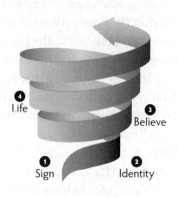

This is why some liken John's way of thinking to a spiral staircase. We can see this by tracing the four key steps mentioned in his book's purpose (from the last chapter) in the rest of the book.

1. Signs to Jesus		2. Identity of Jesus		3. Trust in Jesus		4. Life from Jesus
	➡		➡		➡	

We can start with the first two. Several of the signs in the gospel correspond to Jesus's most famous identity sayings, the "I AM" statements. These are significant in themselves because they allude to God's Old Testament name, Yahweh (which means "I am who I am" – Exod 3:14).

But even when they do not refer to that name, each of the signs still reveals something about Jesus's identity.

The Seven Signs		The Seven "I AM"s	
Turns water into wine	2:1–11		
Heals official's son	4:43–54		
Heals at pool of Bethesda	5:1–15		
Feeds the 5,000	**6:1–15**	**I AM the Bread of Life**	**6:35**
Walks on water	6:16–21		
		[. . . before Abraham was born I AM.	*8:58]*
Heals man born blind	**9:1–41**	**I AM the Light of World**	**8:12; 9:5**
		I AM the Gate for the Sheep/	10:7
		I AM the Good Shepherd	10:11
Raises Lazarus from the dead	**11:1–44**	**I AM the Resurrection and the Life**	**11:25**
		I AM the Way, the Truth the Life	14:6
		I AM the True Vine	15:1

Then compare the three signs directly linked to an I AM saying to John's purpose statement.

Sign	Identity	Trust	Life
Feeds the 5,000	I am the Bread of Life	whoever comes to me . . . believes in me (6:35)	will never go hungry . . . will have eternal life (6:35–40)
Heals man born blind	I am the Light of the World	whoever follows me (8:12)	will never walk in darkness, will have the light of life (8:12)
Raises Lazarus from the dead	I am the resurrection and the life	the one who believes in me . . . whoever lives by believing (11:25–26)	will live, even though he die . . . will never die. (11:25–26)

Even though John repeats the pattern, it does not feel repetitive but cumulative. We feel we are learning more about following Jesus as we read more, climbing the spiralling stairs to a greater appreciation of him.

John's "second book"

All four gospel writers describe the majority of Jesus's miracles in the earlier stages of his ministry. The interesting aspect of John's account is that there are no signs at all after his most spectacular sign, the raising of Lazarus. Even in the first half of the book, there are only a few signs accompanied by long teaching sections.

There is even more extended teaching in the book's second half – after a short transition section. That section includes the meeting of the Sanhedrin at which the religious leaders start plotting to arrest and kill Jesus. During the course of this discussion, the chief priest Caiaphas stuns his colleagues and John's readers alike.

> Then one of them, named Caiaphas, who was high priest that year, spoke up, "You know nothing at all! You do not realise that it is better for you that one man die for the people than that the whole nation perish." (John 11:49–50)

John loves the ambiguous irony of thoughts like that. He spells out its gospel significance explicitly in 11:51–53 – but of course Caiaphas was thinking only of the politics. He felt that killing Jesus would keep the Romans quiet. Again and again, John deliberately uses images or ideas that have more than one meaning. For example, notice how often he uses the image of Jesus being "lifted up" (John 3:14; 8:28; 12:32–34). Jesus could be referring to his being lifted up on the cross, his resurrection ("lifting up" to new life) and even his ascension ("lifted up" to heaven).

The transition also includes Mary of Bethany pouring some expensive perfume on Jesus, an act which he interprets as a burial anointing (12:1–7). It is a shocking explanation, but it fits with what happens next: his triumphal entry into Jerusalem (12:12–19) and the announcement of his imminent death and the division he brings (12:20–50).

After this transition, we return to the slower pace of extended teaching. This time, however, it all takes place during those intense hours with the disciples in the Upper Room. They will be helped to understand what is just about to happen, and how they will survive after he has left them (both by dying on the cross, and at his ascension). There is nothing quite like this much-loved section in the rest of the Bible.

It is for this reason that interpreters have traditionally divided John's Gospel into two "books":

1:1–18	Prologue: The Word was God
1:19–11:44	Book 1: The book of Jesus's signs
11:45–12:50	Transition: Jesus prepares the world for his death
13:1–19:42	Book 2: The book of Jesus's suffering
20:1–21:25	Epilogue: Jesus is alive!

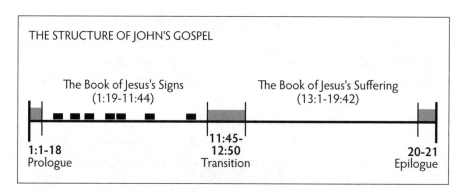

THE STRUCTURE OF JOHN'S GOSPEL

The Book of Jesus's Signs (1:19-11:44)

The Book of Jesus's Suffering (13:1-19:42)

1:1-18 Prologue

11:45-12:50 Transition

20-21 Epilogue

Of course, this is not the only way of dividing up the book – but the exercise of trying to discern how a Bible book is structured is always helpful, since it forces us to work out what the author is doing.

Some tips for preaching from John

What follows is by no means an exhaustive list, but merely a few pointers to consider when preaching a series on John's Gospel.[1]

- **Know where you are**: We need to be aware of where we are in whatever biblical book we are preaching on – but in a book like John, which has such distinct sections, this awareness is crucial. As you handle your specific passage, be sensitive to how much John expects his readers to know already – and even more significantly, what they do not yet know.

- **Big Passages**: It is not usually possible to preach on small passages from John. He does not go in for sequences of short bursts of action of the type found in the Synoptic Gospels. So to do justice to John's account of the miraculous feeding of the 5,000, we would normally have to include the accompanying "I Am" teaching as well (John 6:25–59). But it is also obvious that this teaching forms a sandwich around the miracle of Jesus's walking on water. Because this combination of signs reinforces the link to Exodus link, it would be difficult to miss that out – Jesus is clearly teaching his disciples that he is actually Israel's promise-making God, Yahweh. Yet fifty-nine verses is an enormous passage for one sermon! The challenge is to find a way to draw out the big ideas without getting stuck in all the details.

- **Avoid Lazy Repetition**: The challenge of a sermon series on John (especially when working through his Book of Signs) is to build in variety. Otherwise, we can revert to the four-point structure of John's purpose statement in every sermon. Not only is that unnecessarily repetitive (and therefore boringly predictable), it ignores the cumulative effect of each added angle on Jesus's identity. So perhaps it is wise to focus on the four-point structure in the first *Sign–"I Am"* sermon – and then pick out the ways in which subsequent passages add to it.

---

1. You may have noticed that I often refer to preaching a series of sermons. If you want to know more about how to organize such a series, please see my notes in Appendix 2.

MATTHEW: Tracking Israel's historic journey

 We suggested in the previous chapter that Matthew is especially concerned with growing disciples of Jesus, that is people who would learn from (Matt 28:18–20). If this is the case, we would expect a theme of teaching and discipleship to run through his whole book.

Jesus is the new Moses

Who is the most famous teacher of Israel? Moses must be a strong contender for that title. On Mount Sinai, he taught the people the law of Yahweh. So it is hardly surprising that Jesus follows in his footsteps and delivers the first long passage of teaching in Matthew's gospel on a mountain. The Sermon on the Mount (Matt 5–7) begins with the Beatitudes (5:3–12) and follows them with teaching on discipleship. That sermon has been justly praised in many different cultures in ways that echo the views of the third US president, Thomas Jefferson. Despite rejecting Trinitarian Christianity, he described the Sermon on the Mount as "the most sublime and benevolent code of morals which has ever been offered."

But Jesus is not primarily offering a code of conduct for all to adopt – although the challenges are astonishing. After all, he says that the entry requirement for God's kingdom is righteousness that exceeds that of the Pharisees! (5:20). Their problem was not the seriousness with which they took righteousness, but their preoccupation with its outward appearance.

Rather, in the sermon, Jesus makes extraordinary claims about himself. For example, he repeatedly contrasts other interpretations of Old Testament law ("You have heard that it was said . . ." is repeated five times in Matthew 5) with his own ("But I tell you . . ." comes six times).

It is important to recognise that Jesus never contradicts the law. He is adamant in 5:17–18 that he is fulfilling it and is not abolishing Old Testament ethics at all. He is simply rejecting the Jewish leaders' interpretation and applications of it. To put it another way, it is easy for most of us to obey the letter of the law against murder. A Pharisee would easily be able to include that on the list of sins he had not committed. But the spirit behind the law is not so straightforward. As Jesus put it, "anyone who is angry with a brother or sister," is breaking the essence of the law (5:23).

The Pharisees' arrogance and religious hypocrisy are Jesus's frequent targets in Matthew, and especially in the Sermon on the Mount (6:2, 5, 16). Study these passages to see how this theme is developed in the book:

- Matthew 15:1–20
- Matthew 22:15–22
- Matthew 23

Matthew concludes the Sermon on the Mount with a statement about the crowd's reaction to Jesus's authority, rather than about any resolutions they might have made to live out his teaching:

> When Jesus had finished saying these things, the crowds were amazed at his teaching, because he taught as one who had authority, and not as their teachers of the law. (Matt 7:28–29)

If we read through the rest of Matthew carefully, we will notice that simple phrase "when Jesus had finished" in 7:28 returns four more times (11:1; 13:53; 19:1; then 26:1, which inserts the word "all"). This may seem an insignificant point, and yet in the grand scheme of Matthew's book, it can hardly be accidental. He uses this phrase to mark five blocks of teaching that Jesus gives (either to crowds or to his disciples). The fact that there are five blocks of teaching would have held special significance for Jewish believers, because their Scriptures open with the Pentateuch, the five books of Moses.

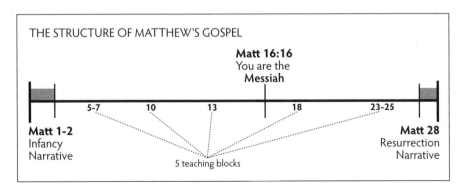

THE STRUCTURE OF MATTHEW'S GOSPEL

Matt 16:16
You are the
Messiah

5-7   10   13   18   23-25

Matt 1-2
Infancy
Narrative

Matt 28
Resurrection
Narrative

5 teaching blocks

So even in the structuring of his gospel, Matthew is making claims about Jesus!

When we see these teaching blocks in the context of the whole book (see the diagram above), it is immediately clear that Matthew does not make Peter's confession of Christ (Matt 16:16) as central to the structure of his gospel as it is in Mark's gospel.

Jesus fulfils the Old Testament story

Given Matthew's comparison of Jesus and Moses, it should come as no surprise that Matthew is regarded as the most Jewish of the four gospels. This point is clear from his opening chapters, for example, which clearly link the New Testament with the Old by means of Jesus's family tree. Matthew is a "big picture" thinker, and he wants us to see Jesus in context.[2]

If given the task of telling Jesus's story, few of us would start with a genealogy – we tend to find them far too dull! But Matthew's genealogy has several fascinating features, if we had but eyes to see them.

For one thing, this genealogy (and its parallel passage in Luke 3) are the last of the Bible's many genealogies. This is no accident. After Jesus, there was no longer any need for them. He is the goal of this history. Everything leads up to him.

Matthew opens Jesus's family tree with Abraham. He then carefully selects the individuals he includes, so as to break the genealogy into three distinct blocks of fourteen:

- Abraham to King David (1:1–6)
- King David to the Babylonian Exile (1:6–22)
- After Babylon to Jesus (1:13–16)

The record proves that Jesus has impeccable Jewish and royal credentials. Or so it seems! But take a closer look and Matthew has surprises in store. Most striking is the mention of four mothers, each from some of Israel's darker moments:

- **Tamar**: The Canaanite daughter-in-law of Judah, who slept with her thinking she was a prostitute. She is the mother of Perez (1:3; Gen 38).
- **Rahab**: The Canaanite resident of Jericho actually was a prostitute, but she saved the lives of Joshua's spies. She is the mother of Boaz (1:5; Josh 2; 6:22–25).
- **Ruth**: The Moabite daughter-in-law of Naomi, who, in desperation approaches (and perhaps even seduces) Boaz in order to ask for his protection. She is the mother of Obed (1:5; Ruth 1–4).

---

2. This section is adapted from Chris Wright's *Sweeter than Honey*.

- **Uriah's wife**: The strangest inclusion in the genealogy is Bathsheba, whom Matthew does not even name. She was presumably a Hittite (like her first husband Uriah), but King David's lust for her led to their adultery and Uriah's murder. She was the mother of King Solomon (1:6; 2 Sam 11).

They are quite a quartet! All four are Gentile, all four are associated with sexual irregularities, and all four are grandmothers of Jesus.

Matthew ingeniously uses his genealogy to pick up where the Old Testament left off and to remind us that Israel's history was not one of perfect righteousness. This is the dysfunctional family Jesus was born into. After all, even the name "Israel" is one that God graciously gave to Jacob after his divine wrestling match – as a replacement for his original name, Jacob, which means "deceiver."

So the genealogy hints at God's amazing plan: there is hope for sinners (even sexual sinners) and Gentiles because there always has been.

Another way that Matthew shows that Jesus fulfils the Old Testament is by quoting the Old Testament prophets. His contemporaries would have been well aware of what they had said and what was expected. That is why Matthew uses the weighty word, "fulfilled." So despite *all* appearances, this baby is very significant indeed.

 Follow up the five Old Testament quotations which Matthew tells us are fulfilled through Jesus.

- Matthew 1:23 ⇐ Isaiah 7:14
- Matthew 2:5–6 ⇐ Micah 5:2
- Matthew 2:15 ⇐ Hosea 11:1
- Matthew 2:17–18 ⇐ Jeremiah 31:15
- Matthew 2:23 ⇐ General theme in Old Testament prophets?

We could say then that Malachi is not really the end of the Old Testament story. In fact, reading the Old Testament without the New is like reading a detective novel without discovering the identity of the murderer! Everything is leading up to that point. Without the New Testament, we would never know the story's climax. But without the Old, we would never understand who Jesus is and why he came.

Jesus accepts an Old Testament identity and mission (Matt 3–4)

It is only in chapter 3 that Matthew's story links up with the start of Mark's story. However, Matthew adds fascinating details not found in Mark, particularly in his account of Jesus's desert temptation.

Matthew 3 is, however, a chapter that raises many questions. For example, if Jesus is without sin, why does he need to be baptized? John the Baptist made it very clear that he baptized people as a sign of their repentance (3:11). So even he is unsure about what to do when it comes to baptizing his cousin (3:14). But Jesus insists on being baptized, saying that he needs to do this to "fulfil righteousness" (3:15). That is a strange phrase, but it rings bells. We have already noticed that fulfilment is important to the Jewish Matthew. If you have read the whole gospel, you will know that righteousness is one of the themes repeated throughout the book.

Remember what we said about looking at the wider context for clues? We will find that Matthew 4 helps us to answer some of the questions raised in chapter 3.

While Mark dealt with Jesus's temptation in just two verses, Matthew goes into great detail (presumably on the basis of what Jesus later shared with his disciples). We learn that Jesus responds to Satan with three quotations. The surprise when following up the quotations (in Matt 4:4, 7, and 10) is that they all come from the book of Deuteronomy, and from only two chapters of that book. Here are the passages that he quotes:

> When the LORD your God brings you into the land he swore to your fathers . . . be careful that you do not forget the LORD, who brought you out of Egypt, out of the land of slavery . . . Fear the LORD your God, serve him only and take your oaths in his name. Do not follow other gods, the gods of the peoples around you; . . . Do not put the LORD your God to the test as you did at Massah. (Deut 6:10–16)

> He humbled you, causing you to hunger and then feeding you with manna, which neither you nor your ancestors had known, to teach you that man does not live on bread alone but on every word that comes from the mouth of the LORD. (Deut 8:3)

Why did he choose these passages?

The original context is crucial here. Moses was preaching to the next generation of Israelites, the people Joshua would lead into the promised land.

Moses's own generation had failed to be faithful to God, so he warns them the next generation not to follow in their parents' footsteps.

The combination of Jesus's "baptism for repentance" and his obedience to God's law (especially as it relates to faithfulness to God in the desert) suddenly gives us an answer to our question. Matthew is making the point that Jesus has come as the embodiment of Israel, the one who will finally do what they were always meant to do, but failed to do. Jesus is therefore the true Israel.

What do we see Jesus doing next? Preaching about God's kingdom and calling twelve disciples (4:12–22). Twelve disciples for twelve tribes in the new Israel. So, yet again, the Old Testament lays the template for Jesus's mission.

LUKE: Tracing the geography of the gospel

 We noticed in the previous chapter that Luke writes his gospel to help people like Theophilus who are dealing with doubts and insecurities. Then he carries on, and does more of the same in his second book, the book of Acts. So all the principles we have discussed for handling the gospels apply equally to Luke's second volume. How can we be sure of this? Well look at the opening verses of Acts:

In my former book, Theophilus, I wrote about all that Jesus began to do and to teach until the day he was taken up to heaven, after giving instructions through the Holy Spirit to the apostles he had chosen. (Acts 1:1–2)

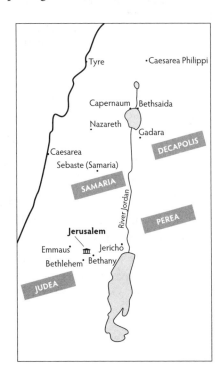

Clearly, this book follows on directly from where he left off at the end of his gospel. The implication is that Acts will narrate what Jesus continued "to do and teach" in the first years of the church. Luke's preoccupation is with the way the gospel moves out from Jerusalem.

When we consider how Luke constructs both books, we can see that the geographical location of each incident is significant for him. For

Mark, the single most important turning point in his gospel is Peter's public confession of Jesus's identity. The same event is mentioned in Luke 9:20, not even a third of the way through the gospel. He omits to tell us its location (Mark 8:27 informs us it happened in Caesarea Philippi), presumably because *all* the events of 4:14–9:50 take place in the racially diverse area around Lake Galilee.

This may seem insignificant by itself. But in Luke 9:51, the geographical focus begins to shift with these momentous words:

> As the time approached for him to be taken up to heaven, Jesus resolutely set out for Jerusalem. (Luke 9:51)

Jesus is heading into the heart of the opposition, the city which by rights should be his. If we then track the geographical focus of the gospel, the surprise is that the book's structure immediately emerges.

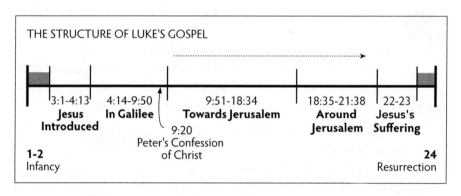

In Acts, we find that Jesus's commission to the disciples follows a similar structure, which we see worked out as the book continues.

> But you will receive power when the Holy Spirit comes on you; and you will be my witnesses in Jerusalem, and in all Judea and Samaria, and to the ends of the earth. (Acts 1:8)

So Luke has clearly mapped out both books together. While his gospel relentlessly moves towards Jerusalem where Jesus will suffer, the book of Acts sees Jesus's message spread far and wide, through persecution of the church and the resolve of the disciples. We can see how the geographical elements in the two books parallel each other if we look at the following diagram.

What are we to make of this?

It seems that the spread of the gospel was an issue that was very close to Luke's heart. He had been a trusted member of Paul's team and so knew first-hand about the challenges of mission in the Gentile world. But it probably was even more personal than that. He himself was a Gentile (unique among all the New Testament writers). He was also a doctor (Col 4:14), which almost certainly means that he had been a slave, like most first-century doctors in the Roman world. It is no wonder that one of his major preoccupations is Jesus's revolutionary welcome to all those who fell outside the old covenant.

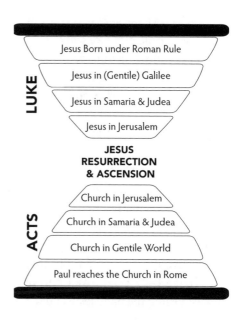

Jesus the man like us and for us

Unlike Matthew and Mark, Luke tends to emphasize Jesus's humanity rather than his divinity (which is not to suggest he ever denies his divinity – far from it!). He seldom uses titles like "Messiah" and "Son of God." Instead, Luke presents Jesus as someone who is prayerfully compassionate and sensitive to everyone around him, especially if they are the kinds of people that the world ignores. A good case could be made for his words to Zacchaeus being a motto verse for the whole book:

For the Son of Man came to seek and to save the lost. (Luke 19:10)

"The Son of Man" is the person Daniel saw in his terrifying vision of a human being who is granted absolute power by God himself (Dan 7:13–14). But what does this Son of Man do with this power? He pours it out in compassion and grace for the sake of those that the world despises, for those who have lost their way. He is a rescuer of the helpless. Luke describes Jesus as Saviour or the one who brings salvation eight times in his gospel, and nine times in Acts – but intriguingly that title is never used in either Matthew or Mark.

Look at Luke's account of how Jesus refers to or treats the
following outsiders:
- **Samaritans**: 9:52; 10:25–37; 17:11–19
- **Tax collectors and 'sinners'**: 5:30; 7:34; 15:1;
  18:9–14; 19:1–10
- **The poor**: 4:18; 6:20 (contrast with Matthew 5:3);
  14:7–24; 16:19–31

The group that stands out from all the others, though, is women. From the outset, Luke regularly and deliberately shows how important they were to Jesus, despite their lower status in first-century society. So whereas Matthew's birth stories tell the story from Joseph's perspective (Matt 1–2), Luke focuses on the perspective of two women: Elizabeth, mother of John, and Mary, mother of Jesus (Luke 1–2). Where Matthew reports that impressive star-followers from the east visited the baby Jesus, Luke reports on the visit of despised shepherds. He deliberately highlights the prophetic prayers of Mary and Anna alongside those of Zechariah and Simeon.

This pattern continues throughout the book. Women are as likely to feature in his parables as men (13:18–21; 15:3–10), and on different Sabbaths, a man and a woman are healed (13:10–17; 14:1–6). While attending a banquet at a Pharisee's house, Jesus shows honour and respect to a woman with a dubious reputation (7:36–50). He is countercultural in his loving acceptance of Mary's devotion to him (10:38–42).

So whenever we preach on episodes that feature these outsiders, it is vital to connect them to the wider theme of the book. Being faithful to Luke means being sensitive to his themes.

Jesus and the Spirit of joy

Luke highlights the work of the Holy Spirit more than any of the other evangelists – even though Jesus teaches extensively about him in John 14–16 and is led into his desert temptations by the Spirit in Matthew 4:1 and Mark 1:12.

In the book of Acts, of course, people are often filled with the Spirit, which leads to bold proclamation of the good news (for example, Acts 2:4; 4:31). But the same thing happens in Luke (1:15, 41, 67). The Spirit brings confidence and joy (which is precisely why Luke wrote his books for Theophilus). He even brings joy to Jesus! (Luke 10:21). We are presumably then to see the Spirit at work whenever joy results (as it does on twelve separate occasions in Luke, and five times in Acts).

Jesus the captivating storyteller

Perhaps the feature of Jesus's teaching that stands out most in Luke is his frequent use of parables. Both Matthew and Mark include some parables, and the closest that John gets to them is his inclusion of Jesus's teaching about his being the Good Shepherd (John 10:11–16) and the Vine (John 15:1–7). But Luke is the one who specialises in parables. He has the same number as Matthew and Mark combined. (Because parables have some special characteristics that may affect how we preach them, the whole of the next section of this book will be dedicated to preaching them well.)

2. From Then to Now: Preaching on the Gospels

So far, we have focused on each gospel individually. Now it is time to make some comments that apply to sermons on any part of any of the gospels.

In our preparation, we must constantly ask three related but distinct questions. Forget one of them, and our understanding of the passage could well be flawed and skewed. Here are the first two questions:

- The historical question: **Why does Jesus do/say this?**
- The literary question: **Why does the author include this episode, at this point in his book?**

If we ask only the historical question without also asking the literary question, we may fail to do justice to what happened by not noticing what the author of the gospel is doing at that point. If we ask only the literary question without also asking the historical question, we may fall into the trap of assuming that the message is not rooted in history, but is merely something that the author made up.

Only after answering those two questions can be begin to approach the third question.

- The application question: **What does this mean for us today?**

If we ask only the first two questions and ignore the application question, we are effectively giving a lecture that does not speak into the lives of our hearers with the Bible's challenges or comfort.

As I said earlier, in some ways, the gospels are the hardest part of the Bible to preach well. The gospels can feel stale for long-standing Christians, who have read the stories many, many times. So how do we preach in a way that preserves the shock value or subversive nature of Jesus's teaching and ministry? How do we recapture the element of surprise in a story whose end we know well?

The biggest challenge, though, is surely the issue of applying the gospel stories to ordinary lives today. For example, what are we to make of this promise from Jesus's teaching the night before his execution?

> Very truly I tell you, whoever believes in me will do the works I have been doing, and they will do even greater things than these, because I am going to the Father. (John 14:12)

Does this mean we can all expect to walk on water, feed thousands, and perform resurrections? Is our inability to do these things simply a symptom of our lack of faith?[3]

Unfortunately, there is not the space to do justice to these issues in a small section. There are other books that deal with them in much greater depth.[4] However, here are several questions we should ask of every gospel passage before we make our application one of naive imitation.

Is this truly good news?

We have already seen that all four gospels are proclaiming a message. So in a sense they have already done the application work for us. However, it is not quite as simple as that. The danger with any sermon application is that we can end up completely undermining the gospel by mistake.

What is it that radically sets the Christian message apart from all others? The great British writer C. S. Lewis once found himself walking into a comparative religion conference, which had drawn scholars from around the world together. The discussion turned to what, if anything, was Christianity's unique contribution to the world. Lewis is reported to have replied, "Oh, that's easy! It's grace!" Eventually the delegates agreed with him. Every religion sets out rules and paths to follow in order to prove or gain merit, except the gospel of Jesus. Only Jesus "dares to make God's love unconditional."[5]

---

3. D. A. Carson in his *Pillar Commentary on John* (Nottingham: Apollos, 1991) helpfully notes that the reason the deeds done by the disciples will be greater is because they occur after Jesus's death, resurrection, and ascension. This means that they are done during the next big stage in God's purposes, a time of clarity and global proclamation. He is not making a crude contrast of quantity (in that the disciples will do far more, because there are more of them) nor quality (as if the disciples can do something greater than raising Lazarus from the dead).

4. For example: Chris Green, *Cutting to the Heart: Applying the Bible in Teaching and Preaching* (Leicester: IVP, 2015) and Murray Cahill, *The Heart Is the Target: Preaching Practical Application from Every Text* (Phillipsburg, NJ: P & R, 2014).

5. Philip Yancey, *What's So Amazing about Grace* (Grand Rapids: Zondervan, 1997), 45.

This truth is the great motivator for Christian preachers. This is precisely what makes it good news. In Luke's words, God in Christ has "come to seek and save the lost." A life for Christ is therefore always lived in dependent gratitude, and never in anxious striving.

Yet when it comes to sermon applications, we can fatally undermine that truth. We may have preached about God's grace with passion and conviction, only to conclude with a list of rules or sins. And those are the things our hearers take away. Suddenly our news is not that good at all. In fact it is bad. It makes God's love conditional on our churchgoing, giving, praying, evangelizing, or Bible reading. Please don't misunderstand me. These are all good things. But they can only be responses to gospel security. All Christian ethics flows out of the good news.

So we must ask of all our applications, is it actually *good* news? Does it reflect the grace of God or undermine it?

This does not mean there will never be difficult things to say. A sermon on, say, Mark 7:1–23 will be challenging and even disturbing. It is a shock to hear Jesus speak of the human heart in such negative terms. But the shock is like the shock of receiving a cancer diagnosis. It is still important to hear the truth (however hard), because only then can we be open to receiving the right treatment. In that context, we could even say that this diagnosis is essential to the goodness of the news.

But for whom is it good news? We sometimes preach as if there are only two types of people listening to our sermons: sinners and Christians, or churched and unchurched. Timothy Keller helpfully points out that there are actually always three types of sermon hearers.[6] He illustrates his point from Jesus's parable of the Father with Two Sons (or the Prodigal Son as it is usually called), arguing that in this parable, *both* sons sin against their father, although in different ways (Luke 15:11–32).

Both sons live for their inheritance, rather than enjoying a relationship with their father. The key difference lies in how patient they are. The younger son wants his inheritance now. He then squanders it all, ending up in a pigsty (a horrific thought for any Jew). The older son is prepared to wait – but assumes he must earn his inheritance by working hard on the property that will one day be his. No wonder he resents his brother's free pass when he finally returns. After all, the money spent to pay for the party will technically be his, since his brother's inheritance has already been spent (15:29–30). But it is only the

---

6. Timothy Keller, *The Prodigal God* (London: Hodder & Stoughton, 2009).

younger son who recognizes what he deserves. He recognizes that he has sinned against his father, and that he is only worthy of being a house slave (15:19).

These two brothers represent the radically different ways we can sin against God.

- Younger Brother: **The rebellious sinner**, who lives the lifestyle of the street and has little time for religion or God. Such people are easily identifiable from their outrageous and at times selfish behaviour. This is just the kind of person who is resented and scorned by older brothers.

- Older Brother: **The religious sinner**, who lives a respectable life and is often seen doing religious activities. He or she would never be caught doing anything outwardly immoral or out of control. But such people want religion on their own terms, and see it as designed to build up moral credits in a kind of spiritual bank account.

Both lifestyles are wrong, for neither has God at its centre.

When preaching to a congregation, we must assume that both types are present (although usually the "older brothers" will outnumber their "younger brothers"). This means that any application that offers a list of rules and regulations might serve to compound the problem. Younger brothers will think they could never belong in this Christian community; they are never going to be good enough. Older brothers will think they are on the right track, and feel complacent and smug. Both need to understand that none of us can ever be good enough for God (a truth that will certainly be offensive for older brothers). Both need to understand that God still loves them, despite this.

The twist for preachers, though, is that there is a third type of person in a church audience.

- A Christian Brother: **The rescued sinner** who understands God's grace and how dependent we are on Christ for all that we hope for. They know that morality is not a currency with which to earn God's favour, but a language in which we respond to God's favour. For rescued sinners, sermon applications are never a cause of anxiety or imposing impossible burdens; rather, they offer but joyful opportunities to channel our love for God.

We must consider how each group will hear our applications, and direct our good news to each accordingly.

How will the news in Mark 7:1–23 be good for these types of hearer?
- The rebellious sinner
- The religious sinner
- The rescued sinner

Is this description or prescription?

In other words, does this passage simply describe what happened then, or does it prescribe what should happen now? Is it primarily for us to learn more about Jesus, or something else?

Take this incident, for example.

> Then Jesus told them to make all the people sit down in groups on the green grass. So they sat down in groups of hundreds and fifties. (Mark 6:39–40)

This comes during the account of the feeding of the 5,000. Does this mean that when the church meets, it should do so outside, and that people should sit on the grass not on furniture? Should we take it even further, and suggest that people should sit down in numerical groups? After all, that is how Jesus organised everybody, and we want to be faithful to him, don't we?

Of course, this is absurd. Mark presumably gives us these details to help us visualize this moment, and because it explains how the disciples knew the size of the crowd.

We should start by assuming that a passage is primarily descriptive, especially when it describes Jesus's activity. We should therefore always begin by asking what we learn about *him*. In the context in Mark, he is clearly overwhelmed by the sense that the people were vulnerable "like sheep without a shepherd" (Mark 6:34). This is an allusion to God's repeated complaint that Israel's leaders were failing to protect the flock of God's people (see, for example, Jer 10:21; 23:1–4; 50:6–7). God said that he would have to come himself to "gather the remnant of my flock" (Jer 23:1–4). As evidence that he is the one who spoke through Jeremiah, Jesus feeds the people in the desert in ways that only God could. There is clearly more than enough material here to preach about. A central application must be that people praise Jesus for who he is and what he came to achieve.

Earlier in the book, we noted that just because Jesus rose early in the morning to pray alone (Mark 1:35), we should not assume that this is an instruction to pray only in the morning. It was presumably a practical solution to his need to spend time with God. In context it also comes before a difficult decision: the need to focus on preaching despite the huge physical needs of the crowds (Mark 1:36–39).

Here are two more examples of Jesus seeking solitary places. How does the context help us to understand his reasons?

- **Walking on water**: Mark 6:46–47 in context of 6:30–56
- **A regular habit**: Luke 5:16 in context of 5:1–26

Is Jesus our model or our Saviour here?

Whenever we read stories of any kind, our natural instinct is to imagine ourselves within them. This is normal, and it is the primary reason that they engage us at the deepest levels. What's more, we tend to put ourselves in the hero's shoes, so that we are at the story's centre.

This is problematic when it comes to the gospels. There are times when Jesus is unique, when the disciples are unique, or when we think ourselves unique when we are not.

When Jesus is unique . . .

Consider these two famous verses.

> Then he called the crowd to him along with his disciples and said: "If anyone would come after me, he must deny himself and take up his cross and follow me." (Mark 8:34)

> For even the Son of Man did not come to be served, but to serve, and to give his life as a ransom for many. (Mark 10:45)

Yes, we are to model ourselves on Jesus, when it comes to the heart-attitude of service, whatever the cost. Taking up the cross is an act of immense courage because it means facing the scorn and cruelty of a world that doesn't care for the things of God. It cannot be done lightly – and at its heart is a willingness to serve, rather than be served, a desire to put God first over everything.

Yet, there is a big difference between us taking up our cross and Jesus taking up his. We model ourselves on his self-sacrifice. But that is where the comparisons must end. There is no sense in which we give our lives as a ransom. We can never deal with others' sin, let alone our own. His death was a unique event in world history (see 1 Pet 3:18).

So whenever we see Jesus at work in the gospels, we must start by asking what is unique about this moment, before we consider imitating it.

When the disciples are unique . . .

We're not in the same place as the disciples in the gospel accounts, so we cannot draw a direct line to them either. So notice their problem here:

> Jesus answered them, "Destroy this temple, and I will raise it again in three days." The Jews replied, "It has taken forty-six years to build this temple, and you are going to raise it in three days?" But the temple he had spoken of was his body. After he was raised from the dead, his disciples recalled what he had said. Then they believed the Scripture and the words that Jesus had spoken. (John 2:19–22)

The disciples lived at a unique moment in human history. Jesus was at work on earth. God's incarnation was a thrilling reality. But there was so much to understand still. They lived with Jesus before his death and resurrection, and struggled to keep up with him. As with this strange claim in John 2, Jesus was constantly sowing seeds that would not bear fruit until after his work on earth was done. It would only occur to them that the temple he was talking about was his body *after* the resurrection.

Or take this example:

> These twelve Jesus sent out with the following instructions: "Do not go among the Gentiles or enter any town of the Samaritans. Go rather to the lost sheep of Israel. As you go, preach this message: 'The kingdom of heaven is near.'" (Matt 10:5–7)

How should we apply this passage? Should we give up our day jobs and all save up for plane tickets to Tel Aviv in Israel as soon as possible?

Well, the context of Matthew's whole book should help us here. In the Great Commission of Matthew 28:18–20, Jesus is clear that his gospel is for the whole world. His disciples (who were the same people he addressed in Matthew 10) are to be at the forefront of this campaign. We can only assume therefore that this earlier passage has a more limited scope because it is part of Jesus's discipleship training programme.

It is clear then we cannot draw a direct line from the disciples' experience to ours.

When our mistakes are not unique . . .

One of the hallmarks of the gospels is how often the disciples come off negatively. New readers are often surprised by this, especially once they realise that these same individuals were the pioneering leaders of the early church. The gospel writers were not afraid to allow themselves to be shown up. Not when standing alongside our perfect Saviour. So, for example, Jesus is exasperated by the disciples' slowness from time to time, as here, after the second feeding miracle in Mark 8.

> Aware of their discussion, Jesus asked them: "Why are you talking about having no bread? Do you still not see or understand? Are your hearts hardened?" (Mark 8:17)

Presumably, it should have been obvious to them that Jesus was performing Exodus-type miracles to point to his true identity and purpose. But they don't get it. The disciples keep getting things wrong – and so do we! Even though we live after Jesus's death and resurrection.

Summary: Is it about doing, knowing or being?

One trend with sermon application is that we too easily reduce it to a narrow list of bullet points. When this happens, it invariably turns into a culture of burdensome legalism whereby believers are expected to pray more, give more, evangelize more, love more, turn up to church meetings more, and so on. It gets most absurd when you hear the fourth sermon in a row calling on believers to read their Bibles more, as if that was the most important thing that the Bible ever teaches!

But the Gospels present quite a specific problem. They simply can't be easily squeezed into such a crudely reduced list. In fact, the key application may not be something to do at all. Sometimes, the evangelist simply wants us to know something, or to believe something. Perhaps we need to reconfigure how we see ourselves in the light of the gospel. After all, isn't the wonder of a message of grace precisely the fact that we do not need to do *anything* to earn God's love; Christ has done everything that could be done to keep us secure in that love.

So here is a list of key application questions we can bring to our gospel passage:

- What is there to praise and thank God for in this passage?
- How does this passage correct our thinking about God, his nature or his plans? Or our thinking about our identity in Christ?
- What do we need to believe as a result of this passage?
- Is there anything we should stop or start doing as a result of this passage?
- Is there anything we need to say to someone as a result of this passage?

 Consider these passages. Are they primarily to teach us about Jesus's identity and mission on our behalf? And/or is there something we should imitate?

- **Jesus calls the disciples** (Luke 5:1–11)
- **Jesus heals a widow's son** (Luke 7:11–17)
- **Jesus raises Lazarus from the dead** (John 11:38–44)
- **Jesus washes the disciples' feet** (John 13:1–17)

6

Acts: Tracing Luke's Second Journey

In many ways, everything said so far about preaching the gospels is applicable to preaching from the book of Acts. This should come as no surprise since Luke was deliberately crafting a two-volume book. Just as he does in his gospel, Luke communicates theological truth through gripping storytelling. We should therefore pay attention to the same seven types of clue that we used for the gospel treasure hunt (see ch. 4).

Still, Acts has some notable characteristics that we should be aware of to ensure faithful handling of this important account of the church's earliest years.

1. Why Luke Focuses on Paul

Few Bible readers give a moment's thought to the strangeness of this book's title. We are too used to calling it the Acts of the Apostles. Yet that title is not strictly accurate. For Luke clearly focuses on Peter in the first few chapters, and then from Acts 7 onwards Saul the Pharisee (soon to be renamed Paul) gradually takes centre stage. After the account of the famous Council of Jerusalem in Acts 15, Peter drops out of the story altogether. But what of Thomas or Matthew or John, or even Matthias (Judas's replacement in Acts 1:26)? Many stories could have been told about each of them no doubt – but Luke is not concerned with them. His purpose in Acts is clearly different from providing a comprehensive account of what Jesus's disciples achieved after the ascension. So what might that be?

Luke's journeys

Luke introduced his gospel by informing Theophilus of his research, when he "carefully investigated everything from the beginning" (Luke 1:3). As Acts proceeds, we are given glimpses of this research, because every now and then he slips in the word "we." At various points, he is a member of Paul's mission team.

- Just after Paul receives his vision of the Macedonian man, we read "we got ready at once to leave for Macedonia" (Acts 16:10).
- Luke then seems to stay behind in Philippi as Paul's team move onto Thessalonica and then Athens (Acts 17).
- But he rejoins them in Acts 20:6, when the team passes through Philippi again. He then travels all the way to Jerusalem with Paul in Acts 21. This no doubt gave him the chance to visit the key places in Jesus's ministry, as well as interview some of the apostles.
- After Jerusalem, he drops out of the story again until he finally accompanies Paul to Rome at the start of Acts 27.

So an obvious answer to the question of why Luke focuses on Paul so much is that he knew him best – and was able to write about him on the basis of first-hand experience. But there must be more to it than this.

Paul's journeys

Yet again, it helps to consider the beginning and end of the book. Remember how it opens:

> In my former book, Theophilus, I wrote about all that Jesus began to do and to teach until the day he was taken up to heaven, after giving instructions through the Holy Spirit to the apostles he had chosen. (Acts 1:1–2)

As we noted before, Luke's description of his gospel here is telling "about all that Jesus *began to* do and to teach." The implication is that in this second volume, he will continue to tell the story of Jesus's activity on earth. Even though Jesus's ascension is the hinge between the two books (Luke 24:50–53; Acts 1:9–11), we are certainly not meant to conclude that he is not active. He reigns from heaven, bringing about his purposes through his church. That is why he gives instructions through the Holy Spirit to the apostles.

After the ascension, the disciples are told to wait for the church's global launch day.

But you will receive power when the Holy Spirit comes on you; and you will be my witnesses in Jerusalem, and in all Judea and Samaria, and to the ends of the earth. (Acts 1:8)

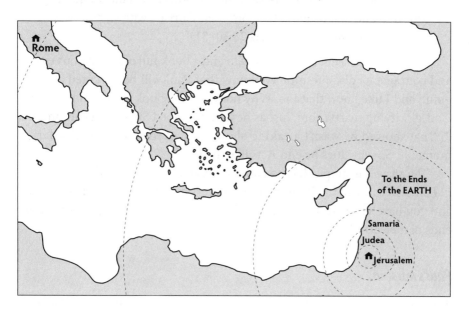

Just as Luke's gospel was driven by the magnetic pull of Jerusalem, the place of Jesus's execution, so Acts radiates out from Jerusalem. If you throw a pebble into a still pond, ripples will be created that flow out in a perfect circle in every direction. It is as if the gospel does the same thing once launched on the world, taken out in every direction from Jerusalem by the apostles and their teams. As we have seen before, Acts is structured around the key moments when the gospel breaks new ground.

- 2:1–12   The first conversions in **Jerusalem** at Pentecost

- 8:1–2   Persecution forces the disciples out of Jerusalem to **Judea** and **Samaria**

- 8:4–25   Ministry and Conversions in **Samaria** (8:14–17)

- 8:26–40   Philip leads an **Ethiopian** to Christ

- 10:1–11:18   Peter leads the **Roman** centurion, Cornelius, to Christ

Now consider the closing verses of the book.

> For two whole years Paul stayed there in his own rented house and welcomed all who came to see him. He proclaimed the kingdom of God and taught about the Lord Jesus Christ – with all boldness and without hindrance! (Acts 28:30–31)

Does that not seem a strange way to end a book full of miraculous events and courageous discipleship? We know that Paul will be executed at some point, and Luke knew that too. Why not close the book with a climactic but God-glorifying martyrdom, just as he had described Stephen's death in Acts 7? That showed he wasn't afraid to show some of the early church's darker moments. So why does he end Acts like this?

The answer is simple. It is no anti-climax at all – because Paul is preaching *in Rome*. Because of the Roman Empire's great might and extent, reach Rome and you have reached the world. In effect, Paul had opened up access to the ends of the earth for the gospel.

Paul's mission

The book's apparent anti-climax is not the only oddity. Another is the fact that Luke gives us three separate accounts of Paul's conversion.

- Acts 9:1–19   Luke's account of Paul's conversion on the Damascus Road
- Acts 22:1–21   Paul shares his testimony with the crowd in Jerusalem
- Acts 26:2–32   Paul shares his testimony with King Agrippa in Caesarea

Why does Luke include the full story each time? He could so easily have given a summary the second and third time. The answer is in fact related to the point we have just considered: his triumphant conclusion to the whole book. The threefold repetition of Paul's testimony gives Luke the chance to focus on Paul's momentous commission from Jesus himself. Each account gives a little more information than the previous one.

- Acts 9:5–6   "I am Jesus, whom you are persecuting," he replied. "Now get up and go into the city, and you will be told what you must do."

- Acts 22:21   Then the Lord said to me, "Go; I will send you far away to the Gentiles."

- Acts 26:16–18   "I am Jesus, whom you are persecuting," the Lord replied. "Now get up and stand on your feet. I have appeared to you to appoint you as a servant and as a witness of what you have seen and will see of me. I will rescue you from your own people and from the Gentiles. I am sending you to them to open their eyes and turn them from darkness to light, and from the power of Satan to God, so that they may receive forgiveness of sins and a place among those who are sanctified by faith in me."

Paul was different from the other apostles – he did not spend any time with Jesus during his earthly ministry. The closest he got was persecuting his people (and Jesus so closely identifies with his people that he regards persecution as a personal attack). But it was his mission that truly marked Paul out. For he had the unique gifts, of mind and character, to be able to pioneer outreach to the Gentile world. And it was that mission that was Luke's great concern for his second volume.

God's kingdom

Do you see why this makes Paul's preaching in Rome a suitable climax? God's kingdom really was extending to the ends of the earth – overcoming all ethnic, social, and religious boundaries – of which the greatest was the Gentile/Jewish divide. Centuries of separation were bound to make that difficult. After all, the division between Jews and Gentiles dated back to the start of the old covenant and God's own revealed call to the Israelites to be separate from the surrounding nations.

This explains why changing this caused such controversy among the first believers. They were predominantly Jewish. All those who were visiting Jerusalem for Pentecost in Acts 2 were Jewish people from all over the then-known world. But each time there was a conversion from a new group, the apostles were required to witness and verify that this really *was* God's work. Without that happening, there was no possibility of other believers accepting each development.

Into the Samaritan world

After Philip preached in Samaria, Peter and John (as the most senior apostles) were sent by the others in Jerusalem to investigate. Once they were convinced that the Lord was indeed at work, they prayed for these Samaritan believers to receive the Holy Spirit (Acts 8:14–17). This was clearly a significant moment in the history of God's kingdom – which is why Peter and John needed to be present.

Into the Gentile world

Philip's next adventure was to be carried away by God into the desert for an encounter with an African diplomat from the region then known as Ethiopia (probably modern Sudan). Not only was he Gentile, but he was also a eunuch – two significant problems to his acceptability before God in the old covenant. Deuteronomy 23:1 barred eunuchs from God's assembly.

Yet it is surely no coincidence that in God's providence he is reading Isaiah. Not only does this great book reveal the wonders of what Christ's death means – and thus giving Philip the perfect evangelistic opening – but it has a very particular relevance for this fascinating man. Just a few chapters after those that Philip explains, we find God offering real hope even for people like him.

> Let no foreigner who is bound to the LORD say, "The LORD will surely exclude me from his people." And let no eunuch complain, "I am only a dry tree."

> For this is what the LORD says: "To the eunuchs who keep my Sabbaths, who choose what pleases me and hold fast to my covenant –

> to them I will give within my temple and its walls a memorial and a name better than sons and daughters; I will give them an everlasting name that will endure forever." (Isa 56:3–5)

If an African eunuch can now be acceptable to God because of what Christ has achieved, then there is surely nobody in the world who is beyond the reach of his grace.

As if to prove the point, Luke's account immediately leaps to another miraculous encounter on the road – this time between Saul/Paul and the risen Lord Jesus. But the next Gentile conversion is the centurion Cornelius. Yet again, Peter is involved – but he takes some convincing. It would take an extraordinary God-given vision to change the habits, not just of his lifetime, but of his entire culture and religion.

God really was expanding the kingdom to include Gentiles. This is what Peter announced to Cornelius's household when he arrived:

> You are well aware that it is against our law for a Jew to associate with or visit a Gentile. But God has shown me that I should not call anyone impure or unclean. (Acts 10:28)

This was not the end of the controversy, however.

When the church in Antioch in Syria sent Barnabas and Paul out to preach on what is now known as the first missionary journey (Acts13:1–3), there were some in the Jerusalem church who were still uncomfortable. They insisted that Gentile converts had to adopt Jewish cultural practices (like circumcision and other old covenant commitments). This led to the crucial Council of Jerusalem in Acts 15. If the pro-Jewish group had won the arguments, missionary work among Gentiles would have been almost impossible – quite apart from the fact that the decision would have undermined all that Christ had died on the cross to win for us.

Paul and Barnabas hurried back to argue the case against making these demands of Gentile converts, and they won the day. James, the apostle who chaired the debate, summed it up with the words, "It is my judgment, therefore, that we should not make it difficult for the Gentiles who are turning to God" (Acts 15:19).

After this, there is no stopping them!

In summary, Luke's fascination with geography continues in his second volume, and both books aim for an ultimate destination that carries great theological significance.

In the Gospel: Jesus is determined to reach **Jerusalem**: the city of his execution and greatest victory:

> As the time approached for him to be taken up to heaven, Jesus resolutely set out for Jerusalem. (Luke 9:51)

In Acts: Paul is determined to reach **Rome**: the city that represents the gospel reaching the ends of the earth:

> After all this had happened, Paul decided to go to Jerusalem, passing through Macedonia and Achaia. "After I have been there," he said, "I must visit Rome also." (Acts 19:21)

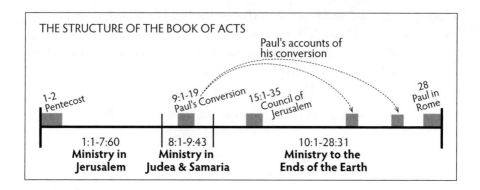

2. The Challenge of Applying Acts

All the challenges of applying the gospels, which we considered in the previous chapter, are still relevant to Luke's second book. But instead of merely repeating the "From Then to Now" section, we will focus on concerns that are unique to Acts.

The most significant issue is the change brought about by Jesus's ascension (found in both Luke and Acts) and Pentecost (in Acts 2). This means that we have far more in common with the disciples in Acts than we have with them when they were trailing Jesus before his death. Like them, we now know that his crucifixion was part of God's plan, and that he would conquer death by rising again. Like them we know that his physical absence (having ascended to his heavenly throne) does not mean actual absence, not least because of his sending of his Holy Spirit at Pentecost. So as Paul taught the Corinthians, it would be impossible for us to claim Jesus Christ as our Lord without the Spirit's work in and through us (1 Cor 12:3).

So what about the church today? Will it be like that of Acts?

Just as with the gospels, the most important question to ask is whether Luke tells his stories primarily as a description of what happened or as a prescription for what should still happen. We can be sure that everything is the former – Luke writes an account of what did indeed take place (some of which he saw with his own eyes). But should we copy what they did, with the expectation that the same things will recur?

The short answer is, "yes, almost certainly!" This is because Luke is writing not simply for Theophilus but for us all, so that we might know and understand the roots of our church. He is showing us how God's kingdom grew out of nothing – just like a mustard seed! And he repeatedly describes three factors that constantly seem to be in place when this happens.

None of this happens by itself of course, and Luke is very concerned to show how God works to expand his kingdom across the world. He points to three key elements.

(i) Kingdom growth: God's Spirit in power

Before his ascension, Jesus tells the disciples to expect the Spirit to come in power. It is intriguing, though, to see what the Spirit will come to do.

> But you will receive power when the Holy Spirit comes on you;
> and you will be my witnesses in Jerusalem, and in all Judea and
> Samaria, and to the ends of the earth. (Acts 1:8)

They are to be witnesses – presumably to give accounts of all that they have seen Jesus do and continue to do. As Luke's book continues, we realise that this witness has many aspects, which go beyond simply opening their mouths.

 Work through these passages to see how the Holy Spirit is at work among Jesus's witnesses:
- Acts 4:32–37
- Acts 5:1–11
- Acts 8:4–7, 18–25
- Acts 14:8–20
- Acts 16:6–10

Again and again, Luke tells us that people are "filled with the Holy Spirit" (Acts 2:4; 6:5; 7:55; 9:17; 11:24; 13:52). And some truly spectacular things happened during the early expansion of God's kingdom. None of it happened without God's being at work. The shocking thing is that he uses flawed human beings as the agents of that expansion.

But in terms of what these people actually do, Luke constantly highlights that the Spirit's most essential gifts were the courage to preach and the power to believe what was preached. This is what happened everywhere.

(ii) Kingdom growth: God's word in preaching

A phrase that Luke repeats throughout the book is "the word of God spread" (6:7; 12:24; 13:49; 19:20). The surprise is that this happens even after persecution, and often because of persecution. The result of Stephen's martyrdom is a case in point.

> Now those who had been scattered by the persecution that broke
> out when Stephen was killed travelled as far as Phoenicia, Cyprus
> and Antioch, spreading the word only among Jews. (Acts 11:19)

This is, of course, just before the church in Antioch sends Paul and Barnabas out to reach Gentiles, and before the Council of Jerusalem endorsed that work. The emphasis all the time, though, is that this is not a message that has been invented or adapted by the first believers; it has been revealed. It is rooted in the Old Testament, and focused on what God did in Christ. As the word about him grows, so faith in him grows.

This is something that has never changed. God is sovereignly able to do extraordinary things and he continues to do so all over the world. Sometimes these victories do closely resemble some of the amazing things that we read about in Acts (especially in the parts of the world where the gospel is breaking in to a society or culture for the very first time). However, what is always the case, in whatever generation or place we work, is that God's word will go out and it will grow.

As we preach and teach God's word as revealed through the apostles in the New Testament, we are part of exactly the same tradition! That is our confidence and conviction – and that is why our call is always to be faithful to that word, over and above any desire or concern for our ministries to look successful in the world's eyes.

(iii) Kingdom growth: God's people in prayer

God is forging a new people, diverse but united in Christ. There will be challenges and problems along the way. There will be persecution and opposition, which will sometimes be deadly. But this is God's extraordinary work.

In Acts we discover what these new believers do when they meet together. Their life together revolves around Christ and his victory, which is why they are determined to study together, praise and pray together, share together. Jesus has changed everything. So it is only right to depend entirely on him.

This provides the preacher with many challenges for the church today, as well as encouragements when we fail or feel weak. For God is the one who can do extraordinary things in the darkest of moments (such as when his preachers are in prison for their faith). That is why we must pray, as the first believers prayed. In fact, prayer is so important to Luke that it is referred to thirty-three times in Acts.

When Peter was arrested by King Herod, what did the believers do?

> Peter was kept in prison, but the church was earnestly praying to
> God for him. (Acts 12:5)

Consequently, Peter was supernaturally freed – and he was then able to join the very meeting that had been praying for his release (Acts 12:12–13).

This does not always happen. When Paul and Silas found themselves in a Philippian jail, they too prayed. But the miracle did not lead to their escape – instead, it led to the conversion of the jailer! (Acts 16:25–28).

There were many twists and turns in this story of kingdom growth. Many times in which the believers came to God in prayer, only to find that God's purposes do not quite fit their expectations or even hopes. For example, there can be little doubt that Paul and his team prayed for the ministry they planned in the Roman provinces of Asia and then Bithynia (Acts 6–8). Luke tells us nothing of how the Spirit of Jesus blocked their paths – only that he did. It must have been very frustrating. But it did lead to the first ever proclamation of the gospel on the continent of Europe (Acts 16:11–12). God knew what he was doing, even if the believers did not.

 What does Luke teach us about the priorities of the first believers when they met together?
- Acts 2:42–47
- Acts 4:32–37
- Acts 6:1–7

In all these ways, therefore, it seems clear that we should preach about the first believers as models to imitate (or to avoid, as with the likes of Ananias and Sapphira – 5:1–11; or Simon the sorcerer – 8:9–24).

However, we must conclude this with one final word of caution.

(iv) Kingdom growth: Unique breakthroughs and revolutions

Some events in Acts are very strange indeed.

One obvious example is the fact that the first believers in Samaria "had accepted the word of God," but for some reason had not received the Holy Spirit (Acts 8:14–17). This seems especially strange in light of Paul's teaching to the Corinthian about needing the Spirit to be able to confess Jesus as Lord. What did those Samaritan converts actually believe? Is this two-stage process of conversion something we can expect today?

Luke tells us very little – but if we see this moment from the perspective of the whole book, then we can see this clearly as a unique event. This is the first time the kingdom breaks out of the closed confines of the Jewish community. As we have seen, it was vital for the most senior disciples (in this case Peter and John) to check everything out and pass on to the others that this was a genuine work of God. No wonder unusual things took place.

Another example is Paul's own conversion story. Should we all expect a "Damascus Road experience"? It was certainly dramatic. Most of us, by contrast, do not have anything like that to look back on – and if we have grown up in a Christian home, we may not in fact recall a specific moment of conversion at all. We can feel a little disappointed as a result. But again, Paul was a unique figure in the history of the church – an apostle commissioned by Christ himself to pioneer the mission to the Gentiles, despite his previous hatred for him and his people. As should be clear from the whole of Acts, and indeed Paul's letters, every conversion is a miraculous event (whether we are able to remember it or not).

In summary, therefore, we are to follow the example of the first believers in their confidence in the sovereign God. He will grow his kingdom through whatever means he wishes. Our responsibility is to depend on him as a community of believers, trusting in what he has revealed, remembering what was won for us at the cross, and living lives of love as we hold out the word of truth. We can never predict what will happen when we do that, but we must always pray that this will expand the kingdom.

For that, Luke's second volume is the perfect inspiration, wherever we live and work.

Who Does He Think He Is?

(Mark 11:27–12:17)

It must be grim being famous: always being recognized; the constant threat of marauding paparazzi; having your every move watched (you can't even blow your nose in public without it being splashed on the front covers). I suppose there are some bonuses. You would be able to walk into a restaurant and immediately get shown to the best table. Or you could get fashionable department stores to open especially for you, as the singer Michael Jackson did a few years ago in London.

But perhaps getting expensive restaurant tables and shops to yourself is not quite what life is all about! And just think of the embarrassment when you expect people to recognize you, and then they don't. You would want to confront them, "Don't you realize who I am?" But that's just wounded pride speaking; does it really matter that much if people don't recognize you?

However, there are occasions when recognizing someone does matter. If you or I fail to spot someone important, it might actually be serious, even dangerous, especially if that failure is deliberate. Perhaps you are driving, and see a traffic cop waving you over. You know what the signal means – you can't fail to spot the authority behind the uniform – but you deliberately reject it.

In the passage we are looking at today, we see people who seem to recognize Jesus's authority – they *do* realize who he is. But they still reject him. In our sermon series on people meeting Jesus, we are now looking at a conversation that gets us into the minds of those who have met Jesus on numerous occasions, but still want to kill him . . .

1. Indignant Authorities (Mark 11:27–33)

After making waves on Palm Sunday and then kicking over the tables of the money changers earlier on in Mark 11, you could be forgiven for thinking that what Jesus does here is quite mad. He goes straight into the lion's den.

> They arrived again in Jerusalem, and . . . Jesus was walking in the temple courts. (11:27)

He goes straight back to the temple which he had been attacking only the day before. Talk about returning to the scene of the crime! So it is no surprise that "the chief priests, teachers of the law and the elders came to him" with a demand. All the Jewish political groups had teamed up to tackle Jesus (despite their differences and even hatred for each other).

The question they asked was perfectly understandable. "Who do you think you are, bursting in here like this? By what authority are you doing these things?" After all, they were the people in charge of the temple – and they had absolutely no recollection of giving anyone a permit to vandalize the place. Even if they had wanted someone to do the job, which they didn't, this supposedly uneducated Galilean carpenter, Jesus, would have been the last person they would have got to do it.

There was something quite ironic about their question. Only two days before, if you remember, Jesus had made a deliberate statement – namely that he is the king who would enter Jerusalem on a donkey, just as Zechariah had prophesied (Mark 11:1–11). More than that, he was the king Malachi had prophesied would be foreshadowed by John the Baptist and then come to his temple to judge it. All in all, Jesus's triumphant entry was his claim to have legitimate authority *over* the temple authorities. They might be indignant, and feel fully justified in their anger, but it was surely dangerous to shake their fists at their legitimate king. Jesus would have been perfectly within his rights at this point to ask "Don't you know who I am?"

But he doesn't. Jesus's timing was impeccable, and the time was not yet right. Instead, he throws the leaders' question back to them. It looks like an evasion, but in fact it is an implicit answer.

> I will ask you one question. Answer me, and I will tell you by what authority I am doing these things. John's baptism – was it from heaven or from men? Tell me!

He didn't decide to mention John the Baptist at random. It is actually very clever – it shows by implication that Jesus regarded his role as being closely connected to John's, just as Malachi said it would be. But more important even than that, it caught the leaders out. Whatever answer they gave would put them in an impossible position. There was no way out. Mark spells that out perfectly:

> They discussed it among themselves, and said, "if we say from heaven," then he will ask, "then why didn't you believe him?"

. . . which is, of course, absolutely true. But the alternative was also too dangerous to contemplate because popular opinion would then turn against them. They were trapped.

Do you see what was going through their mind? Even if they had come to terms with the truth, namely that John *was* the heaven-sent messenger to prepare the king's way, the leaders would never admit to it – why? Because it jeopardized *their own* authority. Vested interests were more important to them than the truth. Power politics was more important than God revealed reality. Let's not forget – in some ways their position was entirely understandable. To come out in the open about John and Jesus was difficult.

We know that some Jewish leaders would eventually be humble enough to admit they were wrong. But, most of them were not prepared to do it at all. They had one purpose in mind.

In verse 33, they look very weak – "We don't know." And so, why should Jesus answer them? He is completely in control of the situation, as ever. He could see exactly where they were coming from. So he immediately launches into a story specifically designed to prove he knows full well what's on their minds. 12:1 makes it clear that this parable is for them.

2. Stolen Authority (12:1–12)

This is a familiar parable. And so it should be, because it's remarkable. But I suspect that we are too quick to assume its significance. Put those assumptions to one side for a minute and try to approach it fresh, remembering the only key to its interpretation in Jesus's day was the Old Testament. But before we even do that, let's get the story's facts straight.

Up in Jesus's home area of Galilee, it was common for people to be working for absentee landlords; in other words, a boss they hardly ever saw. So this is a familiar situation – a guy has laid out a rather fine vineyard and ensures it is well cared for before jetting off on business elsewhere. Now you would think it reasonable for him to expect some, if not most, of the produce from the vineyard to come his way. The tenants would have been bound by their legal contracts to supply it. But in those days, they didn't have email and phones; a businessman could literally be away for years. So their landlord's long absence somehow led them to believe they were beyond his reach and secure in their own lifestyle.

Which explains their reaction to the owner's envoys. Their behaviour is horrific. It is worthy of a Hollywood movie. The violence gets worse with each new person. And Jesus adds in verse 5 that there were others whom he doesn't mention. Eventually, the owner has only one option left – to send his son. And verse 6 makes it poignant, doesn't it?

> . . . a son, whom he loved. He sent him last of all, saying "They
> will respect my son."

It is a vain hope as it turns out.

Now the tenants' logic in verse 7 seems weird, doesn't it? At first sight, it looks as though they thought that by killing the son, the owner would suddenly decide to give them the inheritance instead. That would be absurd. No, their logic is actually shrewd and calculating. They realized that the owner was sending his son as the last resort, and so no one would follow him. That meant that once the owner died, the vineyard would be unclaimed. In ancient law, that meant ownership would come to them. They kill the son, and think they're safe.

But of course, the logic's flawed. The owner could still come back himself, couldn't he? They completely misjudged him. You see, even within the context of the story, what is the most remarkable aspect of what has happened? The tenants' behaviour? Or the owner's? Surely it is the owner's. Why didn't the owner come back and throw the tenants out after the first servant had been wounded? I mean, that was bad enough, wasn't it? That proved their character. If you let your house to tenants, and they beat up your agent when he came for the rent, you'd call the police and have them evicted immediately, wouldn't you? No second chances, let alone a fifth chance. That's basic. Yet this landlord, gives them chance after chance after chance to do the right thing – which they resolutely ignore every time. He shows remarkable patience and trust. Which the tenants presumably misinterpret as weakness.

So Jesus asks the inevitable question in verse 9.

> What then will the owner of the vineyard do? He will come and
> kill those tenants, and give the vineyard to others.

That seems fair enough after everything he's endured, doesn't it?

But what does it all mean? We are told in verse 12 that the leaders recognized themselves in the story. "They knew he had spoken the parable against them." More than that, they felt that they were Jesus's specific targets. So how did they know? Was it just paranoia? Were they right? What was Jesus doing?

Well, here are some words from the Old Testament. And once you have heard them, you'll wonder why there could be any doubt about the story's meaning. They come from Isaiah 5.

> I will sing for the one I love a song about his vineyard: my loved
> one had a vineyard on a fertile hillside.

He dug it up and cleared it of stones and planted it with the choicest vines. He built a watchtower in it and cut out a winepress as well. Then he looked for a crop of good grapes, but it yielded only bad fruit.

Now you dwellers in Jerusalem and people of Judah, judge between me and my vineyard. What more could have been done for my vineyard than I have done for it? When I looked for good grapes, why did it yield only bad?

Now I will tell you what I am going to do to my vineyard: I will take away its hedge, and it will be destroyed; I will break down its wall, and it will be trampled.

I will make it a wasteland, neither pruned nor cultivated, and briers and thorns will grow there. I will command the clouds not to rain on it.

The vineyard of the LORD Almighty is the nation of Israel, and the people of Judah are the vines he delighted in. And he looked for justice, but saw bloodshed; for righteousness, but heard cries of distress. (Isa 5:1–7)

It is impossible to miss the deliberate allusions, isn't it? But those words near the end clinch it:

The vineyard of the LORD Almighty is the house of Israel.

So follow the details through:
- Who is the owner? – God himself.
- Who are the tenants? – the leaders of Israel. They're supposed to cultivate the people of Israel so they produce the fruit of a God-centred life. But how could they, when the tenants themselves were clearly not God-centred but self-centred?
- Who then are the servants? – well, anyone who knows the Old Testament would immediately realize that they were the prophets, whom God sent to call the people back to him. And he didn't just send one, he sent loads of them. And their fate often was frankly no better than that of the servants in the story.
- And who is the son? There are no prizes for guessing that one.

Do you see it? The Jewish leaders get it immediately. And if they understood that they were Jesus's target, then it is not beyond the realms of possibility that they just might have understood who Jesus was as well. Or at any rate, they would have appreciated that Jesus was using the story to defend his actions two days before. What gave him the authority to go into the temple courts and overturn tables? Quite simply the fact that he was the one who was God's last resort. He was God's Son, whom he loved, and yet whom God was willing to send to murderous tenants.

Once we've grasped that, there is something else even more mind-blowing. Jesus brilliantly brings it out in the story. You see, the story presents the tenants as people who hoped to get the vineyard for themselves once the owner had died. But unpack the parable, and the stupidity of the Jewish leaders is clear. How absurd to think that by killing God's Son, they would be untroubled by God in their control of God's people, Israel. The vineyard would be theirs. Absurd! But according to the parable, that was precisely their motive for killing the son, for killing Jesus! So, yes they knew full well who he was. Otherwise, why kill him? It is like speeding up to avoid the police, which you only do because you know they have the authority to stop you. The leaders want to kill Jesus precisely because he is a threat to their independence from God.

Jesus shows how stupid that was, again by quoting the Old Testament. "The stone the builders rejected, has become the capstone," the cornerstone, the most important stone in the new building. "The Lord has done this, and it is marvellous in our eyes?" You see, God is God, however much we might wish it otherwise. And even though on the surface Jesus appeared to be nothing special, the sort of stone that is dug up but appears too full of cracks to be of any use, God will make him the most important stone. And what is the building God is creating? Well, in the light of where they are, it is not hard to imagine that he means the temple – a new temple. Not a temple built with stones. If Jesus, the person who was God, is the foundation stone, then it will presumably be a temple made up of people, people devoted to God. And there was just a hint of that in the parable. Just look at verse 9 – the owner will "give the vineyard to others." Who might they be? Well, leaders over God's people who are focused on Jesus and are both Jews and Gentiles. In other words, to cut a long story short, God's people, the Vineyard, has been reconstructed in the church. In the light of the way Israel's leaders have consistently treated God, that's fair enough, isn't it?

This parable brilliantly demonstrates Jesus's genius, as well as his fundamental claim to have genuine authority from God – because he is God's Son. This is an authority that the Jewish leaders have effectively stolen from God's Son. Dangerous!

God is still God. He deserves nothing less than a life devoted to him. But the Jewish leaders of Jesus's day, and for that matter the whole of humanity, has consistently sought to avoid doing that. God could have kicked them out of the vineyard at any point. But he gave them chance after chance. And remember, there was no reason why he had to do that, except that it was simply in his nature. That's what he is like. He is kind and merciful. Sure, there comes a point when it is too late, when justice demands action. But that never undermines the fact of his merciful nature.

However, the most extraordinary thing of all is that when the leaders eventually do kill him, God uses that death as the ultimate means of bringing forgiveness for people. Forgiveness, that is, for people who won't and can't live for him. That is why the one stone that was rejected has become the most important. For Jesus was both God's ultimate servant messenger AND his nominated Saviour for a rebellious world. But the Jewish leaders didn't recognize that. Or rather, they refused to recognize that. They were too concerned to hold onto their prestige and authority. The irony was that by looking after number one, they actually failed to hang on to anything. They lost it all because they could hardly be trusted as God's trustees.

The danger remains to this day. It happens in churches, where for whatever reason, and in whatever denomination, people end up drawing attention to their own authority and their traditions, and thus obscure Jesus. It can be subtle, and convincing. But God's real king and Saviour gets hidden. It can happen anywhere. If a church starts to focus on its leadership and their vision for ministry, or if we ever start saying things like "No but, we do things this way here" rather than "This is what God has said in his word is the way," we shuffle onto a dangerous path. Jesus would be perfectly within his rights to interrupt us and say, "Look, don't you realize who I am?" He alone is God's servant, God's King and God's Saviour! And what a great God has sent him. The God who gives people chance after chance to return to him. Don't be distracted – turn to the one he has sent to forgive you. Turn to the one who alone has the authority to say your sins are forgiven. Otherwise, we may find that the vineyard he has entrusted to our care gets taken away and given to others.

Section 2

Preaching the Parables

If there is one aspect of Jesus's teaching which is loved and enjoyed more than any other, it is surely the parables. They are vivid and surprising. They are easy to follow, but not always easy to understand. They stick in the mind and can get us thinking for days. Even 2000 years on, this is storytelling at its best.

But there is much more to them than meets the eye. Matthew makes a striking claim about Jesus's teaching style.

> Jesus spoke all these things to the crowd in parables; he did not say anything to them without using a parable. So was fulfilled what was spoken through the prophet: "I will open my mouth in parables, I will utter things hidden since the creation of the world." (Matt 13:34–35)

The quotation is from Psalm 78:2 and seems quite an exaggeration, until we recognize that parables are much more varied than many assume. Here are some examples of things that could be called parables:

- An in-joke: some roar with laughter, others feel excluded because they don't get it.
- A sharp dig at the leaders: bosses don't like it much, but everyone in the market square is grinning.
- A story with a shocking twist that takes your breath away.
- A completely unexpected comparison that you can't stop thinking about.
- A riddle designed to tease, confuse and perplex.

Each of these examples could describe at least one of Jesus's parables. He told many. Depending on how exactly we define the word "parable," there may be as many as seventy in the New Testament. (We have listed some of the most familiar ones in Appendix 1, showing where they appear in Matthew, Mark and Luke.) Some are just single statements, while others are subtle and brilliantly crafted narratives. Jesus was the master of the perfect comeback or gripping story. As we will discover, they served several purposes. And remarkably, they haven't dated (even though they are set in first-century farms or households).

People accused Jesus of being and saying many things – but he was never once challenged for being too academic or inaccessible. That of course does not mean he was simplistic or childish. Far from it. He taught many things that provoked serious thought, both about how to understand them deeply and how to obey them faithfully. If that is true of his teaching generally, it is especially true for his parables. This is the reason for dedicating a whole section of this book to preaching them well.

7

Preaching Jesus's Stories

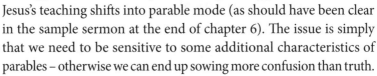

It needs to be said that everything discussed in the previous chapters on narrative still applies. We don't completely change our approach the moment Jesus's teaching shifts into parable mode (as should have been clear in the sample sermon at the end of chapter 6). The issue is simply that we need to be sensitive to some additional characteristics of parables – otherwise we can end up sowing more confusion than truth.

We see that confusion in the many interpreters down the centuries who seem to have taken Jesus's creativity as a cue for their own, which leads them far from Jesus's original teaching! Of course, as communicators of God's truth, we should always seek to use our imaginations as much as possible. (The notion that we might be *allowed* to do this may come as a shock to some!) But our creativity must always be the servant of Jesus's. All the time, we must first seek to understand what he was doing with the parable, and why the gospel writer placed it in its particular context.

1. The Archetypal Parable: Nathan and David

Jesus was not the first parable-teller, of course. Centuries before, another man had been assigned the God-given but fearful task of using a parable to challenge and provoke. At that time, the divinely anointed king was the parable's target, rather than its narrator. So before looking at Jesus's teaching in depth, let us first consider how Nathan's story illustrates the power and effectiveness of parables.

A prophetic precedent

David had untouchable authority. He could do anything he liked. He was God's man for the job, after all. After his adultery with Bathsheba and his subsequent murder of her husband (told with chilling briefness in 2 Sam 11), it looks as though he has managed to get away with his crimes. Only his most loyal lieutenants were in the know (apart from Bathsheba herself), and they were hardly likely to reveal what they knew. David thought he was safe.

Enter Nathan, no doubt with his knees knocking and heart pumping. Those who challenge monarchs tend not to fare well. But his tactic is ingenious. He draws the king into a story of cruel injustice, knowing that it will appeal to his sense of responsibility (2 Sam 12:1–4). He's the king – this kind of thing shouldn't be happening in his kingdom.

> David burned with anger against the man and said to Nathan, "As surely as the LORD lives, the man who did this must die! He must pay for that lamb four times over, because he did such a thing and had no pity." (2 Sam 12:5–6)

Nathan has the king precisely where he wants him.

What appeared to be a clichéd tale of the rich callously abusing the poor, is in fact an indirect charge against the king. "You are that man!" says Nathan in 12:7. This was potentially the most dangerous moment in the exchange. Nathan is careful to evoke God's authority (12:7–13) – how else could he have known about David's secret sins. But this would hardly guarantee the king's appropriate response. It is surely a mark of David's integrity that he does repent, despite the shame of his secret sins being so publicly exposed.

> Then David said to Nathan, "I have sinned against the LORD."
>
> Nathan replied, "The LORD has taken away your sin. You are not going to die. But because by doing this you have shown utter contempt for the LORD, the son born to you will die." (2 Sam 12:13–14)

A purposeful parable

Consider how David might have responded if Nathan had started with a straight accusation. He would undoubtedly have denied everything to begin with; his anger would have been directed at Nathan, rather than his story's rich thief; and Nathan he would quite probably have been punished for insulting the king.

But the parable worked perfectly for several reasons.

- **An involving story**: It is hard *not* to get emotionally involved in this story of a stolen sheep. What the rich man does is blatantly callous and unjust. The fact that the king is meant to stand for justice and truth in the kingdom gets David all the more involved. As one writer puts it, "stories disarm resistance."[1]
- **A subversive story**: The parable is an analogy. In other words, it describes a crime that was *like* David's, but sufficiently different not to rouse his defences too soon. It is only when Nathan eventually points the finger at him that everything falls into place.
- **A provocative story**: It demands a response. It is impossible to remain neutral when hearing this story, which is precisely why Nathan told it. And once David has been exposed, the parable had done its job – there is no need to endlessly analyse each detail for its significance. It is like an arrow fired from a bow that perfectly strikes its target.

It is easy to see why Jesus found parables so useful. His entire ministry and mission were dangerously subversive. It was usually better to draw people into discipleship gradually, rather than stating bald claims about, say, his own divine identity. But just as Nathan's parable only has force in the context of his relationship with David, so it is with Jesus's stories. They only make real sense in context.

2. The Varieties of Parable

Jesus used many types of parable in his teaching. Some commentators describe them as falling along a spectrum, with the simplicity of a one-line saying at one end, and the complexity of a fully worked story at the other. Thus the first, relatively simple, task with any parable is to identify which type it is.

THE RANGE OF JESUS'S PARABLES				
Metaphor Simile	1 Character	2 Characters	3+ Characters	Allegory
Saying	Scenario	Simple story	Complex Story	

---

1. Arthurs, *Preaching with Variety*, 110.

Metaphors

Many cultures like to use traditional proverbs and sayings to make a point. I used to love it when Ugandan colleagues peppered their preaching and conversation with their grandparents' sayings.

Sometimes the meaning of such sayings is quite clear: "When two elephants fight, the grass gets trampled" is a powerful reminder that the victims of war are often not those directly involved in the conflict. Other sayings take a little longer to figure out: "The elephant doesn't find its tusk too heavy to carry." This means that we can bear the burdens we are best suited to. We find similar sayings in the Old Testament book of Proverbs. For example, "The way of the sluggard is blocked with thorns" (Prov 15:19).

The advantage of these sayings is obvious. It is much easier to remember a vivid illustration than an abstract truth.

Jesus liked to use metaphors that work in a similar way. A metaphor is a figure of speech in which a mental picture is used to describe an aspect of experience. Old Testament poetry and prophecy use a lot of metaphors. For example, Isaiah speaks of trees clapping their hands (Isa 55:12). We know that trees don't literally have hands, but we can form a vivid mental picture of a tree doing this. Isaiah is implying that creation shows its joy at the Creator's purposes being fulfilled in the same way we humans do. The picture works, even though it makes no sense if we take it literally.

Similarly, Jesus says in the Sermon on the Mount, "You are the salt of the earth" and "You are the light of the world" (Matt 5:13–14). If we took these words literally, we might roll a person on some meat to season it, or make someone stand next to our chair so that we can read by their light at night. It would be absurd to do that! But Jesus does mean *something* by these statements. We simply need to figure it out. In these two cases, he helps us, although perhaps not as fully as we might wish by adding some explanatory words:

> In the same way, let your light shine before others, that they may
> see your good deeds and glorify your Father in heaven. (Matt 5:16)

The crucial thing is that we do our best to work out from the context what Jesus meant.

Similes

Similes are related to metaphors, but are more explicit comparisons between two ideas that we might never link together. When Jesus uses a simile, he takes a theological truth (for example, an aspect of God's kingdom) and compares it with something familiar from everyday life to make the truth more vivid or memorable. Similes often work very well when they are incongruous and therefore provocative. Matthew groups several similes together in the passage already quoted at the start of the chapter.

- The kingdom of heaven is like a mustard seed (Matt 13:31).
- The kingdom of heaven is like yeast (13:33).
- The kingdom of heaven is like a merchant looking for fine pearls (13:44).

When we read these examples, we must take care before allowing flights of imagination to take hold. Jesus does not leave us to speculate *how* the kingdom resembles these things. In each of these cases, he explains the comparison and tells us what the point of similarity is. He does not want us to imagine that *every* characteristic of mustard seeds or merchants applies to the kingdom. Instead, his point is usually direct and clear, and the last thing we want to do as preachers and teachers is to complicate that.

 Work through Jesus's simile parables in Matthew 13 to see how he focuses their meaning.
- Mustard Seed (13:31–32)
- Yeast (13:33)
- The Hidden Treasure (13:44)
- The Pearl Merchant (13:45–46)
- The House-Owner (13:53)

Scenarios

As you looked at those examples in Matthew 13, you will have noticed that Jesus often expands his similes into what we might call "scenarios." These get closer to what most people think of as parables, that is, stories that illustrate a point. However, these scenarios do not have plotlines, as such, but they do describe immediately recognisable situations, often in some detail.

- There might be an event or action that changes things for the character involved. For example, the merchant finds a pearl and so sells everything he owns to buy it (Matt 13:46).

- There might be a scenario that gets expanded in several ways. A case in point would be the parable of the Seed and the Soils (Mark 4:3–8). There is only one character who is essentially doing one thing: throwing seeds onto the land. The focus on the parable is what happens to the seed once it falls.

Stories

In the first chapter of this book, we looked at the core features of narratives. The more a parable develops into a full-blown story, the more it will share those same features.

One simple way of categorizing Jesus's stories is to subdivide them according to the number of characters involved.

- 2-character stories: Where there are only two characters, Jesus usually invites hearers to compare and contrast them. The Pharisee and the Tax Collector is a prime example (Luke 18:9–14). It is full of surprises as we listen to two men praying in the temple. Another would be the Wise and Foolish Builders (Matt 7:24–27).
- 3-character stories: The majority of the story parables focus on three main characters or groups, often with one of them (God, a father, a landlord) holding some sort of authority over the others. The Lost Son and the Older Brother (or the Prodigal Son as it is more commonly known – Luke 15:11–32) is a case in point, as is the Rich Man and Lazarus (Luke 16:19–31). In the latter, Abraham is the authority figure.

 Where would you place these parables on the spectrum?
- The Two Debtors (Luke 7:41–43)
- The Lost Sheep (Matt 18:12–14)
- The Persistent Widow (Luke 18:1–8)
- The Hidden Treasure (Matt 13:44)

3. The Impact of Parables

It is one thing to distinguish between one-line simile parables and more developed stories, but the key issue is how to interpret, let alone preach, them.

The first place to start is to establish what impact Jesus intended his parables to have on their original audience. He clearly drew crowds by his teaching – and his use of parables was a central factor in that. They provoked his audience but kept them hooked. They lodged important theological truths deep in people's minds, so that they could perhaps recall them for the rest of their lives. They ensured his teaching was always down to earth, rooted in the ordinariness of everyday life. So it comes as a surprise to find this explanation following so soon after his famous Sower story.

Parables as stumbling blocks

> He told them, "The secret of the kingdom of God has been given to you. But to those on the outside everything is said in parables so that, 'they may be ever seeing but never perceiving, and ever hearing but never understanding; otherwise they might turn and be forgiven!'" (Mark 4:11–12)

Most of us naturally assume that Jesus told parables to aid understanding – but here, he seems to suggest that they prevent it! He quotes God's words to Isaiah in which the prophet is warned of the likely outcome of his preaching (Isa 6:9–10). These are clearly difficult verses, but Isaiah's original context indicates that God is not irrationally preventing people from turning back; rather, he is justly giving them over to the consequences of their hardness of heart in refusing to turn. Isaiah's preaching therefore has a confirming function.

Jesus is saying that his parables are a bit like automatic sliding doors, which remain closed, until a sensor detects someone approaching. Only then do they spontaneously open. The key is whether one is moving towards the doors or away from them. If someone's heart is hard and they are not interested in moving towards Jesus, he or she will reject Jesus and regard his parables as lightweight and irrelevant riddles that can be quickly dismissed. On the other hand, for those who are moving towards Jesus, the parables open doors into profound truths.

Of course, the disciples were in a privileged position. They spent more time in Jesus's company than others did, and so they got the inside track on what the Sower story meant (Mark 4:13–20). But Jesus's point here should alert us to how subversive the parables are. They never work in quite the way we expect. But isn't that precisely what we would expect when God tells stories?

Parables as spotlights

But parables are not only stumbling blocks; they are also powerful teaching tools. Jesus used them to illustrate a key truth. He sometimes also deflected hostile questions by telling a story. When he did this, his parable would answer those who were questioning him, but would do so in a way that threw the spotlight back on them.

The context will nearly always help us to establish what point is in his mind.

- Jesus's three agricultural parables in Mark 4 (the Sower and Soils, the Growing Seed and the Mustard Seed) come after some shocks for his followers. As reported in the previous chapter, they had heard religious leaders claim that Jesus was satanic (Mark 3:22) while his own relatives thought he was insane (3:31–34). This hardly bodes well in the early stages of his public ministry. But these parables reassure his followers that there *will* be a harvest despite the lack of fruit (Sower), despite how little there is to do after sowing (Growing Seed) and despite how small it all seems (Mustard Seed).
- The parable of the Good Samaritan is prompted by a lawyer's question about neighbours (Luke 10:25). The story answers the man perfectly, in a provocative way (see the next chapter).

Stories communicate a point far more effectively than a simple statement like "God's kingdom will grow despite so many people rejecting it."

Parables as provocations

As we have seen, Jesus's parables have an uncanny way of catching people out. We may not understand how radical Jesus is being until we have had our hearts exposed to his gaze. It is only then that our intrigue or perplexity can be transformed into discipleship. For in the end, that is Jesus's goal. His parables are designed to provoke a response.

This means we must be alert for the punchline. A parable should catch us off guard, but strike home the moment it is understood. Rather like a great joke, it shouldn't need more explanation. Yet instead of the laughter that follows a joke, Jesus's parables usually provoke us to radical discipleship – or at least stop us in our tracks. We don't see his point coming. They are like those mosquitoes that are entirely silent – so the first we know about their presence is when we suddenly find ourselves scratching a spot.

Of course, this presents challenges to a preacher. It is hard to preserve the element of surprise. Because of the gap between Jesus's world and our own, the range of Bible knowledge in a congregation, and our over-familiarity with the parables, the punchline too often needs explanation. Over-explained parables tend to have as much impact as an explained joke. It's hard to catch people off guard in the way that Jesus did. But that is what we must aim for. There are a number of tactics to achieve this, to which we will return.

Warren Wiersbe captures the impact of parables brilliantly. "I like to think of a parable as a picture that becomes a mirror and then a window."[2]

So initially, a parable describes something normal, even quite dull: a marketplace or a kitchen or losing your car keys. But it has enough in it to grab us and make us think. As we do so, we find ourselves confronted by our reflection in the mirror as we face a truth about ourselves. That is undoubtedly the result of seeing beyond ourselves to the kingdom truths Jesus is illustrating. He exposes just how far our perspective has drifted from God's as our sights are lifted up to God's reality.

Parables as codes? The question of allegories

We have already considered the issue of allegories when we spoke about the danger of treating the gospels as if they were written in code (see ch. 2). The challenge now, however, is that some of Jesus's parables actually *are* allegorical! Perhaps you spotted that in the sample sermon at the end of chapter 6. There it was clear that Jesus's parable of the Vineyard Tenants demands an allegorical

2. Warren Wiersbe, *Preaching and Teaching with Imagination* (Grand Rapids: Baker, 1997), 164.

interpretation, for reasons that we will come to. But should we do the same with his other parables, especially those with more complex plots? Does each parable require a key to unlock the secret code?

After all, look at how Jesus himself unpacks the parable of the Sower (Mark 4:13–20):

- The seed = the word (v. 14).
- Seed on the path = Satan removes as soon as it is sown (v. 15).
- Seed on rocky places = initial joy, but without roots and so quickly falls away (vv. 16–17).
- Seed among thorns = worries of this life and wealth choke the word (vv. 18–19).
- On good soil = hear and accept the word, producing a crop 30, 60 or 100 times what was sown (v. 20).

It is not a complex allegory – its meaning falls into place as soon as the seed is interpreted as the word of the gospel, even if the nuances of the different soils are not immediately obvious. So should we do the same with the parables of the Persistent Widow or the Pharisee and the Tax Collector in Luke 18?

A famous example of parable code-breaking is St Augustine's handling of the parable of the Good Samaritan (Luke 10:25–37). He teases out what each detail represents to produce some rather spectacular conclusions.[3]

- The traveller = Adam
- Jerusalem = the city of heavenly peace, from which he fell
- Jericho = the moon, which signifies Adam's mortality
- Thieves = devil and his angels
- Stripped him = namely of his immortality
- Beat him = by persuading him to sin
- And left him half dead = as a man he lives, but he died spiritually
- Priest and Levite = Old Testament priesthood
- Samaritan = said to mean guardian or Christ
- Bound his wounds = means binding the restraint of sin
- Oil = comfort of good hope
- Wine = exhortation to work with a fervent spirit
- Beast = the flesh of Christ's incarnation
- Inn = the church
- The morrow = after the resurrection

---

3. Taken from Fee and Stuart, *How to Read the Bible for All Its Worth* (Grand Rapids: Zondervan, 2014).

- Two pence = the promise of this life and the life to come
- Innkeeper = Paul

What do you make of that?

To be fair to Augustine, he is applying the grand sweep of the biblical story to the parable, and so writes truth. And his grasp of that story probably went far deeper than we are ever likely to go! Still, even geniuses can head down blind alleys. As several commentators have argued, this could never have been Jesus's meaning. Augustine had to work hard to squeeze biblical truth to fit the parable and he made some arbitrary choices. Why not have Peter as the Innkeeper, since he is the rock on whom the church is built? (Matt 16:18). Most significantly, Augustine's interpretation ignores the fact that the context of the parable is a question about inheriting eternal life and the extent of our neighbourly responsibilities (Luke 10:25, 29). Once we acknowledge the context, the parable gains far greater weight (see the example sermon for this section).

But how can we tell whether we are meant to interpret a parable allegorically or not?

Our starting point should be to assume that Jesus's parables are *not* allegorical. The majority are primarily stories with a point, rather than codes with a key. If they are to be treated as allegories there will be clear signs, such as these:

- **Jesus himself unlocks the code**: As with the Sower and the Soils, Jesus reveals what it means.
- **The audience grasps the significance**: As we saw with the parable of the Vineyard Tenants, the religious leaders "knew he had spoken the parable against them" (Mark 12:12). Of course, by itself that does not indicate an allegorical interpretation – many of the parables have a bite without having to resort to some hidden spiritual meaning. Just think of the Pharisee and the Tax Collector. But the leaders' insight derived from their biblical knowledge.
- **The Bible provides the background**: In the parable of the Vineyard Tenants, Jesus is clearly building on Isaiah's vision of God's vineyard (Isa 5:1–7). He adds details Isaiah did not mention (such as the owner sending his son), but it is not hard to interpret them. Isaiah has already given us the key to the code: the Lord Almighty is the owner, the vineyard is Israel and Judah, the desired fruit are justice and righteousness (Isa 5:7).

It may well be true that some of the parables include some allegorical elements. For example, in the parable of the Two Sons (Luke 15:11–32), the Father does represent God in his grace and mercy – and by extension, the Lord Jesus himself (see his mission statement in Luke 19:10). It follows then that the younger son personifies the life of rebellious licence, while the older son lives a life of religious works.

However, this does not mean we are invited to interpret every detail of the parable as if it represents something else. Instead, we should assume that Jesus includes details like the father's ring and the fattened calf (15:22–23) to make the drama more vivid and effective. Perhaps it would help if we could see these details as being like the props on a stage or film set – they make this fictional world feel real and lived-in. But they should not be the things that the audience concentrates on or remembers.

4. Handling the Parables

 With the gospel narratives, we went on a treasure hunt, following the clues the gospel writers have left for us. We need to follow similar clues when interpreting the parables.

Clue 1: Ask Jesus's audience!

Quiz shows seem to fill television schedules all over the world. So perhaps you have seen the one in which contestants are allowed to ask the studio audience for help when they get stuck on a question. Of course, that never guarantees a correct answer, but if a large percentage of the audience agree on the answer, it is a good sign!

When Jesus teaches, there are naturally no prizes for getting the right answer. But there are certainly consequences. Like every good teacher, he is acutely aware of the people around him, and shapes his teaching accordingly. This is one reason why we must pay attention to who is there when he tells a parable, and even more importantly, to how they respond. This is crucial, even with some of the most famous parables. Their context profoundly shapes their significance.

Take the parable of the Good Samaritan in Luke 10 (which will be the focus of this section's sermon). Jesus does not pluck this story out of thin air. It is prompted by a lawyer who comes to question him. Even though his enquiry could be entirely sincere, Luke tells us that his motivation was not so positive:

> On one occasion an expert in the law stood up to test Jesus. "Teacher," he asked, "what must I do to inherit eternal life?" (Luke 10:25)

This leads to a brief exchange that prompts a second question: "and who is my neighbour?" (Luke 10:29).

We get an inspiring glimpse of Jesus's genius here because his timeless story achieves multiple things simultaneously. What initially seems to avoid the lawyer's concerns actually answers *both* his questions. In so doing, Jesus manages to expose the lawyer's self-righteousness and racism. But that is not all. Jesus also challenges all of us, whether Christian or not, about where we stand with God and other people (especially if they are different in some way). Finally, the story makes us question how anyone can be able to inherit eternal life.

When Jesus puts the final question to the lawyer, it is clear that the man understood exactly what Jesus was up to. He just couldn't bring himself to utter the word "Samaritan" (Luke 10:37). To understand why, read the sermon at the end of this section!

 How does Jesus's audience or intended target help us to interpret these parables?
- The Lost Sheep, Lost Coin, Lost Son (Luke 15:1–3; also 19:10)
- The Lost Sheep (Matt 18:10–14). Is Matthew's context different from Luke's – if so, how does this affect your interpretation of the parable?
- The Ten Minas (Luke 19:11)

We are in danger of misunderstanding these stories not because we lack the key, but because we ignore the context. Sometimes it's obvious. But even where there is no obvious audience, we must see how the parables fit in with the overall thrust of that particular gospel. As ever, context is essential. So for example, Mark 4 groups a handful of agricultural and domestic parables with the parable of the Sower. Each sheds light on how Jesus understands kingdom ministry (especially in the light of its rejection by others in Mark 3).

Clue 2: Enter Jesus's world

We should try to see how Jesus relates to the world of his audience. Are there clues from the stories themselves that help us here? We will probably always feel a wide distance between us and Jesus's culture, but we do at least have his Scriptures in our hands. So we have few excuses for not being immersed in them.

Connecting to the Old Testament

Jesus assumes knowledge of the Old Testament throughout his teaching, and especially in his parables. That is why it is clear that vineyard imagery is used to represent the people of Israel. But that is not the only Old Testament image he uses. For example, when Jesus speaks about sending out invitations to a wedding banquet (Matt 22:1–4), he is drawing on a rich prophetic tradition. Both family weddings and the greatest moments in Israel's history were often celebrated with joyful feasts. It is thus not surprising that Isaiah spoke of God's kingdom in terms of a great banquet. He does so most famously in Isaiah 55, where he says that all and sundry can come to eat and drink their fill, regardless of their ability to pay for it (see Isa 55:1–2 – but see also Isaiah 25:6; 58:14).

Jesus is not the only one to use this imagery. John does the same in Revelation, with his climactic vision of a great wedding feast at Jesus's return (Rev 21:2–4, 9–10).

Connecting to Judean society

Unlike today, when people are moving from the countryside to cities more rapidly than ever before, Jesus's world was largely rural. It was a time when everyone kept a close eye on seasonal weather systems, on harvests and planting. It was a world of rich landowners, peasant farmers and casual labourers who had to look for jobs every day. It was a world where the most vulnerable in society were those who could not work (because they were too young or too old, too ill or too different). No wonder widows, orphans and foreigners often came off worst – as we saw in our overview of Luke's gospel in the previous section.

We must be sensitive to how Jesus builds bridges to his world – and more significantly, to how he challenges it.

- Look out for **countercultural heroes or role models**: A poor man gets named in eternity (Lazarus) rather than the rich man (Luke 16:19–31); a widow models persistent prayer (Luke 18:1–8);

kingdom membership is not based on merit, as the hired vineyard labourers discover (Matt 20:1–16).

- Look out for allusions to the **Roman occupation**: It is hard to underestimate the shock value of Jesus making tax collectors his heroes. They were doubly hated because of their corruption and their collaboration with the Roman enemy. In the parable of the Ten Minas, "a noble man travels to a far country to have himself appointed king" (Luke 19:12). This directly alludes to one of Herod's sons having to travel to Rome before he could take up his throne in Judea.
- Look out for **religious upsets**: Despite Simon the Pharisee's religious authority, he still has much to learn about forgiveness (Luke 7:36–50); a Pharisee not a tax collector is in the wrong with God (Luke 18:9–14); a racially impure (and therefore loathed) Samaritan puts Jewish authorities to shame on the Jericho road (Luke 10:33); the vineyard tenants are thrown out and replaced (Luke 20:9–20).

Clue 3: Spot the breaks with reality

If the only thing Jesus did in his parables was to make connections with his world, they would never have become as popular as they are. His genius was to start in a familiar environment, and then develop his illustration in startling ways. As commentator Leland Ryken puts it, there are "cracks in the realism"[4] of Jesus's stories. So at some point, they will take an unlikely, or even absurd, turn.

Very often, it is precisely this surprising turn that gives the parable its force. We should therefore always look out for them to identify Jesus's main purpose. Here are some examples:

- Is it likely that anyone, let alone a Samaritan, would give so extravagantly to look after a complete stranger? (Luke 10:30–37).
- Would an employer *really* pay all his labourers the same amount, even if some only did half a day's work? (Matt 20:1–16).
- How realistic are the excuses for declining the king's invitation to a wedding banquet in Matthew 22:2–14?

This is not to imply that every parable contains such a twist (the single sentence metaphors hardly have the space for one!); nor does it mean that a

---

4. Leland Ryken, *How to Read the Bible as Literature* (Grand Rapids: Zondervan, 1984), 144.

parable cannot break reality more than once. We simply need to be alert to the possibility of Jesus doing it.

Identifying the cracks in the realism is useful for the preacher. For it is through those very cracks that Jesus exposes the absurdities of the way people actually live. The excuses for not attending the wedding banquet *are* ridiculous – but no more so than the real excuses that people genuinely offer for not following Christ to the heavenly feast. The art of good parable preaching is to help hearers feel the force of that.

 How does Jesus break with reality in these parables?
- The Valuable Pearl (Matt 13:45–46)
- The Three Investor Servants (Matt 25:14–30)
- The Lost Son and Older Brother (Luke 15:11–32)

Clue 4: Feel the emotional force

This relates to the previous point, but is particularly focused on how Jesus's stories leave his audience. What sort of emotions does his story provoke? Does he anger his hearers, or expose them, or simply deepen their curiosity? Is there a moment when the heart skips a beat or when people go "Ahaa!" Once we have worked out what these emotions are, we should aim for our preaching to have the same emotional force as Jesus's original parable.

Take the Pharisee and the Tax Collector (Luke 18:10–14). The divine assessment of these two men in 18:14 will have come as a complete surprise to those listening to Jesus. It breaks the rules of every religious system on earth, let alone the Judaism of Jesus's day. But that is the wonder of the gospel. Our preaching must somehow get that shock across.

Sometimes, Jesus deliberately breaks off before offering a conclusion at all. He does this with the Lost Son and Older Brother. After the lost son's return, the father is overjoyed in complete contrast to his older son. The latter exposes his mercenary heart when he complains about what his brother did and the expense of the family party, while the father shows only mercy and love (Luke 15:28–32).

That is where Jesus stops the story. It is like a movie with a cliff-hanger ending. We perhaps see the father turning back towards the sounds of celebration from inside the house. Then the camera shows the older brother watching him go. And then the film credits start to roll. It is left to us to decide what the brother did next. As such, it is an invitation for us as listeners to consider how we might have acted in the same position.

Clue 5: See with God's eyes

Jesus's teaching is never comfortable. He is quite prepared to ignore the conventions of social etiquette, and is never impressed with people's status. The way he handled the interruption of the so-called "sinful woman" into Simon the Pharisee's dinner party is a case in point (Luke 7:36–50). It could have been deeply embarrassing for Jesus. But he was not unsettled at all. Instead, he used it as a perfect teaching opportunity, even if it meant not sparing his host's blushes. He directs the story of the Two Debtors straight at Simon in order to explain the woman's bizarre action (7:40–43). He is then quite rude in contrasting her welcome with the welcome Simon gave to him. The silence in the room as he spoke must have been very uncomfortable indeed!

Jesus always challenges the world he is in. That is because he brings God's perspective to bear on the world, whether in terms of how individuals think or how societies live. The moment we assume that he endorses what we naturally do and think is the moment we have lost sight of his teaching.

The parables are a brilliant antidote to the problem. Quite apart from the way they get under our skin so well, their big themes lift our sights from our this-worldly perspectives. Here are some of the key themes.

- **The kingdom of God**: In contrast to worldly power systems of nations and empires, God's kingdom (or the kingdom of heaven, as Matthew calls it) is very different. It often starts small (like a mustard seed) and seems unimpressive. It gets rejected by many, but always produces fruit in the end. It is far more valuable than anything the world contains (like the valuable pearl), which is why we should not cling to material and temporary things.
- **The reality of eternity**: Jesus had biblical grounds for calling the man who constructed bigger barns "a fool" (Luke 12:16–20). The man was living without giving thought to the things of God and eternity (in contrast to the wisdom of Proverbs 1:7 and Psalm 14:1). Even though he could never have known the date of his death, he was never ignorant about its coming. The same lack of eternal perspective could describe the successful businessman who ignored the agony of Lazarus begging at his gate (Luke 16:19–31). He should have

known what mattered because, as a Jew, he had access to Moses and the Prophets (16:29).

- **The life of grace**: It is fitting, then, that several parables touch on how people come into the kingdom (the Good Samaritan and the Pharisee and the Tax Collector). Some unpack the liberation that forgiveness brings (the Two Debtors), while others extend the financial image to the responsibility of investing what has been entrusted to us (the Three Servant Investors). It is interesting how often Jesus uses economic metaphors to describe the life of grace! But of course, kingdom values turn worldly economics upside down – hence the apparent "unfairness" of God's grace (because we can't earn it, we all receive the same, regardless of how much work we do for the kingdom – Matt 20:1–16).
- **The finality of judgment**: Jesus's parables maintain in the starkest terms possible that there will be an ultimate reckoning. Whether it is in the judgment parables of the Sheep and the Goats and the Ten Bridesmaids (Matt 25), or the stories of the Wicked Vineyard Tenants (Luke 20:9–18) and the Wedding Banquet Invitations (Matt 22:1–14) it is clear that there will be a division. The expected response is to be *ready* (see Luke 12:38–40; Matt 25:1). This, more than anything else, is what gives Jesus's parables their terrible urgency.

It is guaranteed that any time given to specific study of the parables will have a profound effect. It is impossible to remain untouched and undisturbed. Jesus simply does not share our perspectives on life. But we would be fools to ignore his perspective – however uncomfortable that is.

5. Preaching the Parables

What makes someone a good parable preacher?

It's quite a challenge! But because the majority of Jesus's parables are stories, it stands to reason that it is a matter of being a good storyteller. That may not be a skill we feel we have – but regardless of our gifting, we must take the dynamic of stories seriously. Don't crush the parable dead by extracting a handful of abstract theological lessons to teach. If Jesus thought we needed abstractions, he would have given them to us straight.

So we might as well ask what makes someone a great storyteller, actor or stand-up comedian? Each does it differently, but at the very least, they can all hold audiences captive by the way they speak. That is why it is always worth watching the experts at work, especially when there is silence in the room while they speak. How do they manage to move us to laughter one minute and tears the next? How do they get the timing of the punchline right? We should always try to learn from the performers our church members most enjoy watching and listening to.

It will take years of practice, and each of us will need to learn how to communicate with the gifts we have and as the people we are. However, here are a few suggestions.

Translate the shock

Many cultures around the world have ancient theatre traditions, and producers share the challenge of how to keep those traditions alive. Whether staging a Shakespeare tragedy, or an Indonesian puppet drama, or an ancient Chinese opera, there are essentially two options: the performance can be as authentic as possible, using the closest staging and costumes to their original performances. Alternatively, the plot and drama can be preserved, but put into modern dress and staging, with perhaps some of the allusions changed to fit with contemporary politics. There are good grounds for either approach.

The same goes for Jesus's parables. So in preaching the Pharisee and the Tax Collector to an audience that has never met a Pharisee, should we update the main characters? Should we think about pitting a respected community leader against a notoriously corrupt politician? Or should we find the most despised people group in our own culture to serve as the modern equivalent of the Good Samaritan?

Here it will probably come down to individual taste, for it is difficult to give an absolute rule. Whichever we decide, however, it is vital to take as much care as possible to be faithful to Jesus's purpose as we understand it. Our aim should be to communicate the original shock of the parable more than anything else. If dressing the parable in modern costumes helps to do that, then so be it. Otherwise, we will simply need to explain any first-century allusions as we retell the story. But all the time, we must be trying to recapture that kick-in-the-stomach moment of realization. We want people to feel the shock that Jesus's audience felt.

There is room for creativity here. In fact, the more familiar the parable is to a congregation, the more creativity will be required. Otherwise the shocks will be completely overlooked. This is why more than one preacher has resorted to the radical tactics of secretly dressing up as a homeless beggar and sitting outside the church building as people arrive. It proves that the circumstances of the Good Samaritan or the Rich Man and Lazarus haven't exactly gone out of date.

Preserve the surprise

If the first goal is to find a way to translate the shock, the second is to hold that surprise back for as long as possible! In other words, keep the audience in suspense, especially when they think they know what the parable is about. There are different ways to do this.

The simplest and most common strategy is to retell the story as the gospel writer records it – walking a congregation through it, not in a wooden and dull way, but by reacting to each emotional twist and turn. This needs the lightest of touches, not a heavy-going unpacking of each detail. In this way, you can ensure that the story develops at Jesus's own pace.

Second, we can cling to a conventional viewpoint for as long as possible, until Jesus's parable makes that untenable. So for example, in the Pharisee and the the Tax Collector, it is important to forget (temporarily) everything we know about the Pharisees from Jesus's teaching. For in his day, they were easily the most impressive spiritual leaders around – they were not the "bad guys" they became with the New Testament's influence. So we could build the tension of the parable by emphasizing that the tax collector's posture and reticence were entirely appropriate. Everything was normal – until Jesus's devastating verdict. We could then go back through the story to understand what led to that verdict (for example, by paying closer attention to the egotism of the Pharisee's prayer).

A related tactic is to interpret everything as it first appears, however theologically incorrect. This is something I have attempted to do in the sample sermon for this section (on the Good Samaritan). It occurred to me as I was preparing it that the strangeness of the parable derives from Jesus's apparent suggestion that people are saved by doing good works. So I let that hang in the air as long as possible. Of course, that is only going to be subversive for a theologically educated congregation. For someone from a different religious background, it will seem perfectly normal. How we land the punch, therefore, will differ according to the audience we are addressing.

Deliver the punchline

After all that has been said, this final tip is going to be the hardest to achieve! Just like jokes that lose their bite if they need explanation, so parables can seem limp and lifeless. We need to get the punchline across as clearly as we can.

With the Pharisee and the Tax Collector, it is clear that being religious does not earn God's approval. For it was the "sinful" tax collector who went home restored to a right relationship with God, not the Pharisee. That was a profound shock. Being good, being respectable, being religious, never justifies anyone before God! (Luke 18:14).

This is what we want people to have ringing in their ears as they leave, just as happened when Jesus first taught the story. Grasping and then communicating the punchline, then, is the only way we can have any confidence that our relevant application is faithful to the original passage.

Impossible Love

(Luke 10:25–37)

Lawyers are the same all over the world. They are always poring over case studies, establishing the ins and outs of how the law is applied.

There is a story about one Californian lawyer who was defending a murder suspect. Legend has it that his strategy was to exploit the confusion over when death actually occurs. Apparently, Californian law used to define death as when the heart stops beating. So the lawyer defended his client on the grounds that his victim was not actually dead because the heart had been transplanted and was beating quite normally in somebody else!

Well lawyers in Jesus's day also loved playing with case studies – a fact Jesus exploits to devastating effect with the case of the Neighbourly Samaritan. Jesus is throwing out a challenge: argue your way out of this one!

Here's another thing about lawyers: they thrive on teasing questions. And this famous story in Luke 10 can only be understood when we see the questions on either side of this case study. Notice the structure. See how it starts:

> On one occasion an expert in the law stood up to test Jesus. "Teacher," he asked, "what must I DO to inherit eternal life?" (10:25)

Then by the time you get down to verse 37, Jesus has answered it. Like many lawyers, it's taken him a while – but he gets there in the end. Notice the crucial word:

> Verse 37: Jesus told him, "Go and DO likewise."

The man wants to know what to *do* to get to heaven. Jesus tells him. Do the same as the guy in our case study. Well, there we have it in black and white: Be good, boys and girls – and heaven is yours! But framed within this question and answer is another set of questions. Did you notice that at the start, Jesus's response to the lawyer's initial question was another question?

There is a joke about the rabbi who was once asked "Why do rabbis always answer questions with another question?" The rabbi stroked his beard for a while and eventually answered, "Why shouldn't rabbis always answer questions with another question?"

Well in response to the verse 26 eternal life question, Jesus asks for a summary of Jewish law. And the lawyer's answer is perfect – A++! Love God; love your neighbour. Love is the best summary you can get. So in verse 28 Jesus commends him: you've answered correctly. DO this and you will live! There it is again. Get to heaven by being good.

Then the lawyer deflects him with another question in verse 29. Something's troubling him about the loving the neighbour bit. So he asks "Who is my neighbour?"

Now, we know next to nothing about this lawyer. He's clearly no fool. But Luke hints at his mindset. In verse 25 we're told he's trying to test Jesus. Fair enough. That could be neutral – he's just checking him out; or it may be a trap. But the biggest clue is in verse 29: he wanted to justify himself. He wanted to know how to get right with God. DO is the operative word.

If you think about it, this isn't a surprising question for a lawyer to ask. If you spend your entire life thinking about the law, you're always questioning limits, testing boundaries. What's in, what's out? These are crucial legal questions. Hence the neighbour question. Who should I love? Are there limits? Who is my neighbour? If he genuinely wants eternal life, he needs an answer to this question.

So Jesus takes him on. And he always gives as good as he gets. Even if Christians you know aren't up to it, Jesus always was. The lawyer asked for something to do – Jesus gave him something to do. And it's rather more than he bargained for. You see, this is no children's bedtime story. It is a legal case study with punch.

1. Love without EXCUSES

Jesus turns what started out as an assessment of his own legal know-how into a test of the lawyer's legal obedience. And just as love is the key to the law, so love is the key to the case study. But what sort of love does Jesus mean? His answer is deeply disturbing. Even today.

The road from Jerusalem to Jericho is exceptionally dangerous. Still. In less than twenty-seven kilometres, it descends 1,000 metres with plenty of sharp bends in the road and plenty of hiding places from which to attack unwary travellers. So it was the perfect setting for a case study involving an assault.

A solitary walker was easy prey – and it's not surprising that he ends up at death's door. He's unconscious. He's hardly breathing. He's hardly moving a muscle. His life is literally seeping away with his congealing blood as every moment passes. A truly gruesome scene – but on that road, a common one. Only one conclusion to draw: he's dead. Flies buzz around the corpse, vultures circle high above. Except it's no corpse, is it? He's alive. Get up close, and you can see, you can hear, the faintest of breaths. But you need to get up close.

Now, for all its dangers, the Jericho road was a busy one. Many priests actually lived in the beautiful and fertile area around Jericho, famed for its wonderful date palms. The climate there was so much better than the climate in Jerusalem! So when they had finished their temple duties, they would leave the dust and chaos of the city and make their way home – via the Jericho road. Priests travelling on this road were an everyday sight. Jesus's case study is credible.

Verse 31 explicitly says "a priest happened to be going down the same road" – he was probably returning home after doing his shift at the temple. It's always easier going home downhill after work. Today there are still many parts of the world where people must walk long distances for work. This was one of the first things to strike us when we first went to live in East Africa. Whenever we went upcountry, even if in the middle of nowhere, we would see people walking – usually for miles.

So put yourself in the priest's shoes – no doubt tired, hungry, keen to get home. Perhaps there was something good on television he didn't want to miss. As he made his steady progress, the first things he probably noticed were the vultures. A sure sign – he knew what to do; he knew his Bible.

The biblical law was explicit: Contact with dead bodies made a priest ritually unclean (Lev 21:1–3). Even though it's weird and hard for us to get our heads around it today, being unclean made his temple job difficult. A corpse was about the biggest threat to purity imaginable. Even a moment's contact was enough. And if he did become unclean – well he'd have to turn right around, trudge all the way back, and go through all that temple ritual to get sorted all over again. It was just not worth it.

What's more, it could be a trap. The man might only be pretending to be dead. That sort of thing happened in Uganda quite a bit, and happened to friends of mine – someone lies on a deserted road faking injury so that his mates can rob anyone who stops to help. So the priest walks straight past the corpse. Who wouldn't? "The guy's dead anyway. It's not my job. I'm not a funeral director. I don't have the time. I just can't afford to let a corpse make me unclean."

Except it's no corpse, is it? The guy's alive. But you'd only know that up close. But the priest simply won't take the chance. Far from checking to make sure, he actually walks to the other side. Who can blame him? He had every excuse in the book.

Next up: a Levite in verse 32. He was also a temple employee, but junior to the priests. So Jesus is working down the Jewish social order. I'm sure the audience got the point. "You just can't trust today's leadership – they don't care about anyone except themselves." You can see the knowing glances as they smirk to each other. And guess what – no surprises here. The Levite does exactly the same. Again, who can blame him? He had every excuse in the book – the book being the Bible!

So when Jesus said "Do likewise" at the end – he clearly doesn't mean be like the priest and Levite. Far from it. Jesus obviously sets them up as a contrast.

But Jesus's legal expert could have related to the priest and Levite, don't you think? They had every excuse NOT to get involved. The lawyer knew his Bible and not to touch corpses. Except this wasn't a corpse, was it. The man was alive. And the law says nothing about becoming unclean through contact with someone dying – only someone dead. This man in the ditch needed help. FAST. The priest and Levite merely AVOIDED their responsibility to love. They used the Bible to give them excuses NOT to love.

Don't we all do the same, whether we're Christians or atheists or from another faith altogether? We find excuses. We justify our actions. In fact, when we put our minds to it, we can justify any action. We're all lawyers at heart. Perhaps we do it out of wanting to use our time strategically. There are bigger priorities, we say. I've got a really important political meeting to go to (which will equip me to usher in justice more effectively). Or I've got to get to my church prayer meeting. I can't do everything. Someone else will have to look after this guy.

True, these are all good things. But Old Testament temple purity was fairly important too. In fact it was God's idea. So do you see the problem? They're excuses. Excuses NOT to love. After all, you could hardly say that helping a dying man in a ditch is a strategic use of time. Sometimes, you see we must be prepared to love – not because it's a means to an end – but because we are to love our neighbours as ourselves; loving, come what may; loving without excuse! But the story continues . . .

2. Love without BOUNDARIES

Your average listener would have guessed what was next. We've had a priest, then a Levite. Now of course – it's an average Jewish man, an ordinary citizen like anyone else in the crowd. HE would obviously be the good guy. So far, so predictable.

But Jesus wasn't predictable. He doesn't go for a Jew at all – he chooses to use a Samaritan in his case study. Outrageous. Jews and Samaritans had centuries of history, centuries of baggage. "Even a Gentile would have been better, Jesus! But a Samaritan – come off it! Your story was pretty realistic before that. Now you've blown it. Samaritans are a bunch of no-good, corrupt, stinking outsiders who were probably responsible for the attempted murder in the first place. They're all the same – you can't trust them."

But Jesus says that's where you're wrong. You can trust them. This one, anyway. He's the hero. He realizes the man's alive. He gets up close to check. He does everything he can to help.

Note that Jesus avoids telling us anything about the wounded man. We know absolutely nothing about him. We don't know whether he was Jewish, Samaritan, or from Timbuktu. Because it didn't matter. It didn't concern the Samaritan. What mattered was that he was a *man* – a fellow human being about to die. The Samaritan showed love regardless of race barriers and cultural barriers. This truly was love without boundaries.

Do likewise? Love without boundaries. Love that is blind to colour or caste? What about love that is deaf to accent or language? The love that Jesus demands must transcend every conceivable barrier – whether it be of class, race, sexuality, looks, abilities. You name it. And it must go beyond the individual level. Where is the love for our fellow human beings? Where is the love without boundaries? Where is the love for those on the margins of society?

3. Love without ACCOUNTS

The Samaritan goes beyond the call of duty. Jesus's storytelling is vivid. In verse 33, he says: "He came where the man was" – in contrast to the temple officials he got up close – "and when he saw him he took pity on him." He wasn't thinking here; he was feeling. He wasn't strategizing; he was overwhelmed. This man is DYING! How could he not help? He picked him up and took care of him. More than that – he didn't just save his life (which would have been wonderful in itself), but he did everything he could to get him back on his feet again. At great personal expense.

He just happened to be carrying a rudimentary first-aid kit of bandages, wine and oil. He used them up. He then lifted the man onto his donkey – so now he was going to have to walk himself. He took the man to a nearby hostel.

Realizing the man needed more than rest, he went to a cash machine and returned with the necessary funds. Two silver coins – equivalent to 2 months' rent – and that's just for starters! This is extravagant love – for someone that the Samaritan, like us, knew nothing about. He was just a dying man in a ditch. That is all. A remarkable act of extravagant love and practical compassion. It is love without excuses, without limits, without accounts. Jesus doesn't tell us when the practical giving to this man stopped. We just know that the Samaritan would return to give MORE!

Former UK Prime Minister Margaret Thatcher once commented that "no one would remember the Good Samaritan if he only had good intentions – he had money too." That's certainly true – but it is ironic that her comment was made in the 1980s, a time that was infamous for excesses of money-grabbing, not money-giving. Sure, the Samaritan did have money – but he had something far more significant than money. He had love – love without limits. Costly love. You don't have to be rich to have that. But you can be rich and not have that. What matters is what you do with your wealth.

This truly is a legal case study with punch. It's supremely challenging. But I want you to notice how Jesus ends it. We would expect him to ask, "So, who is my neighbour?" The answer would be obvious – the man in distress and dying in the ditch, he's my neighbour. The lawyer would have agreed: he'd have been forced to condemn the priest and Levite, despite undoubtedly sympathizing with their excuses. A tough pill to swallow, but one he'd have accepted. A dying man is my neighbour.

But that's not actually the question Jesus asked, is it? Jesus's question is much tougher.

Who was a neighbour TO the man in the ditch?" (Luke 10:36)

That's very different! And again the answer is simple – but this time it's not so much a bitter pill as an impossible pill to swallow. See the lawyer's response? "The one who had mercy on him." He can't even bear to say the word "Samaritan" – it gets stuck in his throat. The question isn't complicated to answer – it's just impossible to accept. It's too stomach-turning that a member of a hated minority could possibly be an exemplary citizen. I guess it might be equivalent to a highly respected human rights campaigner passing by on the other side while a convicted terrorist is the story's hero. But in Jesus's case study, when he said "Go and do likewise," it is the *Samaritan* who is the model – it is the Samaritan that Jesus had in mind. Do what *he* did!

And that's the end. We hear no more about the lawyer so we have no idea how he responded. But he got answers to his questions, didn't he? What must I do to inherit eternal life? Well – DO what the Samaritan did. Love like him without excuses, without boundaries, without accounts. Well – that's impossible, isn't it? It's too much. The Samaritan in the story is just *too good*.

And that's precisely the point, isn't it? This love is too much – it is unsustainable. Nobody is actually like that. Not in REAL life. And thus, Jesus proves that it is impossible to work your way to heaven – it is impossible to DO anything to justify yourself. For heaven's standard is nothing less than perfection – perfect love for God, perfect love for neighbours. How can it be otherwise? Anything less would turn heaven into hell.

The only way to inherit eternal life is God's way: Jesus died on the cross to do what we could never do. It is only through his death on the cross that we can be justified and made right with God. It is only through what he DID, not through what we DO, that we can inherit eternal life. This case study ingeniously exposes our need to receive this sort of love because of our total failure to give this sort of love.

Jesus loves us like the Samaritan loved – he loves us without excuses, without boundaries, without accounts. That is what makes the Christian message *good* news.

But it is imperative that we don't leave the parable there. So I want to close with a challenge to those here who already follow Christ. Because once we have been justified by his amazing act of love on the cross, how can we not respond with the same sort of love? How can we not go and do likewise? Not to earn his favour but because we have his favour. This parable is not merely an illustration of the love that Jesus showed us. It is far more – it is a piercing challenge to those of us who complacently do not love others as Jesus loved us. Which is why this parable hurts. None of us can remain untouched. Because Jesus still tells each one of us here to "Go and do likewise." Love without excuses, without boundaries, without accounts. And if you find your Christian friends not doing that, you'll have an inkling of how much they need Jesus's love themselves.

He did for us what we could NEVER do by ourselves.

Section 3

Preaching the Letters

Hi! It's me . . . Yes, I'm finally on my way . . . Yup . . . Won't be too long now.

I'm on the bus, actually . . . Yes, I realize that, but I didn't have much choice. There was a problem at the station. It was absolute chaos . . . Oh, and I ran out of power on my phone. That's why I had to borrow this phone.

No, I've not forgotten . . . It's safely in my bag. It'll be fine. I promise. I'll get it to you in good time.

OK? . . . Got to go. See you soon . . . Bye

I have lost count of the times I have tried to avoid listening to a stranger's public phone conversation. Perhaps you're the same. We don't want to be nosey, but if people insist on speaking loudly, we can't help it. I remember sitting at an airport departure gate and overhearing a surgeon describe in gory detail the operation he was scheduled to perform that evening. Fortunately most of what he said was meaningless to me – but it was still grotesque.

Usually it requires little imagination to work out what the person on the other end is saying. Like the half-conversation I opened this chapter with. One or two details are impossible to work out (such as what is in the bag or what relationship the speaker has to the other person), but the rest is clear. After delays on a difficult journey, the person has managed to make contact with someone and give a new estimated time of arrival.

The New Testament letters give us a chance to eavesdrop on some ancient conversations. When you stop to think about it, that in itself is astonishing. It is almost as if the gap of 2,000 years falls away, so that we can hear someone like the Apostle Paul speaking in his own words. This is not to deny that some details will seem strange and alien, and of course, we only have half of the conversation in our hands. We still need to guess what the writer was responding to or how those he was writing to reacted. But there are many things that we can work out with reasonable confidence, and we gain insights into each writer's passion. Those writers still speak to us today.

Some of those letters were written to individual congregations in a specific city (like Corinth or Rome), or in a wider area (like 1 Peter, or the letter to the Colossians which was to be shared with the Laodiceans – Col 4:16). Others were written to individual friends (like Timothy or Titus). They are arranged in the New Testament with Paul's letters coming first (with letters to churches ahead of letters to individuals), and then letters written by others (the "General Letters"). We will focus primarily on Paul's letters, but will give some additional tips for the General Letters as we go.

8

Understanding the Occasion of the Letters

While all the Bible's human writers had clear reasons for putting pen to paper, the letters are the parts of the Bible that are most closely tied to a specific time and place. That is why they are sometimes called "occasional" documents, which simply means that they were written for particular occasions. Unlike the prophetic books in the Old Testament (and the gospels), which were compiled over long periods, the letters were generally written in response to some news. Sometimes this was good news that had reached the writer, and sometimes it was news of some sort of church crisis. As we read them, we can perhaps imagine Paul pacing up and down a room as he dictates to a secretary[1] who desperately tries to get the words down on paper.

What this means is that even though it is likely that we will only be preaching on a small section of a letter, it is vital to have a grasp of the whole letter's overall background and purpose. It is only by understanding this background that we can have any confidence in our handling of an individual passage.

In the rest of this chapter, we will be focusing on this big picture understanding of the letters.

1. Have Right Expectations When Reading the Letters

The fact that each letter was prompted by a specific occasion has three important implications for us:

---

1. See Romans 16:22, where Tertius identifies himself as the secretary, while in Galatians 6:11 Paul suddenly starts writing in his own hand.

Expect answers, but not necessarily to our questions.

The clearest evidence that the letter writers are answering questions comes in 1 Corinthians. From the start of chapter 7, Paul works through a list of questions that had probably been sent to him in a letter from the church in Corinth. The clue that this is the case is the phrase "Now about . . ." Here are a few examples:

- 1 Corinthians 7:1   Now for the matters you wrote about . . .
- 1 Corinthians 8:1   Now about food sacrificed to idols . . .
- 1 Corinthians 12:1   Now about spiritual gifts . . .

Similarly, each letter in the Bible was intended to help Christians deal with some situation in the world in which they lived. But the world in which the ancient Christians lived is not identical with the world in which we live. We have different contexts, and different questions. So we must not expect the letters to speak to our situation directly. Rather, we need to identify the context in which they were originally written and look for parallels to our own situations.

Expect great theology, but not necessarily systematic theology

Without exception, the letter writers apply revealed truth to the situation they are addressing. They are writing theology. But don't expect to find a complete summary or analysis of a particular topic in one place. The context of the letter's recipients rarely demands that. Perhaps the closest that Paul gets to doing this is his teaching on the Spirit and his gifts in 1 Corinthians 12–14. But even then, we would have to draw on other passages like Galatians 5 and Romans 8 to get the bigger picture. So we should never assume that a paragraph is the writer's (or indeed, the Bible's) full revelation on the subject.

In other words, the letters are not chapters in a work of systematic theology or a dictionary.

Expect pastoral reality, but not necessarily direct relevance to us

The letters are relevant to us – but not directly so. For example, when Paul asks Timothy to come quickly to him, bringing his clothes and the writing materials he left behind in Troas (2 Tim 4:13), none of us would even think of suggesting that members of our congregation should jump on a plane to Turkey to go and look for them. That would be ridiculous! It was clearly a personal instruction for Timothy and nobody else. It gives us glimpses into Paul's suffering while in prison in Rome, and perhaps the quality of partnership between him and Timothy, but little more.

Less obvious, perhaps, but just as unique to Paul, is his account of his conversion in Galatians 1. He tells us that immediately after his dramatic encounter with Christ on the Damascus road, he went south to Arabia. He only met the apostles three years later (Gal 1:17–20). He does not include this detail as if it is some sort of model to follow – like many other aspects of his conversion, this is unique to him. He mentions what happened only because he is using these strange events to underline his authority as an apostle. This was presumably what gave him the authority to oppose Peter to his face (Gal 2:11).

What do these verses tell us about the occasion of their writing?
- 2 Corinthians 7:8–10
- 1 Thessalonians 2:1–2
- Titus 1:5–6
- James 5:1–4

The preacher's first task is thus to work out what prompted the writing of the letter in question. This is an essential place to start. If we do not do this, we risk reducing the letters to mere reservoirs of beautiful sayings or moral wisdom. The result will be a sermon of great superficiality, irrelevance and perhaps even heresy.

So how can we go about discovering a letter's occasion?

2. Research the Background in the Book of Acts

Before working on the text of the letter, it is always worth checking Luke's second volume, the book of Acts, for useful background information. Because Luke was one of Paul's companions, this will be especially relevant for Paul's letters. Acts sometimes tells us about the recipients of the letter and even about the actual circumstances in which a letter was written. As the table shows, for some letters Acts offers very specific information; for others, we only have a general picture of the period or context to draw from.

Paul's Letters	Acts Background
Romans Paul has not yet visited Rome when he writes, but plans to (Rom 15:23–33)	**Acts 27:1–28:31** Final journey to Rome
1 & 2 Corinthians The letters were written in the period soon after Paul's extended time in Corinth	**Acts 18:1–18** Visited during Third Missionary Journey; we are introduced to Apollos, Priscilla and Aquila
Galatians Probably written in between the two Corinthian letters, after getting reports that false teaching was gripping the church. Paul explains his confrontation with Peter (Gal 2)	**Acts 10:9–48; 13–14** Peter's vision, which enabled him to visit the Gentile Cornelius's house. Paul visited Galatia during First Missionary Journey, and probably challenged Peter before the Jerusalem Council of Acts 15
Ephesians Written in Rome a few years after Paul's visit, probably at the same time as Colossians (with which it has many similarities)	**Acts 19:1–20:1; 20:17–38** *(and Acts 28:16–31)* Paul lived there for two years during his Third Missionary Journey; he later met the elders at Miletus en route to Jerusalem
Philippians Written from a Roman prison; the church was the first planted in Europe and clearly meant a great deal to Paul	**Acts 16:11–40** *(and Acts 28:16–31)* Church planted during Second Missionary Journey with remarkable first converts
Colossians Paul never visited Colossae – but this church in the Lycus valley had good links with the Ephesian church, through the one who planted it, Epaphra.	**Acts 19:1–20:1** *(and Acts 28:16–31)* Paul's two-year ministry in Ephesus impacted the whole region (19:10), which is how the gospel came to Colossae
1 & 2 Thessalonians The first letter was written very soon after Paul had to leave Thessalonica; the second a few months later	**Acts 17:1–10** During Second Missionary Journey; could only stay three Sabbaths (between two and four weeks)

1 & 2 Timothy	Acts 16:1; 17:14–15; 18:5; 19:22; 20:4
The first letter was written after Paul was acquitted in Rome, the second after his second imprisonment	*(and Acts 28:16–31)* Timothy was clearly a trusted member of Paul's long-term team, which is why he was given tough jobs like helping with the problems in Corinth (1 Cor 4:17)
Titus Although Titus is not mentioned in Acts, Paul clearly trusted him enough to oversee the development of leadership for the Cretan church	**Acts 27:7** *(and Acts 28:16–31)* Paul visited Crete during his final journey to Rome
Philemon He was Onesimus's Colossian slave-owner probably converted through Paul's Ephesus work	**Acts 28:16–31** Paul presumably had Onesimus's help during his Rome imprisonment, but feels he should now send him back

Map showing important cities and regions in Paul's ministry of preaching and letter-writing.

In this section on the letters, it may be helpful if we concentrate on one letter, and take most of our examples from that. So I have decided to focus on how to go about preparing a sermon on Paul's letter to the church in Philippi.

To help you get an idea about how to link Acts and the letters, let's look at how Acts 16 helps us with Philippians.

When we read that chapter in Acts we are reminded of how remarkable the events that took place during Paul's brief visit actually were. His team knew they were meant to be there because of the famous invitation in Paul's vision of a man from Macedonia (Acts 16:6–10). Of course, that did not prevent them from experiencing hardship and opposition. But what stands out is the obvious diversity of the first converts:

- Lydia, a prosperous businesswoman and trader
- a demon-possessed slave girl
- a tough Roman veteran who was a jailer

Paul was forced to leave the city (after insisting on his rights as a Roman citizen) but not before doing all he could to give the new Christians there as firm a foundation as he could. It was an extraordinary and eventful visit that gave rise to the very first church in Europe, a church that would always know that it had been born in the fires of persecution.

While Paul is the most prominent person in Acts, the book also contains information that is useful when reading the General Letters, that is, the letters written by other writers. Although we cannot tie those letters as closely to specific events, Acts does give us a better feel for the world in which they were written. It was a time when Christians could often feel under siege, battling tensions within their communities (such as false teaching and division), while enduring persecution both from Jewish groups who had rejected Christ and from the Roman imperial rulers. No wonder life was tough for them.

The authors of the General Letters write to sustain, encourage, and sometimes rebuke, those to whom they are writing.

- The identity of the author of **Hebrews** is unknown, but the overarching message of the letter is clear. Resisting the pressures from the Jewish community to return to the fold, these Christian converts are to persevere with Jesus because he is superior to anything that the old Jewish religion has to offer (Heb 10:19–25).
- **James** writes to believers who are "double-minded," trying to live with one foot in the world and one foot in God's kingdom (Jas 1:8; 4:8).

Even though their attitude is understandable in a hostile world, it is inconsistent and unstable (Jas 1:2–7).

- **Peter**'s letters were written to people living in the Roman provinces of what is now north-western Turkey. The Christians were few in number, spread out and isolated (1 Pet 1:1, 6), circumstances which made enduring persecution for their faith so much tougher.

- **John** was traditionally associated with the church in Ephesus, and he writes his first letter to reassure believers who have had their confidence undermined by false teaching (1 John 3:19–24). His second and third letters are more intimate, dealing with the need to live lives consistent with the truth and love of the gospel (2 John 6–7; 3 John 4).

- **Jude** is primarily concerned with the dangers and consequences of false teaching. He urgently appeals for perseverance in the face of these challenges (Jude 21, 24).

3. Get a Sense of the Whole Letter

Read the whole several times

 Imagine you are away from home for a long period and you receive a long letter or email from a loved one. It would be odd if you decided to restrict yourself to reading just a paragraph a day after breakfast. No! You would want to read it all at once, perhaps quickly the first time to get the general gist, and then more slowly after that.

So why don't we do that with the letters in the Bible? Even the longest, Romans and 1 Corinthians, will only take a little more than an hour each.

When you read right through the letter at one sitting, you will find that you get a much better grasp of the whole letter. Even our favourite passages were never written in isolation, but always as part of a whole. So the more we read each letter, the better our familiarity with its details and our grasp on the reason for its writing.

Have specific goals for each read-through

It sometimes helps to jot ideas or observations down on a blank sheet of paper as you read through the whole letter. Perhaps you can have different questions or goals for each read-through:

1:   Are there any details that relate to the letter's background in the book of Acts? It is good to start with this while the relevant Acts passage is still fresh in your mind.

 Reread Acts 16:6–40, and then read through the whole of Philippians. Are there any details in the letter that correspond in any way to what we learn from the book of Acts?

You might then want to work through some of the other goals on other read-throughs, if you have time.

If you are used to preaching in another language, perhaps you could work through the letter in that language, before comparing your notes with mine below.

2:   Identify key individuals or groups mentioned in the letter. What do we learn about their relationships to each other or to the author? Does the writer mention opponents? How do they show their opposition?

3:   Look for words or ideas that are repeated throughout the letter or regularly in an individual chapter. When put together, do they point towards what the letter is about?

4:   Look for clues to what prompted the letter to be written in the first place?

5:   Can you begin to see the main building blocks of the letter? Are there sections that work together to form a general argument? Or does the writer go from one separate point to another?

Remember – this is simply a method of gathering preliminary impressions before studying the passages in detail. It will be useful, because your mind will continue to make connections with the wider letter as you do so.

Here are some of the details that stood out for me as I read through Philippians several times.

1st: Any links with Acts 16?
- Partnership in the gospel from the start (1:3–6)
- Not intimidated by persecution (1:20; 1:28; 2:15–16)
- Divisions are common in every church – but perhaps especially in one with such diverse early converts (4:2–3)
- The only people in Macedonia who supported Paul at the start were the Philippians (4:15–16)

2nd: Key people mentioned
- Paul and Timothy, writing from prison in Rome (1:13–14, see also 2:19–24)
- Epaphroditus had generously been sent by the Philippian church to work with Paul, but has had to return (and so carries the letter – 2:25–30)
- Euodia and Syntyche, two key women in Philippi (4:2–3)

Two different opposition groups:
- in Rome, there are those who 'stir up trouble' for Paul (1:17)
- In Philippi, the 'dogs' (3:2)

3rd: Repeated words/themes
- Proclaiming/defending the gospel
- Partnership in ministry
- Standing firm in unity within the church
- Persecution and opposition outside the church
- Joy in Christ
- Following holy, sacrificial examples
- Eternal perspective of life after the grave

4th: Clues to the occasion
Paul writes to:
- reassure the Philippians that his imprisonment is not actually a setback (1:12)
- put their own suffering in the context of God's purposes (1:28–30)
- remind them to work hard for their unity in Christ (1:27; 2:1–4; 4:1–3)
- explain why Epaphroditus was returning home so soon (2:25–30)
- warn them about the false teachers (3:2)
- thank them for their generous gift which had been sent by Epaphroditus (4:10–19)

5th: Clues to a structure
I couldn't finalize a clear structure at this stage – but a few things struck me:
- The Jesus song of 2:5–11 echoes throughout the letter (before and after it comes) – in particular, Timothy and Epaphroditus are held up as living examples of those who live according to Jesus's pattern (2:12–30)
- Paul deals with the two opposition groups very differently (he tolerates the Roman one, but is scathing about the Philippian group)
- The issue of Euodia and Syntyche's disagreement comes up near the end – could it be that everything in the letter is building up to Paul's appeal for them to reconcile?

These notes are by no means the finished product, but are early impressions from reading through the letter. There is still much work to be done.

Take note of the beginnings and ends

Letters were structured slightly differently in the ancient world. Today we might put the recipient's name and address on the envelope (with perhaps a return address), and then start the letter on a separate sheet with our own address and greeting. We would usually leave our name and signature until the end.

Ancient letters worked the other way around, primarily because they were written on scrolls. It wasn't possible simply to flick to the end to see who the letter was from (as we would do today). So putting all the relevant information in the opening lines, meant there was no need to open up the whole scroll. This was the standard formula:

- Writer's introduction (with perhaps a summary of credentials or title)
- Recipients and their location
- Standard greeting
- Prayers of thanksgiving or blessing, followed by a general introduction
- The main body of the letter, which can vary greatly in length

Another standard formula tends to govern the letter's close:

- Practical arrangements (either for the letter or the sender)
- Greetings from others
- Final summary or postscript, and/or prayer or praise

Sometimes there are variations from this structure, which may themselves help with interpretation. For example, at the start of Galatians, Paul seems in a rush to get right to the point (Gal 1:6). There are no warm, personal greetings or appreciation for the believers in Galatia; instead, he immediately starts expressing his alarm at what has happened there. False teaching seems to have taken over and the need for action is desperate (1:6–10). Contrast this with the encouragements he offers to the Thessalonian believers (1 Thess 1:2–10).

Just as we saw with the gospels earlier, it is useful to take note of how Bible books start and finish. The endings can be especially useful for identifying clues as to why this particular letter was written. For example, does the writer end his letter with comments that link up to anything that he said at the start of the letter?

What do we find if we compare the opening and closing verses of Philippians?

- **Opening**: Paul (joined by Timothy) writes to a church they both know and clearly love. But notice how Paul emphasizes his inclusion of all the church members. In 1:1, he writes to "all God's holy people in Christ Jesus at Philippi"; 1:3 "my prayers for all of you"; 1:7 "feel this way about all of you . . . all of you share God's grace"; 1:8 "I long for all of you."

- **Close**: Paul thanks the Philippians for the financial expression of their partnership in his ministry, which reinforces his deep connections with them (4:10–18). Once again, he emphasizes the inclusivity of his affection: "Greet all God's people in Christ Jesus" (4:21); "All God's people here send you greetings" (4:22).

So even these verses appear to endorse Paul's appeal for gospel unity.

What can you glean from looking at these introductory and concluding verses?
- **Romans** 1:1–6 and 16:25–27
- **1 Corinthians** 1:1–9 and 16:19–24
- **Titus** 1:1–4 and 3:12–15
- **1 Peter** 1:1–9 and 5:8–14

It should be clear by now that none of this work requires you to use a commentary. It is simply a matter of coming to the text with the right questions. We can never do everything on our own (and it would be foolish to ignore the work of those who have spent months or even years considering these texts), but we can usually do much more than we think we can.

4. Imagine the Other Side of the Conversation

Having read through the letter a few times, we are now in a stronger position to speculate about what was being said at the other end of the phone line, as it were. It requires only a little creative imagination to figure out what people were saying and doing to provoke the letter, and what the writer hopes will result from the letter. The answers to these two questions will help us draw together what we have discovered so far about why the letter was written.

What happened before Paul wrote Philippians?

A number of things can be established.

- The Philippian church wanted to support Paul in his ministry. They did this in two ways: by sending one of their key members, Epaphroditus, to join his mission team (2:25), and having him deliver a generous financial gift to Paul (4:18).
- Epaphroditus told Paul some of the church's news, both positive and negative, and spoke about internal and external threats to the church. Within the church, there were splits in the congregation. At that time, believers did not meet in church buildings but in people's homes. So if the owners of those homes stopped talking to each other, the impact on the whole fellowship would be terrible. This is presumably what makes the disagreement between Euodia and Syntyche so painful (4:2–4). Meanwhile, some false teachers had arrived and were trying to force Gentile converts to take on Jewish culture as part of their Christian discipleship. Paul is adamant that adding extra requirements to all that the Lord Jesus has achieved on our behalf fatally undermines what Jesus has done (3:1–14).
- Epaphroditus had been seriously ill and so Paul was sending him home. But he does not want the Philippian Christians to jump to the conclusion that Epaphroditus has not supported Paul adequately or has quarrelled with him when they see him returning home so soon. So Paul stresses that he is sending his friend back because of his health, not because of any disappointments with his ministry (2:25–30).

What Paul hoped would happen after the Philippians read this letter

Our answers to the previous questions help us to establish what Paul hopes for. This is important because it points us towards the letter's application for his original readers/listeners.

- For the Philippian Christians to stand together in unity in Christ by working hard to sort out their differences with Christ-like sacrificial love, and to reject the false teaching which undermines their confidence in Christ.
- For the Philippian Christians to persevere with gospel hope in the face of hardship and hostility from the outside world.

- For the Philippian Christians to continue to be generous gospel partners, just as they had already been by sending Epaphroditus and financial support.

It needs to be emphasized that no part of this exercise has required the use of commentaries. That does not mean we now understand everything in the text, but it does mean that we each have it within us to grasp the big ideas once we have the Bible open and our minds and hearts engaged.

5. Draft a Tentative Outline

At this stage, nobody should expect to have grasped every aspect of a biblical letter. That can only come after studying each of its passages in detail. However, we can still attempt to draw up a tentative outline of the letter, which can serve as a useful guide to the letter's bigger picture once we start to get immersed in the details of the passage we will be preaching on.

If you have been working on Philippians throughout this chapter, then before reading further, see if you can draft an outline of the whole letter by yourself.

Remember – do not automatically copy the paragraphs or headings used by your preferred Bible translation. They are not indicated in the original text, but are added by the translators. Which means they can get things wrong!

Here is my tentative outline for Philippians so far.

- *? 1:1–11*   *Greetings and prayer*
- *? 1:12–26*   *Paul's hope in Christ in the midst of suffering*
- *? 1:27–2:18*   *Church life modelled on Christ*
- *? 2:19–30*   *Two brothers who minister like Christ*
- *? 3:1–14*   *Gospel confidence only possible in Christ*
- *? 3:15–4:3*   *Follow Paul's example for unity in Christ*
- *? 4:4–23*   *Final instructions and greetings*

This outline is good for now, but it definitely needs more work. We will be doing some of that work in the next chapter, as we consider how to look in depth at an individual passage.

9

Studying the Details of the Letters

When it comes to working on a Bible passage, a useful technique is to print or write it out so that you can make notes on it. This gives us a freedom to work with the text in a way that we would not with our published Bible. This technique is especially useful when working on a passage in the letters, since they tend to be shorter and construct arguments from point to point. Underlining and notes can help us to see how that argument develops.

Some people make their notes by using different coloured pens to highlight or underline words and phrases of interest; others scribble observations, questions and thoughts in the margin. It doesn't much matter how you do it, as long as you do it.

Here I suggest we work through a short passage from Philippians 1:12–18 to see how the whole process moves from detailed study to a possible sermon structure.

1. Highlight the Significant Details

At first sight, a Bible passage can feel like a jumble of text and sentences. We might understand what each word means by itself, but it is hard to see how they all fit together. So we need to tackle the passage by asking a series of simple questions.

- What words or ideas get repeated?
- Are those repeated words developed in any way?
- What images or metaphors are used?
- Are there any difficult words/ideas to understand?
- What is shocking or surprising?

Start marking up the copy of the passage that you have written or printed out. It does not matter much how you do it, as long as you can understand how you have done your own notes! I usually use one colour or type of line for each repeated word or phrase.

 Try and do your own mark up of Philippians 1:12–18, before looking at mine.

Your notes may end up something like this. Each of the types of markings link similar words. So I have put "Christ" in a box (to make the word stand out); "gospel" has a wavy line, while "preach" and "proclaim" both get a double line. And so on.

> ¹² Now I want you to know, brothers and sisters, that what has happened to me has actually served to advance the gospel. ¹³ As a result, it has become clear throughout the whole palace guard and to everyone else that I am in chains for Christ. ¹⁴ And because of my chains, most of the brothers and sisters have become confident in the Lord and dare all the more to proclaim the gospel without fear.
> ¹⁵ It is true that some preach Christ out of envy and rivalry, but others out of goodwill. ¹⁶ The latter do so out of love, knowing that I am put here for the defense of the gospel. ¹⁷ The former preach Christ out of selfish ambition, not sincerely, supposing that they can stir up trouble for me while I am in chains. ¹⁸ But what does it matter? The important thing is that in every way, whether from false motives or true, Christ is preached. And because of this I rejoice.

A repeated word is obviously important. So sometimes, simply identifying those repetitions is all that is needed to get to the heart of the passage. At other times, it needs more work. But this is certainly the best place to start.

In this passage, Paul's central focus leaps out at us: Preaching the gospel. He mentions it four times. But we still have a few questions.

- Is preaching the gospel the same as "preaching Christ"?
- Why does he focus on his suffering here? He describes himself as being "in chains" three times.
- Why does he highlight the other preachers who are causing him trouble?

So far so good, but we still have work to do. The challenge now is to find out how the passage's logic flows.

2. Create a "Flow Diagram"

It may seem an obvious point, but we should remember that New Testament letters make sense and are not a jumble of unrelated ideas. They were written for a purpose and so they always have a logic to them (even if it sometimes takes time to identify it). If the letters had not made sense, they would never have been shared beyond the first believers who received them. True, Paul does sometimes break off in mid-sentence to start a new idea (as in Phil 3:1–2), but he does come back to the point, and actually, these detours do tend to serve his main purpose.

So how do we find that logic? One of the best ways to do that is to create a flow diagram.[1] This is a useful tool for establishing the most important ideas in a passage, those on which all the other thoughts depend. We end up with something that gives the argument visual shape.

Perhaps we can see the flow of a passage as being like a great river. When we lived in Uganda, we used to live around an hour's drive from the source of the River Nile at Jinja on Lake Victoria (although friends in Rwanda and Burundi would claim the true source as being in their mountains, from which streams flow into the lake). By most reckonings, the Nile is the world's longest river. At its Ugandan source, it is already wide, and it will travel nearly 800 km before it reaches the Mediterranean Sea. All along the route, there are hundreds of tributaries and streams.

Imagine driving cross-country in the region, and coming across a wide river. We could easily assume that it must be the Nile. But after examining the map, we discover that it is actually a smaller river that feeds into the Nile, not the Nile itself.

We can make the same sort of mistake when reading a Bible passage. We come to something that appears to be an important theme – but when we start investigating, we discover that it is just a sub-theme, flowing into the real main theme.

A sentence flow diagram can work like a map, helping us sort out which is the main river of the idea and which are the streams feeding into it.

---

1. Not all languages are suited to this method. I am told, for instance, that it is quite difficult to use in languages like Chinese and Korean.

Here is how to go about creating a sentence flow diagram:

- Return to the passage printout on which you have already picked out repeated words. Highlight all the linking words like "because," "and," "therefore," "so," and so on.
- If you can spot where the main sentences stop and new ideas start, mark it on the text with a slash mark.

This will result in a page that looks something like this.

/ ¹²(Now) I want you to know, brothers and sisters, that what has happened to me has actually served to advance the gospel. ¹³(As a result) it has become clear throughout the whole palace guard (and) to everyone else that I am in chains for Christ. ¹⁴ And (because) of my chains, most of the brothers and sisters have become confident in the Lord (and) dare all the more to proclaim the gospel without fear. //
¹⁵ It is true that some preach Christ out of envy and rivalry, (but) others out of goodwill. ¹⁶ The latter do so out of love, knowing that I am put here for the defense of the gospel. ¹⁷ The former preach Christ out of selfish ambition, not sincerely, supposing that they can stir up trouble for me while I am in chains. // ¹⁸ (But) what does it matter? The important thing is that in every way, whether from false motives or true, Christ is preached. (And) because of this I rejoice.

Now, on another sheet (turned sideways, so it is in landscape format), write the passage out by hand, but not in the format usually found in books. Follow these instructions:

- Start each new sentence on the left.
- Every time there is a conjunction (a linking word), or a new clause in the sentence, drop to the next line, leave a small indent, and start writing the rest of the sentence there. (Sometimes you run out of room – as I did with verse 12 – and need to drop a line anyway. If that happens don't indent.)
- Carry on writing until you reach the next conjunction or clause. When you reach it, pause and consider whether it also flows from the previous main idea. If it does, then place it directly below the previous clause. (See verse 13, where "throughout the whole palace guard" is parallel with "and to everyone else." Both flow out of "it has become clear.")
- If it is a new thought, or a new level of dependence, then when you drop a line, add another indentation. (So again in verse 13, "that I

am in chains for Christ" flows out of the previous two clauses, but
is on a different level to them.)

- When you start a new sentence, return to the left margin.

12 Now I want you to know, brothers and sisters,
    that what has happened to me has actually served to advance the **gospel**.
        13 As a result, it has become clear
            throughout the whole palace guard
            and to everyone else
                that I am **in chains** for Christ.
        14 And because of my **chains**,
            most of the brothers and sisters have become confident in the Lord
            and dare all the more to proclaim the gospel without fear.

15 It is true that
    some **preach** Christ out of envy and rivalry,
    but others [preach] out of goodwill.
        16 The latter do so [preach] out of love,
            knowing that I am put here for the defense of the **gospel**.
        17 The former **preach** Christ
            out of selfish ambition,
            not sincerely,
            supposing that they can stir up trouble for me while I am **in chains**.

18 But what does it matter?
    The important thing is that
    in every way,
    whether from false motives
    or true,
        Christ is **preached**.
            And because of this I rejoice.

Looking at the diagram, we can see that our earlier sense of the centrality
of preaching is reinforced. It features in each of the three sections of our
passage. It also appears that preaching the gospel and preaching Christ are
interchangeable, which suggests that they amount to the same thing. After all,
the heart of the Christian message is not an idea or philosophy to guide us in
life but a person to rescue us from death.

3. Summarize the Passage in One Sentence

As we draw all these threads together, we can begin to identify the passage's
structure or skeleton. At first sight, it appears that Paul is making three separate

points. But a closer look at 1:15–17 and 1:18 suggests that the latter is simply a summary of the previous verses. So there are in fact two ideas here:

- 1:12–14 – Paul's imprisonment serves gospel proclamation, it does not hinder it
    - He can preach to the palace guard and beyond (v. 13)
    - His continued ministry gives others courage to preach (v. 14)
- 1:15–18 – Paul's joy at gospel proclamation, even when motivated by selfish ambition
    - Some preach Christ out of goodwill (v. 16)
    - Others preach Christ out of selfishness (v. 17) – but they both preach Christ!

In both cases, we see Paul's remarkable ability to see beyond the pain and stress of his circumstances (persecution from outside the church, hostility from within the church). He can see God's good purposes for the gospel in it all, which explains how his joy can be genuine. So a summary sentence for this short passage might go like this:

Paul rejoices when Christ is preached, whatever the circumstances.

This summary gives us a pointer for how to apply this passage in a sermon. Paul himself offers a striking discipleship model for persevering in ministry during tough times. Not everyone in a congregation will have a formal ministry role, few will find themselves having their ministry discredited by other believers, even fewer will be imprisoned for their faith (hopefully). But all followers of Christ have the responsibility to live for and proclaim Christ. These verses inspire us to look beyond our circumstances, just as Paul was able to do. In fact, following his example is a key theme of Philippians as a whole.

Join together in following my example, brothers and sisters, and just as you have us as a model, keep your eyes on those who live as we do. (Phil 3:17)

 Nobody will be able to grasp all the parts of this process without repeated practice. Here are some suggestions for passages to work on (perhaps with some friends or colleagues).
- Romans 5:1–11
- 1 Corinthians 15:1–11
- Ephesians 2:1–10
- Colossians 1:15–20
- 1 Peter 1:3–9

---

4. Return to the Big Picture

We are not quite ready to work directly on constructing our sermon yet. We still need to check that our interpretation of this passage fits within the letter's overarching flow. We also need to be open to adapting our understanding of the whole letter in the light of any new insights we have gained from this detailed study. This is part of the normal dialogue between the big picture and the details which we considered at the start of this book.

So what connections can we make to the rest of the letter from these verses? We have already considered the importance of following good discipleship models in the Christian life. Is there anything else?

- The centrality of Christ to the gospel is clear throughout the letter. In particular, 2:5–11 shows how Jesus models sacrificial love and saves rebels at the same time. Preaching the gospel is the same as preaching Christ.
- Paul appeals to the Philippians to continue in gospel ministry in the face of hardships (1:28; 2:15–16).
- He also reminds them to rejoice with him in the midst of his suffering (2:18).
- Personality clashes should not prevent gospel partnership, which is why he appeals to Euodia and Syntyche to be reconciled (4:2–3).
- Gospel unity is paramount; but this does not mean unity or partnership with anyone and everyone. The people causing trouble for Paul here are clearly different from the false teachers of Philippians 3.

There will undoubtedly be other connections, but these are enough to make the point, and to show how the passage is embedded in the letter.

We can now ask whether our outline of the whole letter needs to be amended at all. After the detailed study of this passage, it makes sense to tighten up the title of that section like this:

- *? 1:1–11*   *Greetings and prayer*
- **1:12–26**   **Paul suffers for preaching Christ because of his hope in Christ**
- *? 1:27–2:18*   *Church life modelled on Christ*
- *? 2:19–30*   *Two brothers who minister like Christ*
- *? 3:1–14*   *Gospel confidence only possible in Christ*

- *? 3:15–4:3*   *Follow Paul's example for unity in Christ*
- *? 4:4–23*   *Final instructions and greetings*

If you are planning to preach through the whole of the letter, it is going to be possible to refine the entire outline. It is never set in stone, but is part of an ongoing conversation with the text.

Now, we are ready to work on constructing the sermon's content. But that is the topic of another book!

Gospel Economics

(Philippians 3:1–11)

I don't know about you, but one of the things I find most confusing in the modern world is how the worlds of finance and money work. I have very little to do with them on a day-to-day basis. Yet, wherever we live in the world, our lives can be significantly affected by economic issues. When the countries that produce oil decide to raise the price of oil, it affects the cost of a bus or taxi ride. Or perhaps your government has suddenly decided to ban the use of banknotes with only a few hours' warning (as India did in November 2016 for the commonly used 500 and 1,000 rupee notes). The result was chaos right across the country. When I am travelling with Langham, I am suddenly very keen to know how much different currencies are worth; and when we lived in Uganda, we constantly juggled three currencies: British pounds, US dollars and Ugandan shillings. It's almost impossible for ordinary people to come out better off in that situation.

But the Bible has its own unique financial principles, which we must all grapple with. If worldly financial policies can lead to unemployment and financial ruin, biblical economics is even more serious. The stakes are even higher. Every business (whether a small market stall or multinational corporation) needs to keep an eye on how much money they actually have, whether in a bank or in products. Every year, they need to do their accounts and work out whether they have made a profit or a loss.

The interesting thing is that Paul wants us to do our accounts as well – but not in quite the same way. He wants us to work out whether we are making a spiritual profit or loss – he actually uses the language of profits and loss as we will see. For in Bible terms, a loss can lead to spiritual ruin and ultimately death. The problem in Philippi is that these early believers had been thrown off balance. They felt utterly confused by the different teaching they were hearing. But Paul was desperate for them to get things clear in their minds: nothing less than the health of their Christian discipleship was at stake.

Some people think that this section in chapter 3 was added at a later date, and was not part of Paul's original letter. They say that these verses don't fit with the overall themes of Philippians. Superficially, they have a point. After all, although chapters 1–2 have been challenging, their tone has been consistently positive and encouraging. That encouragement seems to continue in 3:1.

> Finally, my brothers, rejoice in the Lord! It is no trouble for me to write the same things to you again, and it is a safeguard for you.

Then suddenly, in the next verse, Paul launches into what seems like a deranged outburst:

> Watch out for those dogs, those men who do evil, those mutilators of the flesh.

A rude awakening if ever there was one!

But despite that, the links with the previous chapters are strong and vital. These words still fit within the context of 1:27, and the appeal to "conduct yourselves in a manner worthy of the gospel." And Paul states that he is repeating truths that he has already discussed them. This is because these truths are essential. Some teachers have clearly come to the city to bring a message to the Christians that is convincing and challenging. They call themselves Christians, they are no doubt friendly and they do seem to have a point. But Paul insists that his friends should have nothing to do with them. Not because he doesn't like the teachers, or because he's trying to build his own little empire. But because the message of Jesus, the Crucified Lord, is at stake. There must be unity in the truth, but what they are teaching is a distortion of the truth.

Because the Philippians are likely to have been confused, Paul has to make his case. That is what chapter 3 is all about.

1. Do Your Spiritual Accounts (3:1–6)

Credit is important to almost every area of life. Your bank account needs to be in credit if you are going to be able to pay your rent and feed your family. You need to have a good credit score if you want to borrow money to buy supplies for your business or to build a home for your family. When it comes to getting a job, employers will want to know about your work experience and whether you are recommended as an employee by reliable people. Similar questions may be asked by your future in-laws if you want to marry someone. You need to be "in good credit" with other people if you are to get that job or to marry into that family. And you need to have good "credit" at your work if you hope to get a promotion.

The concern to build up credit comes naturally to us, whether in terms of our finances, our relationships or our achievements. So it is no surprise that people also want to try to build credit with God. They assume that God wants us to build up an impressive list of holy deeds. One survey of 7,000 under 25's from Protestant denominations in the USA found that 60 per cent of them agreed that "the way to be accepted by God is to try sincerely to live a good life." Almost 70 per cent agreed that "God is satisfied if a person lives the best life they can."

Trying to earn spiritual points with God is the natural religion of humanity. So when some people claiming to be Christian come along with a plausible, apparently biblical argument for doing so, it's easy to understand why the Philippians got confused. But Paul does not mince words in verse 2: they are "dogs, evil-doers, mutilators of the flesh."

So what was the big problem? It all hinges on the fact that for Jews, circumcision was an important marker to show that a man was a Jew and so belonged to God's people. God had commanded that his people do this in Abraham's day (Gen 17) – and the practice continues among Jews to this day. Now preachers had come to Philippi insisting that Gentiles converts to Christ must become culturally Jewish and must also be circumcised. Those who taught this were called the circumcision party, or Judaizers. Fair enough, you might think. Circumcision had always been the sign you were part of God's people, hadn't it? What could be the problem with that? It's there in the law after all.

But Paul strongly disagrees – and expresses how strongly he feels by a rather gruesome play on words in which he parallels flesh mutilators in verse 2 and circumcision in verse 3. He states in verse 3 that *Christians* are the true circumcision group, whether they've been physically circumcised or not, whether they're Gentile or not.

The Jews had sometimes referred to Gentiles (whom the old covenant law tended to exclude from God's people) as "dogs," because dogs were ritually unclean animals. But shockingly Paul says that it is the *Judaizers* who are the dogs, the unclean ones outside God's people. God true people are those who worship by the spirit of God and who glory in Christ Jesus.

That's a strong claim. So why say it? Is Paul getting things out of proportion? No. It's all a matter of confidence and where you think your credit lies.

You may not have heard of Barings Bank in London. But if you were a financial investor in the 1980s and 1990s, any connection to Barings Bank would have impressed you. If you were somehow offered the chance to invest some money in the bank, it would have been a rock-solid investment, no doubt about it. After all, Barings was London's oldest privately owned merchant bank founded in 1762. It had all that tradition; all that experience to draw on. They could be trusted.

Who could possibly have guessed that in 1995 the whole lot would collapse in spectacular fashion? All because of some reckless and extravagant trading by an English employee called Nick Leeson. He cost the bank $1.4 billion. That kind of money is unimaginable. Thanks to his efforts, he himself ended up with a six-and-a-half-year prison sentence in Singapore, while the entire bank was sold for just £1 to a Dutch bank which agreed to take on its debts. A solid investment? It would have seemed like it before Nick Leeson started working there. It would have seemed like the perfect place to keep your savings. But the reality was very different. There was no security there at all. Their accounts would have showed huge debts and massive losses.

There is a chilling parallel to the mindset of the Judaizers. They may not have invested money in a bank, but they had invested their time, energy and passion in trying to please God by keeping his law. They thought this was the perfect investment.

Paul understands the Judaizers perfectly. After all, before his conversion to Christ, he was like them. He was the perfect model of the devout Jew – and he was absolutely confident that this was enough to put someone's spiritual account into spiritual credit. As he says in verse 4:

> I myself have reasons for such confidence. If anyone else thinks he
> has reasons to put confidence in the flesh, I have more.

Then we read a long list of spiritual credits, which can be divided in two: the first deals with whatever came to Paul by virtue of his birth:

- He was circumcised at exactly the right time according to the law.
- He was born into the people of Israel.
- He was member of the tribe of Benjamin – a great honour since Benjamin was the only one of Jacob's sons born in the promised land. The tribe remained loyal to the house of David, and contained Jerusalem within its territory.
- Despite growing up in Tarsus (in southern Turkey), Paul was a thoroughgoing Jew, "a Hebrew of Hebrews"– with all the right education. As he says elsewhere, he was even taught by the hugely famous Rabbi Gamaliel (Acts 22:3).

In verse 5, he turns to what he has achieved.

- He was a Pharisee – which means that the law was of supreme importance to him. So much so that he believed it was right to seek

out and destroy any group that threatened the authority of the law
– that's why he persecuted the church.

- But Paul's supreme achievement comes at the end of the paragraph:
when it comes to legalistic righteousness, he was faultless.

Do you believe him?

Well, for all the doubts we might have, Paul clearly had no doubts – even
after his conversion. That's the whole point. For as far as the law was concerned,
he had kept all its external demands – to the letter. He wouldn't have been
interested in internal failures, which only he and God were aware of. Outwardly,
he was totally obedient. He couldn't be faulted. Never underestimate that
achievement. His concern for godliness puts us to shame. We get nowhere close.

The shock is that Paul has since experienced a complete revolution in his
thinking. Don't imagine that he now denies his old legalistic righteousness.
Not at all. He could still boast about that if he wanted to. But he won't, because
he now realizes it gets him nowhere. God may have provided all that law
and tradition, but its purpose was never to make people righteous. Paul had
invested in the wrong thing. It's like buying minutes for your phone only to
discover the code was fake, or saving up all your 500 rupee notes in order to
buy a present for the family just as the banknote gets cancelled.

2. Escape from Your Debts (3:7–9)

> Whatever was to my profit I now consider loss. (v. 7)

It's as if someone has come along, and provided a totally different interpretation
of the figures. While you thought your business was doing well, it was actually
losing money once all the expenses were included in the accounting! That was
what Paul had discovered in spiritual terms. But he wasn't confused, because
this new analysis convinced him. It fitted with what he knew in his heart – and
with the way Jesus saw reality. When Paul got converted on the Damascus
Road, his whole world was turned upside down, and he uses stunning language
to prove it.

> What is more, I consider everything a loss compared to the
> surpassing greatness of knowing Christ Jesus my Lord, for whose
> sake I have lost all things. I consider them rubbish that I may gain
> Christ, and am found in him. (v. 8)

The NIV translation is far too polite. The Greek word translated "rubbish"
actually refers to excrement and rotten food. You know that smell if you have

ever been near a poorly maintained latrine or cesspit. It can make you feel like throwing up.

That gives you some idea how Paul feels about his old way of life. He found it repulsive. Rather like the things left to rot in drains and gutters. He wasn't neutral about it – he couldn't be. Why? Because he had realized that all his old religious credit left him in the red. It all left him spiritually bankrupt before God.

> Not having a righteousness of my own that comes from the law, but that which is through faith in Christ – the righteousness that comes from God and is by faith. (v. 9)

You see, he may have been faultless if you take the law on its own terms – if you judge it on externals. That's all human beings can do, isn't it? You can't read my heart, and I can't read yours. BUT . . . God can. And if righteousness is about being in a right relationship with him, then we're ruined. No amount of good deeds will change the heart.

Once Paul saw that, he had no doubts. He yearned for a heart that could truly be right with God. And there is only one way that can happen – if God gives him a new heart. It's as simple and as seemingly impossible as that. And how do we receive it? By trusting Jesus as the only one who can perform the operation. Because he simply hands it to us – righteousness with God, righteousness that we don't need to earn, righteousness that we could never earn however much we tried. That is the only way it is possible to come out of spiritual debt.

Now can you see why Paul is so violent in his denunciation of the Judaizers? It is simply because they imply that we can't trust Jesus to do everything we need to get right with God. The law *is* a divine gift – but it was never designed to make people righteous. It was designed to be a marker for people who had been made righteous. To show that they belonged. And when Jesus comes along, he says you don't need those old covenant signs anymore[1] – instead, by his Spirit, Jesus brings a circumcision of the heart, just as Jeremiah had anticipated (Jer 4:4). Returning to physical circumcision is like putting your confidence in things *we* do. Paul was never going to budge on that – to add to the gospel is to destroy the gospel. It shifts the responsibility from Jesus back to us.

So never forget that our instinct is always to build a spiritual résumé, a list of all the things we feel proud of. That just seems to be human nature.

---

1. This is one of those instances where a grasp of the Old Testament background is essential for interpreting the New Testament.

Even if we've been Christians for a while, we still try to build up all sorts of achievements that we imagine will impress God somehow. We can do it even when we fully understand faith-based righteousness. Do you find yourself thinking that if you've had a personal time of prayer and Bible study today, then God should bless you more and the day should go better? Then if it doesn't, do you blame him? Are you tempted to feel superior if you're from an old Christian family with famous ancestors? Do you have even the remotest suspicion that because you come to a Langham Preaching seminar or read a Langham Literature book, that God must be especially pleased with you? After all, what could possibly be better than that!?

Well, forget it all – that attitude stinks. It's what made Paul vomit. Our confidence can *only* come from Jesus. Not because we're zealous or from a good family or theologically educated – but because of God's totally undeserved kindness to spiritual rebels and bankrupts.

It's all a matter of how you look at it, ultimately. Do we look at things the world sees as personal achievements: in other words, does what we do earn us credit? Or do we look at our achievements the way God sees them: as useless excrement, adding up to nothing? Because in Bible finances, God turns everything upside down.

3. Make an Eternal Investment (3:10–11)

If Jesus has done everything for us, is there anything left for us to do? Listen to what Paul says:

> I want to know Christ and the power of his resurrection and the fellowship of sharing in his sufferings, becoming like him in his death, and so somehow to attain to the resurrection from the dead.

If you have read earlier parts of Philippians, I wonder if that sounds familiar. Back in 2:5, Paul said, "Your attitude should be the same as that of Christ Jesus." And then he went on to describe all that Jesus gave up – even submitting to death on a criminal's cross.

Now Paul is saying that in his own life, he wants to be like Jesus in his death. Now, I should say that I always found verse 10 hard. It always seemed unreal to me for Paul to *want* to share in Christ's sufferings! I could understand someone prepared to live with suffering, but it's quite another thing to *want* it.

But Paul is not claiming to enjoy pain. What matters is not the suffering so much as the sharing with Christ. He wants to follow Jesus wherever he leads, because Jesus has turned his life upside down. As a result of the gospel, Paul no longer regards life in the same old way. He is no longer concerned for worldly prestige or credit; his sights are set on far greater matters: being with Jesus forever. He wants to "gain Christ," for as he said back in chapter 1, for "to live is Christ, and to die is gain." This way of life is possible now because of the power of Jesus's resurrection working in his life. It simply wouldn't be possible otherwise. So he looks forward, prepared for whatever life has in store for him.

In Bible terms, that is investing in something that counts because it lasts for eternity. Jesus once said "whoever wants to save his life, will lose it, but whoever loses his life for me and for the gospel will save it" (Mark 8:35). The question that faces all of us is not how holy we are being, how spiritual or devout. The proper question is whether or not believe Jesus's interpretation of our spiritual accounts? Do we believe, as Paul did, that we are making a genuine gain or profit by following Jesus in this life? Even if it includes sharing his suffering and pain in some way? Or should we try to do some extra work on our own, in case Christ's work isn't enough? As a kind of spiritual insurance?

Paul trusted Jesus wholeheartedly and passionately. And if the gospel of grace is true, can we do anything else?

Section 4

Preaching Revelation

There are many reasons for leaving the book of Revelation to the end of this book – the most obvious being that it comes at the end of the Bible! That is an entirely appropriate place for it because it draws all the Bible's key themes together in a satisfying conclusion. It forms the perfect climax.

Yet the primary reason for leaving it till last is that the style of the book makes significant demands on the preacher, so that all the skills and experience gained from handling the rest of the Bible will be essential.

Before we start, it is necessary to point out some of the unhelpful effects that Revelation can have on people. It sometimes seems to bring out the worst in people when it was originally written to bring out the best! This shows itself in three unhelpful ways.

Terror!

The book is filled with the stuff of nightmares. It describes a world of terrifying monsters and elemental forces, a universe where people feel like ants in a world of giants. It describes the end of the world in lurid colours and frightening detail. No wonder some do everything they can to avoid reading it. If someone's biblical diet consists of the gospels and Paul's letters, then this reaction is hardly surprising.

Yet terror is the very emotion that Revelation was intended to remove! It was written for times when the *real* world seems filled with monsters and dark forces. So whenever we study and preach on this book, we must remember that it was written to build CONFIDENCE, not fear!

Obsession!

Some discover that the book of Revelation is the perfect foundation for a life's work! There are so many fantastical and weird details that the rest of the Bible can seem dull and colourless by comparison. So it can become an unhealthy obsession, and even the sole focus for biblical study.[2] No other book attracts anything like the same dedication.

One way this obsession shows itself is through combing newspapers or websites for indications of a fulfilled prophecy. There is no doubt that the Bible has deep relevance to current affairs, and so it is right that we keep our eyes open to what is going on around us. But there are a few pitfalls to doing this when working with apocalyptic literature, as we will see. So above all, we need to remember that this book was written to make us PATIENT, not psychic!

Confusion!

Perhaps for most people in our congregations, Revelation is simply a mystery. It is unlike any other book we have ever read, and that uniqueness is precisely the problem. We have nothing to compare it with. It is a bit like exploring an alien planet, with terrain and plants that are unrecognisable. Everything seems confusing and disorientating.

The result is that many people start the book but never reach the end. It seems readable and encouraging to begin with, but things take a turn for the worse after chapter 7 (unless we have given up after chapter 3, that is). But there is great wisdom in its placing in the Bible. It draws threads together from the whole Bible, and we should always keep the rest of the Bible in mind as we read it. Like all other sixty-five books, it was written to be UNDERSTOOD, not avoided!

We should receive Revelation as a God-given gift, to be treasured, trusted and rejoiced in. This is a book that is as needed today as it has ever been – especially in the many countries around the world where Christians are openly persecuted for their beliefs and lifestyles.

One way to hold back these different emotions is to consider what the Bible expects us to think and know as we approach the book of Revelation. So this will be our focus in the next chapter. Then we will consider some of its unique characteristics in the following chapter. We will then be in a much stronger position for applying and preaching Revelation to a contemporary congregation.

---

2. For example, some people are overly focused on the idea of the Rapture and the Millennium. I cannot discuss these ideas in detail here, but have included a few notes on the topic in Appendix 3.

10

Approaching the Book of Revelation

The title "Revelation" is a direct translation of the book's opening words in Greek, of which the first is *apokalypsis*. The word literally means "unveiling," the bringing to light, or revelation, of things previously hidden. This is entirely appropriate. John's book is full of details that would be impossible to guess or predict without this unveiling. Our lives are bound by time and space – this book lifts our eyes and ears to reality beyond, to eternity and the very presence of God. It is truly breathtaking.

It is as if the curtains concealing a theatre stage are pulled back, and we discover what is *really* going on in God's universe. Or perhaps we could think of God as a great painter. He has just completed his masterpiece, but it has been kept under wraps. Until now. The coverings are pulled back, and now the world can see the work in all its glory. It is a work of genius, even if at times it is an uncomfortable one.

We should remember, however, that the Apostle John did not invent apocalyptic writing. He was drawing on an ancient and honoured heritage found in several parts of the Old Testament. The most famous is the second half of Daniel, but there are other, shorter, passages that could also fit in this category. Because this heritage had such distinctive features, the word *apocalyptic* has come to be used of all writing that uses this style.

Bible commentator Paul Barnett makes this helpful comment about the style:

> [Apocalyptic literature] usually arose when things seemed dark, and evil had the upper hand. God's people are suffering and injustice is dominant. All the indications are that they are on the

losing side. Apocalyptic texts, however, tell them that they are on the *winning* side and that God will conquer in the end.

The apocalyptic writer was a visionary who saw beyond the present miseries tot he end of all things when God would punish evil people and vindicate innocent sufferers. Apocalyptic writing is highly charged and usually deeply symbolic. Often the language is coded to throw would-be persecutors off the scent.[1]

 Before we look at Revelation in depth, read some of these passages to see if you can identify some of the common features of apocalyptic writing? Don't worry too much about trying to interpret their meaning or significance at this stage. Simply make a note of the distinctive apocalyptic features.

- The key Old Testament apocalyptic books
  - Daniel 7–12
  - Isaiah 24–27, 33–35
- Ezekiel 38–39
  - Zechariah 12–14
- Other apocalyptic passages in the Old Testament
  - Jeremiah 33:14–26
  - Joel 3:9–17
- Apocalyptic passages in the New Testament
  - Matthew 24 (& Mark 13, Luke 21)
  - 2 Thessalonians 2

---

1. Biblical Assumptions about Revelation

Having pointed out some unhelpful approaches to apocalyptic literature, it is important to get on the right track by identifying certain assumptions we can make when we approach the book of Revelation.

---

1. Paul W. Barnett, *John The Pastor: Encouragements for a Struggling Church* (Milton Keynes: Paternoster, 2015), 7-8

a) Jesus laid the groundwork for Revelation (Matt 24)

Jesus himself sometimes used an apocalyptic preaching style. This is clear when we read the last of the five teaching blocks in Matthew's gospel (Matt 23–25). It is fair to say that those verses lay the groundwork for Revelation, which would be written a few decades later. At this point, we need to highlight just two important features of Matthew 24.[2]

The experience of distress and deception: In talking about the "end times," Jesus is adamant that there will be terrible experiences, from which his followers are not exempt:

> For then there will be great distress, unequalled from the beginning of the world until now – and never to be equalled again . . . For false messiahs and false prophets will appear and perform great signs and wonders to deceive, if possible, even the elect. (Matt 24:21, 24)

Not only are Jesus's followers not exempt from persecution, they may well be the specific target for it (as John makes clear in Revelation). Suffering is a reality for believers, and so are spiritual fraudsters. This means we should never be surprised to hear of people claiming messianic status or divine authority. Jesus told us that this would happen.

It follows that any interpretation of Revelation must take these realities into account. Any interpretation that suggests that followers of Jesus are immune to suffering cannot be correct. That is a direct contradiction of Jesus's own teaching.

The need for trust, not timelines: It's hard to know how much clearer Jesus could have been about his return:

> But about that day or hour no one knows, not even the angels in heaven, nor the Son, but only the Father. (Matt 24:36)

Not even Jesus knew when the second coming would take place! It is astonishing how often people forget this. As he teaches in the subsequent verses, the crucial point is that his return is guaranteed. It is a future fact. Yet it will still come as a surprise. Surely that suggests any attempt to identify a specific date is going to be doomed to failure?

---

2. One issue that sometimes arises in relation to Matthew 24:40–41 is "the rapture of the saints" (although that is not what Jesus is talking about in Matthew). I have included a brief note on it and on the topic of the Millennium series in Appendix 3.

So, however you understand the big picture of Revelation, please don't aim to become a "Second Coming Countdown guru." That path may lead to fame, fortune and television shows, but it is not faithful to either the spirit or the letter of what Jesus taught. Instead we should simply trust in the fact of Jesus's return and encourage our people to do the same. We should be content with being ignorant about dates or timelines, because Jesus was!

b) The Bible gives the background for Revelation

One of the most accessible commentaries on Revelation is Michael Wilcock's 1975 contribution to The Bible Speaks Today series, *The Message of Revelation*. In it, he summarizes the whole of Revelation under the heading: "The Book We Could Do Without." That may seem a strange thing to say, but it makes a lot of sense. His point is that there is actually nothing new in Revelation. As he says:

> Revelation is a "pledge of his love." We could do without it; it tells us nothing we could not learn elsewhere in Scripture. But Jesus has given it to us . . . to quicken the pulse and set the soul aflame over the gospel which all too often we take for granted.[3]

So we should always be wary of brand new interpretations of Revelation that don't fit with the rest of Scripture. They simply can't be correct. It is a weird and wonderful book – but it as much the result of the Holy Spirit's inspiration as Proverbs, Colossians or Isaiah.

2. Revelation Is the Bible's Blended Book

As we have seen throughout this book, it is always wise to allow the Bible's writers to inform us of their purpose instead of presuming to know it ourselves. John informs us of his reason for writing this book in the very first verses – and in so doing highlights the fact that it blends several different biblical styles together.

Revelation is an apocalypse (1:1)

To say that Revelation is an apocalypse does not mean that it is full of doom and disaster (as the popular understanding of the word would suggest). As we

---

3. Michael Wilcock, *The Message of Revelation* (Nottingham: IVP, 1975), 220.

have just noted, the first word of the book is *apokalypsis* meaning "unveiling." This informs us from the very start that Revelation is a book proclaiming what cannot naturally be seen or heard. The spiritual battles and eternal consequences described here are invisible to the naked eye.

Think of it as giving us a glimpse of human history and the end of days from the perspective of God's throne room. What a privilege it is to have this book in our possession!

Revelation is prophecy (1:3)

Prophecy is another word that does not quite mean what people think it means (at least when it refers to Bible books). Many assume that prophecy simply entails predictions of the future. Yet that does not quite fit. Even a brief glance at the great books of Isaiah or Jeremiah, for example, shows that they have far fewer explicit predictions than we might have hoped. The prophets of old tend to have been far more concerned with their present context than the long-term future.

This explains why it is often said that biblical prophecy is as much forth-telling as it is foretelling. In other words, it speaks into its own era with a message from God that is relevant to the hearers. The message may include some predictions, usually because these are necessary to encourage the present faithfulness of believers. That's the crucial point. Their focus is on their immediate hearers, not some remote future brother or sister.

We should remember that fact as we interpret John's Revelation. He was a believer living under the Roman Empire in the first century. That shapes everything in his book, and his proclamation of God's perspective on that time is precisely what qualifies the book as prophetic. Ultimately, in New Testament terms, prophecy is about witnessing to the supreme truth – Jesus is Lord! Now and Always. That is the big theme that runs through every paragraph of Revelation.

Revelation is a letter (1:4)

One of the most famous sections of the book contains seven letters to the seven churches (Rev 2–3). However, the whole book can be seen as a letter to those same seven churches (as 1:4 makes clear). The whole thing was to be circulated around each of them – perhaps a bit like the news or prayer letters that people in ministry often send out to friends and supporters.

Because Revelation is a blend of these different types of biblical literature, there is wisdom in gaining experience in handling each of them before embarking on serious study of the book.

3. Revelation Is the Bible's Final Occasional Book

This point should not come as a surprise after recognizing that Revelation was in fact written as a letter. Just as Paul wrote each of his letters for specific people on specific occasions, so does John in Revelation. One of the first errors that is commonly made when interpreting Revelation is to ignore this fact. We always need to be aware of its original context.

The book was written specifically for believers in seven cities in Asia Minor (modern western Turkey). These cities were not fictional or part of John's heavenly visions; they were important stops on the major trade routes in the region. Each church faced significant, though different, battles. But the primary source of their problems was the Roman emperor. Which emperor it was depends on the exact dating of John's exile on Patmos and when he made a record of his visions. One option is the Emperor Nero (AD 54–68), but the more commonly suggested enemy is the ruthless Emperor Domitian (AD 81–96).

In the light of this background, should we restrict the book's relevance exclusively to the first century?

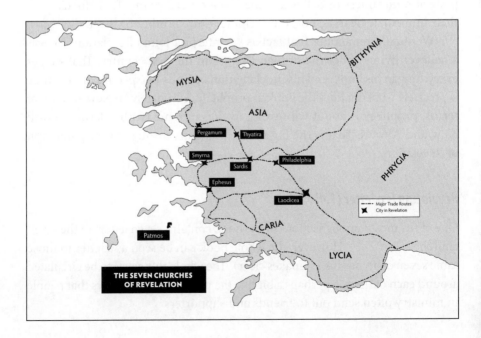

A history book: Is Revelation only about the first century?

We might assume that, like much Old Testament prophecy, the majority of the future descriptions in Revelation are prophecies for John's present or *near* future. That is why some interpret the book solely in terms of the events around the time when John wrote the book. They claim that everything described in Revelation has already happened. In other words, today's readers are living *centuries* after the events it describes. There are spiritual lessons to learn for faithful discipleship (just as there are with the Old Testament history books, for example), but there is little direct application to contemporary or future events.

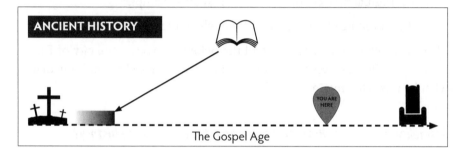

But this is not a commonly held view. For starters, this approach does not explain why so much of the imagery (especially later in the book) seems so catastrophic. It is hard to resist interpreting it as the end of the world as we know it. Suggesting that John is simply using exaggeration to describe dark times is possible, but seems unlikely.

So perhaps we should see Revelation as having a primarily future relevance?

An end-times book: Is Revelation mainly about the long-term future?

John did seem to expect his book to be relevant beyond his own lifetime, but he could have been mistaken. After all he was told:

> Do not seal up the words of the prophecy of this scroll, because the time is near. (22:10)

Yet there are many details and images that seem to refer to the end of the world, as we have already noted. Consequently, some take the opposite view to the Ancient History view. They suggest that John provides us with a countdown, a timeline, to the climax of history. Our job is to keep our eyes open for the moment the clock starts ticking and prophecies start being fulfilled.

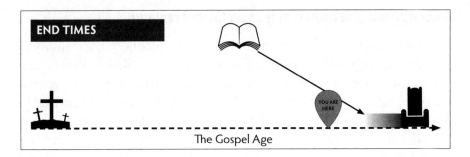

But this also is too simplistic. It does not do justice to details that clearly relate to John's original first-century context. Take this example:

> The seven heads are seven hills on which the woman sits. (17:9)

That must refer to the source of all the believers' woes – the city of Rome, famously built on seven hills. John's readers would have known immediately what he was referring to.

A timeline book: Does Revelation describe stages in human history?

So perhaps a better approach is to combine the previous two approaches. Perhaps Revelation offers a timeline between the first century and Jesus's return at some unspecified time in the future. If so, then Revelation offers us an outline of the various stages of human history from the perspective of heaven. The reader's task is therefore to identify which detail refers to which event down the centuries.

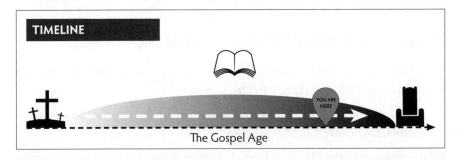

As a result of adopting this approach, generations of Christians have confidently identified Revelation's details in terms of contemporary events and individuals. The beast (often identified as the antichrist of John's letters) has been identified with Saladin during the time of the medieval Crusades, and with the pope in Luther's day. Or is he possibly Napoleon in the nineteenth century? Or the British Empire? Or Hitler or Stalin or Mao or Pol Pot or the European Union or a presidential candidate or a multinational corporation or . . . or . . . or . . . ? Take your pick!

That illustrates one problem with this approach. Another is that, as we have already seen, Jesus warned us against trying to identify the timing of his return. He wants us to concentrate on trusting his faithfulness instead of second-guessing his movements.

One more option remains, and it is one that undermines all three of the options we have described.

A universal book: Revelation is for all generations

Could it be that John's book genuinely is for all time? It has relevance to every generation, not in the sense that each can find itself described in the book's timeline (as if it offered a birds-eye view of human history). Instead, it offers an overview of God's sovereign work over the world, confirming spiritual truths that are true throughout these last days. It thus has universal relevance for every people group at every time.

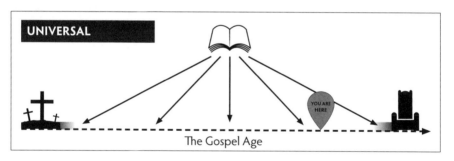

John naturally uses imagery from his contemporary world (hence the allusions to the Roman Empire) and he also points ahead to some of the unique, cosmic events at Jesus's return. But the passages between those points fit with any century in history.

That explains why some of the symbolism is hard to link with specific people or events. It also explains why the end of the world seems to happen more than once (which itself suggests that the book's chapters cannot be a consecutive account of world history)!

So when John wrote, "the time is near," he meant it only in the sense that it is near from God's perspective. After all, as Peter tells us, with God a day is like a thousand years and a thousand years are like a day (2 Pet 3:8).

Revelation really is a book for all time and all peoples – just as the whole Bible is. This means that when we teach it, we should ensure that we have understood its first-century roots but should interpret it in such a way that it is relevant to all believers everywhere.

11

Getting to Grips with Apocalyptic Writing

We can now consider how to understand and teach some of the unique features of apocalyptic writing. While there are certainly a few complex details, there is no reason to feel intimidated by it. Apocalyptic is much more straightforward than it might at first seem. The key is simply to recognize how its features were intended to work.

1. Read as Word Pictures (Not Drawing Instructions)!

It is not hard to see why apocalyptic has inspired some of the world's great artists. For example, John describes in Revelation how he is taken from scene to scene by his angelic guide and told to "look!" As we read his book, we naturally find ourselves longing to see what he can see and to picture it in our minds. It is only as we stop to think about some of these scenes that we are suddenly confronted by their strangeness, if not impossibility. Take this for instance:

> Then the angel showed me the river of the water of life, as clear as crystal, flowing from the throne of God and of the Lamb down the middle of the great street of the city. On each side of the river stood the tree of life, bearing twelve crops of fruit, yielding its fruit every month. (Rev 22:1–2)

Each of these elements is straightforward enough. It's only when we try to imagine what it might look like that it gets tricky. A river in the middle of the heavenly city's main avenue? And then how does this tree stand "on *each* side"?[1] Perhaps it forms a bridge of some sort, with huge extended roots coming down? It is clearly a special tree, though, because it can be harvested monthly, instead of the normal annual crop.

Should we just put this down to a new form of heavenly tree species? Or could there be another purpose here? It surely makes far more sense to focus on what each element *means*, rather than how each element *appears*. Our first instinct should be to interpret Revelation, not to draw it.

So the point about the heavenly tree of life in Revelation 22 is that its fruit is accessible (it has roots on both sides of the street) and abundant (it has multiple harvests).

But that is to move too quickly to interpretation. Before moving on, here are a few other "impossible" or fantastical images.

- "The hair on his head was white like wool, as white as snow, and his eyes were like blazing fire . . . His face was like the sun shining in all its brilliance" (1:14, 16). This awe-inspiring vision of Christ is contradictory if taken literally. It is impossible to look directly into the sun, so John would never have been able to see his hair or eyes!
- "The locusts looked like horses prepared for battle. On their heads, they wore something like crowns of gold, and their faces resembled human faces. Their hair was like women's hair, and their teeth were like lions' teeth" (9:7–8). This is the stuff of ancient myths and legends!
- "And I saw what looked like a sea of glass glowing with fire" (15:2). There is no need to conjure up burning oil slicks here!

Identify the images

Apocalyptic is not the only Bible literature to make use of pictures and images, of course. Poetic writing uses them all the time, frequently lifting an image from one aspect of life and placing it alongside another, often in surprising ways. This always lends the image new depths and significance, and is never meant to be taken literally (as we saw when considering the parables). Thus the kingdom of God "is like a mustard seed." We do not take it literally, but *"literarily"* (if I can put it like that). In other words, we interpret it as its literary genre demands.

---

1. Some translations try to smooth over the image by translating it as "trees" standing on each side. However, John's original Greek is very clearly singular – there is one tree of life, on both sides of the river.

The difference is that apocalyptic literature takes the imagery a step further – it extracts us from the realms of the ordinary and thrusts us into the realm of the supernatural, the kinds of worlds that myths and legends from cultures across the world describe. This is why we are confronted by fantastical beasts with multiple heads and horizons filled with people in every direction. But our approach should be no different than it is when we come across imagery in Bible poetry or parables. We simply seek out the possible significance of the image from the context.

John's first readers would have understood his book much like we understand political cartoons today. They have bite and sometimes spark controversy – but their target is immediately obvious. The same is true of Revelation. Of course, we are so far removed from John's time that this causes us some difficulty. On the few occasions where we don't get clues from the rest of the Bible, we might need help from commentators who have spent a lifetime in study. For example, they would know that Rome was built on seven hills, which immediately throws light on a number of John's symbols about the empire that persecuted the first Christians (see Rev 17:9). However, we can take comfort from the fact that we very rarely need to turn to commentators.

Sometimes, though, no work is required at all, since John in fact explains the significance of his images:

> I turned around to see the voice that was speaking to me. And when I turned I saw seven golden lampstands, and among the lampstands was someone like a son of man. (Rev 1:12–13)

> The mystery of the seven stars that you saw in my right hand and of the seven golden lampstands is this: The seven stars are the angels of the seven churches, and the seven lampstands are the seven churches. (Rev 1:20)

But why are there seven of all these things? Why is this type of writing so obsessed with numbers.

Understand the numbers

Numbers also require interpretation, but for some reason, the care that people bring to interpreting other Bible details seems to abandon them at this point! We should treat the numbers no differently from the images. They are not necessarily literal, but they are usually significant. Just as the images are not included so that we can draw them, neither are the numbers there so that we can calculate the end of the world!

So let us consider the number that crops up throughout John's book: the number seven. There is no need for blind speculation about what this means, nor even a knowledge of classical history, however, because its symbolism of "seven" is clearly derived from the Bible.

In Genesis 1–2, God rested on the seventh day, after six days of creating. This is foundational, setting the pattern for the human working week (Exod 20:8–11). Rest in the Bible comes with completed work, and so seven denotes completion, fullness, perfection.

So when John sees seven lampstands as representing seven churches, we are meant to see this as representative of the whole of God's church. This explains why only a few churches are mentioned – for we know that there were other congregations in the Roman province of Asia Minor that could equally well have been included. As becomes clear as we read through the letters in Revelation 2–3, the challenges facing these seven churches are representative of the primary challenges faced by Christ's church in a hostile world. This implies that the whole book, and not just chapters 2–3, is for the whole of Christ's church on earth, both then, and now. It is not just a book for those caught up in the fires of persecution.

This interpretation of the number seven sheds light on one of Revelation's most talked about numbers:

> This calls for wisdom. Let the person who has insight calculate the number of the beast, for it is the number of a man. That number is 666. (Rev 13:18)

Ancient Hebrew and Greek did not have separate characters for numbers (as modern languages do) – instead they used the first letters of the alphabet with a marker to show that the letter was to be interpreted as a number. If we were to represent this in the Roman alphabet, it might look something like this: 1 = a', 2 = b', 3 = c' and so on. This meant that names could always be assigned numerical significance too. For example, some ancient graffiti discovered in Pompeii in southern Italy read, "I love her whose name is 545." When the Roman Emperor Nero's name is taken from Hebrew into Greek, and the numbers allocated to the letters are added up, we end up with 666. Nero was a terrifying persecutor of the church, so it is hardly surprising to find him described as the beast.

But intriguing though this background knowledge is, it is unnecessary for establishing the number's significance. Believers would certainly have considered 666 the ideal number for the beast – since each digit is just less than seven, the number of perfection. By that token, God's number would be 777. This fits with one of Revelation's constant themes – God's enemies try to imitate God and his purposes, but never manage to pull it off. Such is the fate of the fraudulent trickster. He is superficially convincing, but his true colours always show themselves in the end.

But why shouldn't we take these numbers literally? After all, when John is shown the believers in heaven who have been sealed with God's seal, he is specific: there are 144,000 (Rev 7:3–8). This number that has been taken literally by various groups throughout the last two thousand years.

As so often, we should study a verse's context before plunging into our interpretation. What do we read immediately after this paragraph?

> After this I looked, and there before me was a great multitude that no one could count, from every nation, tribe, people and language, standing before the throne and before the Lamb. They were wearing white robes and were holding palm branches in their hands. (Rev 7:9)

What do we discover if we compare these two groups?

Revelation 7:3–8	Revelation 7:9
I heard . . .	I looked . . .
144,000	Countless multitude
All the tribes of Israel (12,000 from each)	Every nation, tribe, people, language
Sealed on the foreheads, servants of our God	Wearing white robes, holding palm branches

John's experience has been full of surprises. In 5:5 he is told of "the Lion of the tribe of Judah," but when he looks, he sees a "Lamb looking as though it had been slain" (5:6). Here, he is told of 144,000 sealed believers, but when he turns to look, he sees the vast multitude. We are clearly meant to identify these two sections as describing the same group of people: God's saved ones. A single people group has become a global, united nations, just as God promised Abraham (Gen 17:3–6).

But why 144,000?

As is clear from the Old Testament, God created Israel with twelve tribes, each descended from a son of Jacob. So twelve has a similar significance to seven – both are numbers of completion. In order to give a sense of the size of the crowds, the numbers are multiplied by 1,000. Thus we find 12 x 12,000 comes to 144,000.

Can you work out the significance of these numbers?
- **24 elders on 24 thrones** (4:4). *Clue*: 12 is significant in the New Testament as well as the OT!
- **42 months** (11:2). *Clue*: = 3½ years, (half of 7), suggesting it is not an infinite length
- **10 days** (2:10). *Clue*: a round, limited number

Tell the Time(s)

Apocalyptic writers often treat time and history in a non-literal way. This is why they often seem to divide periods of time into neat packages. Real history is messy and confusing – but because writers like John are given a heavenly perspective on it all, they can see the patterns that make some sense of it all. From a pastoral perspective, this is crucial for those who are enduring terrible persecution. It offers vital meaning and hope for resolution at precisely the moments when none seems even conceivable.

This does not mean that all these neat packages fall in chronological order. They might describe the same event from different angles. A case in point is the sequence of seven seals and seven trumpets.

The Seals
- 6:12 "I watched as he opened the sixth seal."
  - 6:13–7:17 the consequences of opening the sixth seal
  - 7:10 "a great multitude that no one could count"
- 8:1 "When he opened the seventh seal, there was silence in heaven for about half an hour."

The Trumpets
- 9:13 "The sixth angel sounded his trumpet"
  - 9:14–11:14 the consequences of sounding the sixth trumpet: the angel and little scroll, followed by two witnesses (10–11)
- 11:15 "The seventh angel sounded his trumpet, and there were loud voices in heaven."

When we compare the seventh seal with the seventh trumpet, there is quite a surprise. The former leads to silence, the latter to resounding praise. But in their different ways, both point to God's completed work of salvation. Just before the seventh seal is opened, the elder instructing John speaks of the moment when every tear is wiped away (7:17 compare with 21:4). The subsequent silence is presumably because there are no longer tears. This only happens at the end – when Jesus returns.

John is then immediately carried away to the trumpet sequence. At the end, the praises of heaven rejoice that the Messiah's kingdom has begun, along with the judgment of the world (11:15–18). There follows a breathtaking, if brief, moment when the temple courts of heaven are opened up, presumably to allow people into God's presence.

This is made even more impressive by the reminders of God's presence with his people on Mount Sinai – the lightning, thunder, and earthquake (Exod 19:16–19). In Exodus times, God's holiness meant that access to him was impossible for sinful people. Now, even though the same natural phenomena occur in his presence, the court is accessible to his people.

In their different ways, both the seventh seal and seventh trumpet usher in the eternal age of God's kingdom, heralded by Jesus's return. This surely cannot happen twice! Nor can the judgment of the dead – even though this is described again in 20:11–15.

Even though the accompanying diagram looks intimidating, it helps to show that when we read Revelation we are not dealing with consecutive moments along a timeline. They are different angles of the same events. If we

AN ATTEMPT TO COMBINE 3 OF REVELATION'S JUDGMENT CYCLES

tried to establish the actual order of these events, it makes sense to suggest that the two heavenly crowds (the 144,000 in 7:1–8 and the great multitude in 7:9–17) provide the brackets to John's visions of six seals, seven trumpets and seven bowls.

But how do we understand the significance of all this imagery when put together? What resources do we have to help us here?

2. Use the Bible (Not the Newspaper)!

The truth is, your daily newspaper is **less** important for understanding Revelation than many think. This is not to deny the possibility of current events resonating or fitting with what we read. I would go so far as to say that it is sadly inevitable that they will. That is the nature of the last days in which we live. The point is that John could never have known anything about Nazism, Communism, the European Union, Al Qaeda, ISIS or credit cards and bar codes. These may, or may not, be apocalyptic fulfilments.

Far more significant for interpreting Revelation is the Bible's library itself. The previous sixty-five books are the best resource we have. We should not, however, seek out an individual passage to be a kind of interpretative key, as if that one passage will unlock everything there is to know in Revelation. Instead, we should see this book as having been inspired, influenced and shaped by *everything* written before it.

Drawing on the Old Testament

Bible scholar Bruce Metzger has calculated that of the 404 verses in Revelation, 278 are quotations from or allusions to the Old Testament. That is well over half the verses. This will come as no surprise if Revelation is indeed the book "we could do without."

There is not enough space here to point to the background for every allusion. That work can best be done by using a Bible concordance to look up previous uses of the images or ideas.

Incidentally, it is worth being aware of one potential danger of using concordances. That is the danger of making false links just because the same word is used in different places. We must always take time to ensure that the specific image we are studying is used in the same way in a cross-reference. Take the word "salt" as an example. Jesus tells his followers to be salt (and light) in the Sermon on the Mount (Matt 5:13). Presumably he sees salt as something positive. A concordance will inform us that salt is also mentioned in Genesis 19:26, where Lot's wife is turned into a pillar of salt. But it would be wrong to conclude that this was a positive thing for her, let alone a model for us! Her becoming salt was not positive at all – it was a punishment! Jesus's use of "salt" is completely different and coincidental at best.

The most significant precedent for Revelation's judgment imagery is surely the Egyptian plagues (Exod 7–13). This table gives a comparison between those plagues and Revelation's trumpets and bowls.

10 PLAGUES Exodus 7:8–13:16	7 TRUMPETS Revelation 8:6–11:19	7 BOWLS Revelation 15:1–16:21
Nile becomes blood (7:17–21)	Hail and fire mixed with blood; earth, trees and grass burned up (8:7)	Foul and evil sores (16:2)
Frogs (7:25–8:15)	Burning mountain falls into the sea (8:8); sea life dies; ships destroyed (8:9)	Sea becomes blood (16:3)
Gnats (8:16–19)	Blazing star on rivers and fountains (8:10); waters poisoned, many die (8:11)	Rivers and fountains become blood (16:4)
Flies (8:20–24)	sun, moon, and stars darkened; day and night in darkness (8:12)	Sun allowed to scorch people; People curse God; do not repent (16:8)
Cattle disease (9:1–7)	Star falls from heaven to earth, opens Abyss; locusts emerge (9:1–11)	Kingdom of beast in darkness People curse God and do not repent
Sores (9:8–12)	4 angels at Euphrates released and cavalry kills (9:13–19); no repentance (9:20–21)	Euphrates dries up; kings of whole world come to Armageddon (16:12–16)
Hail and thunderstorm (9:22–26)	Kingdom of this world becomes the kingdom of Christ (11:15–18)	Earthquake splits Babylon into 3; cities destroyed (16:17–21)
Locusts (10:12–20)		
Darkness (10:21–29)		
Firstborn dies (12:29–30)		

John's visions do not match Exodus's details exactly – but when placed side by side, it is clear that they supplied a precedent for the imagery of divine judgment. His visions were shaped by his biblically-shaped imagination.

 Can you identify the judgment imagery that found its way into John's book in these passages?
- Psalm 78:43–52
- Psalm 105:27–36
- Amos 4:6–13

The more fantastical imagery in John's visions (such as multi-headed monsters and angelic figures) originates in Old Testament apocalyptic writing, especially Daniel and Ezekiel. This list gives just a taster.

• Use of significant numbers	Ezekiel 3:15–16; 40:20–23	Daniel 9:25–26
• The threat from the sea	Ezekiel 32:2	Daniel 7:2–3
• Terrifying animals and wild beasts	Ezekiel 14:15–21	Daniel 7:2–6
• The heavenly throne room	Ezekiel 10:1–5	Daniel 7:9–10
• Earthly powers and kingdoms	Ezekiel 27–28	Daniel 8:19–27
• A message for all nations	Ezekiel 38:23	Daniel 7:14

The similarities do not stop there. Both Daniel and Ezekiel were written against the backdrop of Israel's exile in Babylon. That city looms large throughout the Old Testament and became the ultimate symbol for everything that stands in rebellion against the Creator, from the Tower of Babel/Babylon onwards (Gen 11). It therefore comes as no surprise that this continues through to John's visions, even though we know that he clearly had Rome in view as the great enemy of his day (Rev 17).

The final area of Old Testament resonance comes in the many songs of heaven that John hears. Singing formed a vital element of Israel's spirituality and worship of God, so we would expect it to feature in heavenly visions. Israel's songbook, the book of Psalms, is an obvious source of inspiration for John. But there are some even older precedents.

A powerful example comes again from the book of Exodus. After God has rescued the people from Egypt, Exodus 15 gives us the songs of Moses and his sister Miriam (which would eventually be incorporated into the Psalter as Psalm 106). This is a song of praise, but the grounds for praise are very different from those in many of our contemporary songs and hymns. This song praises God for his rescue of Israel, certainly, but the primary focus is on his simultaneous acts of judgment on Egypt. There are clear reminders of this in the songs of Revelation (see 11:15–19; 19:1–9).

Drawing on the New Testament

As a contributor to both the Gospels and the Letters, John unsurprisingly draws on aspects of the New Testament. Again, there are far too many links to highlight them all here. So we will concentrate on one of the central discipleship themes in the letters in particular, which is "the now and the not yet" (the idea that some of the promised blessings of being in Christ's kingdom have been fulfilled for believers now, but not all – there are still some for which we must wait patiently). The teaching in Revelation is entirely consistent with this.

To understand this point, it is worth seeing how the New Testament understands the idea of the Day of the Lord, which is a recurrent theme in the Old Testament prophets. Even a brief reading of the prophets demonstrates that they shared a belief in the inevitability of God coming to earth to act with justice and mercy once and for all. His coming would be a single, global, and even cosmic, event (Isa 13:6–9; Ezek 30:3; Amos 5:18).

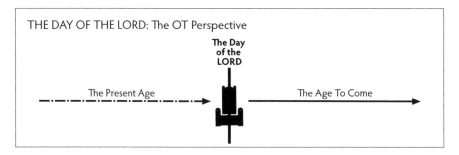

But when Jesus started preaching, it became clear that it did not quite work like that, from his perspective. Early on in Jesus's ministry, we see him teaching in the synagogue in his home village of Nazareth and standing to read the passage set for that Sabbath: Isaiah 61. If we compare what Luke records as the reading with the original passage, it becomes clear that Jesus does a very strange thing. He stops in the middle of a sentence in Isaiah 61:2. He announces the fulfilment of "the year of the Lord's favour" (Isa 61:2a), but omits "the day of vengeance of our God" (Isa 61:2b). The way Luke describes this moment underlines Jesus's deliberate action with the vivid details of his rolling up the scroll and sitting down and the expectant hush of the audience (Luke 4:20–21). He did not make a mistake. So are we to assume that Jesus does not believe in a final judgment? Or is something else going on?

The answer is linked to what happens to the Day of the Lord. Jesus divides this great day in two – creating a new, "in-between" period. It begins with his first coming, and ends with his second. Hebrews 1:1 refers to this period as "the last days," and it is a time of great tension. This is because we have so many of the joys and blessings of Christ's kingdom already granted to us, but not everything is rosy or positive. This is also a time of great evil and confusion.

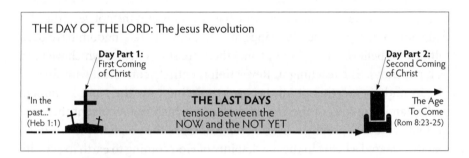

THE DAY OF THE LORD: The Jesus Revolution

Day Part 1: First Coming of Christ

Day Part 2: Second Coming of Christ

"In the past..." (Heb 1:1)

THE LAST DAYS tension between the NOW and the NOT YET

The Age To Come (Rom 8:23-25)

Judgment: now and not yet

In his letter to the Romans, Paul speaks of divine justice in two ways. In Romans 1, God's judgment is a present and ongoing reality, whereby he "gives people over to their sin." In other words, they face the consequences of their own actions because of God's *lack* of intervention (Rom 1:24, 26, 27). Then in Romans 2:16 he speaks of a day when judgment will happen once and for all across the whole world (see also Rom 3:20). We live in the tension between the two, and the delay between our present and that final day is itself a sign of God's grace and mercy (Rom 3:26).

We find the same tension between Now and Not Yet in the book of Revelation. There are times when God does intervene in the present time in judgment – a case in point is Jesus's letter to the church in Ephesus (Rev 2:4–6). But the focus of John's book is on the lead up to, and the events of, the great day of Jesus's return (Rev 20:11–15).

Blessings: now and not yet

In Romans 8 Paul brilliantly handles the tensions that the Now and Not Yet causes in regard to blessings. He is clear that if we are believers in Christ, we have already been given God's Holy Spirit, who brings us many blessings in this life. We have the privilege of divine sonship and the ability to cry "Abba, Father" (Rom 8:15). Yet at the same time, we find ourselves constantly struggling with our failures and sins, as well as the suffering from living in a fallen world. This is why we groan in frustration, like the rest of creation, longing for the day when we will truly have "the redemption of our bodies" (Rom 8:22–23). We rely on the Spirit's prayers in the midst of our groans (Rom 8:26). In other words, we have many grounds for tears in this present life, but look forward to the glorious day when we will enjoy all of God's heavenly blessings (Rom 8:17). Until then, we are protected in Christ (Rom 8:31–39).

Revelation deals with this same tension. There is a recurrent image of God's people being sealed by Christ, marking them out as belonging to him. Christ blesses us in our earthly lifetimes, by his presence with us (remember his standing among the lampstands in Revelation 1). But our belonging to Christ never prevents us from suffering. In fact, the opposite is the case, for the beast and his cohorts sets out to destroy God's church. We see the gruesome image of Babylon the prostitute getting drunk on the blood of God's martyrs (Rev 17:6).

The whole purpose of Revelation (and indeed, all of the Bible's apocalyptic literature) is to prove that God's enemies never have the last word. God does. Or, to take the title of one preacher's published sermons on the book, "The Lamb Wins!"

12

Applying the Book of Revelation

The real danger with preaching Revelation is getting so caught up in the details that we lose sight of the book's overarching purpose. So it makes sense to preach through quite large sections of the book. For example, we might take just one talk to cover the seven letters to the churches, another for the seals and trumpets, another on the tactics of the beast (from several different chapters), and so on. We could, of course, also break up the series into a twenty-one-week series on the book (with a chapter a week), but that would probably be far too much for most congregations.

If figuring out all the signs and symbols in apocalyptic writing can be overwhelming at times, then thinking about application feels even more intimidating. We can scratch our heads in desperation, especially if we have concluded that contemporary political figures do not directly correspond with Revelation's characters. The key to applying this book, as with the rest of the Bible, is to consider why John wrote it in the first place.

He himself was suffering persecution, exiled to the tiny island of Patmos. This is why he could write as "your brother and companion in the suffering and kingdom and patient endurance that are ours in Jesus" (Rev 1:9). His purpose, then, was primarily pastoral. He didn't write to entertain or thrill, or even to terrify. He wrote to reassure and encourage, to stiffen the resolve of the doubting and hurting.

As we have already seen, ancient Jewish apocalyptic often arose at times of great distress and persecution. Darkness had fallen and glimmers of relief were nowhere to be found. The aim was to lift the reader's gaze to a reality that exists beyond the visible world – so that we share God's line of sight.

The challenge is to identify what this perspective means for our local congregation in the normality of everyday life.

1. Revelation Is for All Churches at All Times

We have already considered why Jesus chose to address his letter to only seven churches in Asia Minor. He could easily have included the church in Colossae, for instance. The seven that are included are intended to provide a composite picture of the entire body of Christ. No one church congregation can ever do that, but the congregation-specific letters of Revelation provide an extraordinary picture of the church's diversity and complexity.

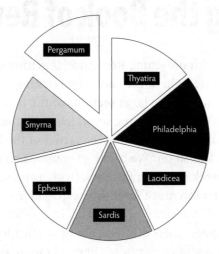

We can see this very clearly when we study Jesus's letters as a group. The first thing we notice is that each of the letters follows a relatively fixed structure (as we saw earlier with the New Testament's main letters).

- Each is addressed to a church's angel (or messenger).
- Jesus is identified (often with imagery from Revelation 1).
- "I know . . ." Jesus walks among the lampstands and so knows what the church is experiencing and how the believers live.
- "Yet I have this against you . . ." Jesus calls on the believers to change course in a particular area.
- "Whoever has ears . . ." Jesus reminds those who remain faithful what is in store for them in the future.

This structure makes it quite easy to compare the letters with each other – the differences really do stand out. So here is a summary of just some of the details, to help us see Jesus's verdicts clearly.

Church		Commended for . . .	Warned about . . .	SUMMARY LESSONS
Ephesus	2:1–7	Hard working; intolerant of evil	Forsaken first love	LOVING JESUS
Smyrna	2:8–11	Enduring poverty and slander		ENDURING SUFFERING
Pergamum	2:12–17	Faithful in a hostile city	Tolerant of false teaching	SOUND TEACHING
Thyatira	2:18–29	Continued growth in good deeds	Tolerant of immorality	HOLINESS
Sardis	3:1–6		Spiritual reputation groundless	SPIRITUAL LIFE
Philadelphia	3:7–13	Waited patiently in a hostile city		PATIENT WAITING
Laodicea	3:14–22		Lukewarm and worldly	TRUSTING GOD'S RICHES

Several letters do not fit the structure outlined above exactly. We can see that Jesus has nothing to commend in two of the churches (Sardis and Laodicea), while two receive nothing but encouragement (Smyrna and Philadelphia). Those two were also facing the fiercest persecution, so their lives were not exactly straightforward.

The most powerful aspect of these letters, however, is their combined impact. If we summarize the key applications for each church and bring them together, we get a sense of what Christ expects of any and every congregation. None is perfect, all need work, none can be complacent. The letters give any preacher of Revelation, and indeed anyone in pastoral ministry, a compelling checklist of areas for application. For as Christian communities, we are to do all we can

- to love Christ,
- to endure suffering,
- to teach sound (healthy) truths,
- to seek to be holy,
- to check for genuine spiritual life (rather than only having a reputation for it),

- to wait patiently for Christ's return, and
- to trust in God's provision for us.

This is precisely what gives the book of Revelation its universal relevance and urgent importance. For example, we might be working and ministering in a culture that is tolerant or supportive of religious freedom. Persecution is not part of our daily experience. But our churches may face other challenges – such as a complacency about their devotion to Christ (like the Ephesian church in 2:1–7) or tolerance of false teaching (like Pergamum in 2:12–17). For others, persecution is horribly real. Life is lived one day at a time because it is impossible to know what will happen next. The truths of Revelation are then a lifeline. The knowledge that the persecutors will not have the last word and that every human system that challenges God's authority must collapse changes everything (as it must have done for the believers in Smyrna and Philadelphia). So we should have no concerns about applying Revelation to our modern contexts – there will always be connections to be made.

2. Revelation Helps Us to See the World from God's Perspective

Another feature of apocalyptic writing (no doubt provoked by the darkness of its original circumstances) is that everything gets magnified. The colours and sounds become more vivid and intense, and the world is divided into clear blocks of good and evil, those for God and those against God.

This is what Jesus anticipated in some of his Last Day parables, a case in point being the parable of the Sheep and Goats (Matt 25:31–46). The shepherd places the sheep on the right, and the goats on the left, in what is an absolute and irreversible division (25:33). That will only seem right if we understand that God's justice is perfect, without error or partiality, and eternally good.

But we must understand some important things about God's perspective. So before closing this chapter with four positive applications, there are two crucial negative points to bear in mind.

Not a call to judge . . .

There is a danger that we presume we can decide who are sheep and who are goats. What absurdity and arrogance! Jesus does not teach about that last day to invite us to share in his exclusive task but to warn us to be ready for him by trusting and obeying him.

This is the point of one of his earlier stories, the parable of the Wheat and Weeds (Matt 13:24–30). The farmer sows good seed in anticipation of reaping a bumper harvest. But as so often happens, weeds (which the farmer says were sown by an enemy) sprout and grow together with the wheat. The farmer warns his farmhands that they must wait for harvest time before trying to separate the wheat and the weeds so that they do not accidentally pull up some of the wheat. This is crucial for those of us who live before that final day. It is not for us to decide who is a sheep or a goat, nor to imagine we are in a position to separate out wheat from weeds. Both of those tasks are God's alone.

This is not to say that we can afford to sit back and relax while we wait. Even if it can never be our job to decide on somebody's eternal fate, we must still be alert.

... but a call to discern

In his gospel, John includes an awkward conversation that Jesus had with some Jewish believers who objected to the implications of his teaching. He was not exactly diplomatic with them. He goes so far as to suggest that their unwillingness to accept his claims indicated that their true father was the devil.

> You belong to your father, the devil, and you want to carry out your father's desires. He was a murderer from the beginning, not holding to the truth, for there is no truth in him. When he lies, he speaks his native language, for he is a liar and the father of lies. (John 8:44)

Jesus is clear, then, that the spiritual battle is real – and it is a conflict between truth and lies. This is played out throughout Revelation. Of course, it is not always easy to tell which is which. People would never be taken in if the lies were unconvincing. That is precisely why Christ's followers need to be alert.

It is interesting, therefore, to see how the enemy repeatedly tries to replicate who God is and what he does. Satan never succeeds (hence his number is 666), but he gets frighteningly close.

In the accompanying table, I have attempted to draw together some of the enemy's deceits as they appear in the book of Revelation. In the left column we can see God as he reveals himself and his plans through the gospel. On the right, we can see Satan's repeated but failed attempts to do the same.

TRUE		COUNTERFEIT
GOD THE TRINITY		**THE SATANIC TRIPLET**
The Father and Creator	Originating plan	The Dragon (12:3, 9) • Creates Beast (13:1)
Christ the Son	Executing plan	The Beast • Dragon (seven heads with crowns, ten horns) • Beast II (seven heads, ten horns with crowns)
Spirit as Witness • book of Acts • promotes worship of Christ • another counsellor (John 14:16–18) • guides into truth (John 16:13)	Bearing Witness / Spreading Lies	**Beast II / False Prophet (13:11–18; 16:13)** • works miraculous signs (13:13) • promotes Beast worship (13:12) • exercises authority of first beast (13:12) • deceives (13:14)
THE CHRIST		**THE BEAST**
19:12	Diadems	13:1
19:11–13, 16	Name	13:1
12:5, 10	Power	13:2
1:17–18	Resurrection	13:3, 12
1:6	Worship	13:4
Exod 15:3, 11f	Praise	13:4
7:3; 14:1	Seal	13:16
5:9	National Allegiance	13:7f
GOD'S PEOPLE		**SATAN'S PEOPLE**
Followers of Christ – marked (14:1) • Endure persecution **Pure Bride of Christ (19:7–8)** • Separates from the prostitute		**Followers of Satan (13:16)** • Persecute the church **The Prostitute (Rev 17–18)** • Seduces the church

All this fits perfectly with Jesus's own apocalyptic preaching that we have already considered (Matt 24). He warns of those who will deceive many by claiming to be the Christ (Matt 24:4–5).

This discernment must lead to determined trust in God and his purposes. Even in the times of darkness, or perhaps especially at those times. As we will see in the passage chosen for this section's sample sermon (Rev 11), terrible things have, do, and will happen to God's people. Such things suggest that the enemy is winning.

But as John says twice – after the second beast appears (13:18) and after the vision of the Babylonian prostitute drinking the blood of believers (17:9) – "this calls for wisdom." If nothing else, Revelation must help us to be wise and alert to the reality of the spiritual battle confronting us all. But it must also convince us that it is not a hopeless battle. For the book gives us a glimpse of the story's end, and it is truly glorious.

3. Revelation Keeps Us Trusting in the Story's End

John's breathtaking visions enable him to see the entire world and all of human history at a glance. The most significant truth to flow out of that is the privilege of knowing the end of the story in advance. We do not discover what tomorrow will hold for each of us, but we are given enough insight to be able to trust that if tomorrow is tough, God can and will ultimately redeem the situation. He will overcome all his enemies and bring the greatest good out of the greatest evil.

This glorious truth should have at least four consequences, which are challenges for non-believers and comforts for believers.

Patient in the tensions

A repeated phrase in the seven letters at the book's opening is "the one who is victorious" or "the one who overcomes" (Rev 2:7, 11, 17, 26; 3:5, 12, 21). The significance of that phrase can best be summed up in the words Jesus gives to the church in Philadelphia, a church that Jesus commends for their faithfulness.

> I am coming soon. Hold on to what you have, so that no one will take your crown. (Rev 3:11)

The point is, they are to hold out for Jesus's promised return – which is guaranteed, despite its unspecified timing. But the wait will not be endless.

God is at work, even in the midst of horror and suffering. And he is "coming soon." This idea is picked up later, at a point of real terror and anxiety.

> This calls for patient endurance on the part of the people of God
> who keep his commands and remain faithful to Jesus. (Rev 14:12)

In my experience of ministry in several different contexts, a huge proportion of pastoral problems would be significantly eased if people understood the tensions of the "Now and Not Yet." We need a much clearer grasp both of what Christ Jesus has *already* given us and of the promises we must still wait for. This is the only way to align our expectations for life in this world with God's perspective. The book of Revelation is a brilliant gift from heaven for doing just that. It allows room for neither escapism nor total despair. Instead, in spite of storms or confusion, it calls on us to be patient amidst the tensions, and not to deny the reality of these tensions. None of it is easy. The book is a healthy reminder of that. But its call is clear. We are to hold on and walk on.

So if our preaching of this book does not lead to patient endurance in the face of all the tensions of life in the last days, then something has probably gone wrong.

Confident in our hope

Patience is, of course, only possible if we have confidence in the promises of the future. From its opening lines, John's vision is designed precisely to instil such confidence. So we read that Jesus gives to John for our benefit a vision of "what must soon take place" (Rev 1:1). This phrase is repeated on the final page of the book (Rev 22:6), and thus frames everything in between.

There are some terrible scenes in the book, without a doubt. Some of the horrors inflicted on God's people in chapter 17, for example, are chilling. But even these serve to remind us that God has the last word. This is true even, or especially, at the moments of gravest tensions. The so-called battle of Armageddon in chapter 16 is a case in point. There the scene is set for the ultimate cosmic battle between God and all earthly rulers.

> Then [the impure spirits] gathered the kings together to the place
> that in Hebrew is called Armageddon. (Rev 16:16)

It has the makings of an extraordinary show down. And then . . . nothing happens. Without any effort at all, God ends this rebellion in an instant. John does not even see how it is done. All he knows is that once the seventh bowl is poured out,

out of the temple came a loud voice from the throne, saying, "it is done!" (Rev 16:17)

This is a deliberate echo of Jesus's last words on the cross, despite not being precisely the word he used in John 19:30. God shows his power over Babylon and the world in various acts in the subsequent verses, but there is nothing about the battle. It is as if he simply needs to click his fingers, and any opposition disintegrates. The battle of Armageddon, ironically, is no battle at all.

To cap it all, there is the glorious, thrilling vision of eternity in Christ's presence in the final two chapters. In complete contrast to the dull, ghostly and insubstantial visions of heaven that many people hold, this window into perfection is solid, spectacular and awe-inspiring. A world without sin or suffering, as proven by the tears that are wiped away. A world of cosmic harmony and interdependence, because of the God who lies at its very centre.

> And I heard a loud voice from the throne saying, "Look! God's dwelling-place is now among the people, and he will dwell with them. They will be his people, and God himself will be with them and be their God. 'He will wipe every tear from their eyes. There will be no more death' or mourning or crying or pain, for the old order of things has passed away." (Rev 21:3–4)

John has offered his readers a glimpse of this spectacle, and God's good purposes as we wait for it. This is all about confident hope. So if hopeful and confident Christian service is not the outcome of our preaching from this book, then something has probably gone wrong.

Praise for God's purposes

We have already considered the songs of Revelation and their Old Testament precedents. It is fascinating how central praise is to the whole vision. There are places and times for lament and pleading to God, and the Bible wonderfully offers us words to help us do that.

But for all the terrors and horrors of Revelation, it is striking how little lament there is in the book. More often than not, John's ears are filled with the sound of heavenly praises for all that God plans and achieves. Of course, there is no need for lament within God's eternal throne room. That is only needed in a fallen world. But John is given the celestial perspective on that fallenness. There is no denial that our world is fallen, but the praise focuses on God's all-powerful justice that must and will condemn all that is evil. That is why there is the famous Hallelujah Chorus in Revelation 19 just after the fall of Babylon is declared.

So if our preaching of Revelation does not lead to the praises of God for his good, just and powerful purposes, then something has probably gone wrong.

Jesus at the centre

Jesus Christ is at the heart of everything in Revelation.

- He is the one who dictates the letters to John. He is the one who dwells among his church, and who writes letters to each of the churches (Rev 1–3).
- He is the Lion who is the Lamb, the one who uniquely is worthy to open the scrolls of human history and who deserves heaven's praises because he suffered on the cross (Rev 5).
- He is "the Root and Offspring of David, the bright Morning Star" who has revealed this extraordinary vision and achieved the grounds for hope in a fallen world. He is the Judge and Saviour who alone is worthy of worship (Rev 22:16–21).

In short, he is on the throne of the universe. He is the one who lived, died, rose from the dead and will return. He is the "Living One [who] was dead" and is alive forever, which is why he calls on us not to be afraid but to trust him (1:17–18).

If our preaching of Revelation does not lead to the adoration of Jesus Christ, then something has probably gone seriously wrong.

There are many challenges to preaching this book – and we have hardly scratched the surface. It makes great demands on our minds and hearts, on our creativity and imagination. But what a treasure it is for a church that is under pressure and perhaps struggling to hold onto what is important or central.

The Breath of Life from God

(Revelation 11)

When you are travelling by bus, you expect the driver to know the route to your destination. If he keeps stopping to ask for directions at every crossroads, you start to feel a little uneasy. Does he know the road at all? It is even worse if he seems to be driving recklessly the rest of the time. Is he going to take you over a cliff in the dark when he suddenly encounters a tight turn that he did not anticipate?

I well remember an eight-hour overnight bus trip I had to take in Peru. We travelled up and up into the Andes Mountains, even reaching a point at Ticlio where the road is at a height of almost 5,000 metres (16,000 feet). I was very grateful that I was not the driver! Not only because I did not know the route, but also because I was affected by altitude sickness. It was good to be able to trust the driving to a professional who knew the area. I even managed to get some sleep!

The original readers of Revelation were in a somewhat similar situation. Their Christian journey was uphill, in unfamiliar territory. They were experiencing brutal persecution. But this book is designed to sustain them by revealing that God is actually in control. The road may be long, and full of potholes, and wind around dangerous precipices, but God is the driver. He knows the road, and he knows what he is doing. They can trust the driver!

Which makes Revelation 11 a shock. Even though we have seen some weird and gruesome scenes in previous chapters, we were not too disturbed because God was in control. But in chapter 11, it's as if the bus has been hijacked and the driver thrown out! Someone else seems to be at the wheel, directing our journey.

Many commentators think that this chapter is more difficult to interpret than some of the other chapters. Yet that is no reason to be discouraged since its main thrust is fairly plain.

1. When God's Mission Seems Bitter (11:1–10)

There is no shame in admitting it: God's mission can sometimes seem bitter. If we feel that, we are in good company. After all, see what John's angel guide told him when he gave him the scroll of God's purposes to eat:

> It will turn your stomach sour but in your mouth it will be as sweet as honey. (Rev 10:9)

In chapter 11 of Revelation, we see the sourness of this God-given ministry – but only after we have seen John's first job. He is like a construction site foreman, out with a measuring stick and architect's plans.

God's people are protected (11:1–2)

> I was given a reed like a measuring rod and was told, "Go and measure the temple of God and the altar, and count the worshippers there." (v. 1)

It is as if John is leading some sort of celestial roll call. And it's no surprise they're gathered in the temple around the altar – for that is an image of being in intimate relationship with God. With God, there is protection. He is a stronghold and refuge, as the Psalmist used to sing.

But the next impression we get is less comforting. They're surrounded. Tensions are high and the threats to God's people very real. So the angel gives John these instructions:

> Exclude the outer court; do not measure it, because it has been given to the Gentiles. They will trample on the holy city for 42 months. (v. 2)

One small oddity is that the NIV translation describes these attackers as Gentiles. That seems to contradict everything in the previous chapters about how God is calling his people from every nation. But here it is being used simply as a label for those who are not members of God's people (regardless of their ethnicity). So perhaps it is best simply to use a legitimate alternative and translate the word as "nations" rather than "Gentiles."

But then we have another of those peculiar Revelation numbers: the holy city will be trampled "for 42 months." Well, there's a bit of mathematical fun here – because in verse 3 we find another number, "1,260 days." The average calendar month lasts 30 days, so 1,260 days amounts to 42 months. And that is not a random number – for 42 months is then exactly 3½ years. Which is half of 7 – the number of perfection.

But don't worry too much about the numbers. The crucial point is to understand that God knows the time periods – they are fixed. This temple siege will not last forever.

God's preachers have perseverance (11:3–6)

What happens next is extraordinary. The people are huddling inside their God-given refuge under incredible pressure. Then look at verse 3:

> And I will appoint my two witnesses, and they will prophesy for
> 1,260 days, clothed in sackcloth.

It seems crazy, doesn't it? Why would anyone want to go out into that? Why take the risk?

If the people in the temple felt the need to defend themselves, then surely it would have been much more sensible to send out their champion fighters to take on the threat – just as young David took on Goliath back in the old days? But no. The people's champions do something much more absurd. They go out to preach! And they go on for months. God has it all planned.

But why are they described using the imagery of olive trees and lampstands in verse 4? Olive trees provided the oil to light lamps in the ancient world – and so it is natural that they go together. And that is the clue to who these two witnesses are. Remember the lampstands back in chapter 1? They represent the seven churches. It is highly likely then that the two witnesses, and the lampstands, and olive trees represent one thing: the church of God.

But hang on. If this is the one church, why are there two witnesses? Probably because the ancient court system always required two eyewitnesses to confirm any evidence. So the idea here is that God's church has God's authority to be his witness. Despite what some commentators may say, it is unlikely that these are identifiable individuals. But the imagery is clearly identifiable.

Look at the effect of their message: Fire comes from their mouths (v. 5); they shut up the sky so it will not rain (v. 6). Who does that sound like? Isn't that just like Elijah as he preached to the prophets of Baal on Mount Carmel? His God-given words had the power to bring fire and drought as he exposed the Canaanite idolatry.

Then take the end of verse 6:

> They have the power to turn the waters into blood and to strike
> the earth with every kind of plague . . .

Who is that? That must be Moses, back before the exodus from Egypt.

Moses and Elijah: two great saints used by God to speak when his people was under threat. John's point here is that God protects them to do their work of witnessing. God has clear sanctions for those who want to harm them.

So far so good. But did you notice where the witnesses are preaching? In verse 4 they "stand before the Lord of the earth." This is not simply a matter of facing the hordes. They are walking right into the lion's den. For the "Lord of the earth" is not actually the Lord Jesus at all, but the one who has implacable hatred for Jesus and his people.

Standing before him takes immense courage. It reminds me of the great Festo Kivengere, who was Bishop of Kigezi in south-west Uganda during the 1970s and 1980s. During the dark years of Idi Amin's terrible dictatorship, Festo felt impelled to confront the president *personally*. In his own command post in Kampala. On four or five occasions. Festo challenged Amin to stop the killing of thousands of people. His message was truly prophetic – and dangerous. He only survived because friends helped him to flee to Rwanda just as Idi Amin's men came to arrest him.

This is what the church is called to do – to bear witness to the good news of God's kingdom – a kingdom of truth, justice, grace and love. That inevitably puts the church on a collision course with earthly rulers. No wonder the Lord of the earth is furious. The only reason that the two witnesses survive for 3½ years is because God protects them. But then everything seems to go horribly wrong.

God's preachers are destroyed (11:7–10)

> Now when they had finished their testimony, the beast that comes
> up from the Abyss will attack them, and overpower and kill them.

You weren't expecting that, were you? It's as if the bus has been hijacked and the enemy has won. What's going on? Can this really be God's mission? It doesn't make sense. I don't fully understand it. I don't understand why God needs to allow it. Why does it have to be like that?

One thing is certain, though. It fits with church history. It fits with present reality. It fits with the foreseeable future. For it is a fact that people die for their faith.

Bishop Festo survived the Amin regime, but his boss Archbishop Janani Luwum most certainly did not. He had a similarly prophetic ministry to Bishop Festo's and repeatedly challenged the president. His final provocation was to send a formal note in 1977 protesting the countless deaths and disappearances in Uganda. After that, he was charged with treason, forced to appear in public with Amin, alongside two other "suspects," and was then apparently killed in a "car accident" on his way to an interrogation centre. But when his body was released to his relatives, it was riddled with bullets. His reputation as a courageous Christian leader was confirmed a few years later, though. In 1998, he was included in the ten twentieth-century martyrs whose statues stand above the Great West Door of London's Westminster Abbey.

As if Revelation 11 couldn't get worse . . .

> Their bodies will lie in the street of the great city which is figuratively called Sodom and Egypt, where also their Lord was crucified. For 3½ days men from every people, tribe, language and nation will gaze on their bodies and refuse them burial. (11:8)

This is an outrage – in the Middle East, as in many other parts of the world, burial was supposed to take place soon after death. Leaving a corpse in the street was the ultimate insult. But notice – this is also for a fixed period. They will lie there for just 3½ days, after their 3½ year ministry.

Verse 10 is even more macabre.

> The inhabitants of the earth will gloat over them and will celebrate by sending each other gifts, because these two prophets had tormented those who lived on earth. (11:10)

It's almost like a grotesque distortion of Christmastime. Instead of sending Christmas cards to friends and family, people send out "Rotting Witnesses" cards and exchange "Conquered Church" presents. This image has all the horror of ISIS videos of killings in the Middle East. Why are people behaving like this? How can they do this?

They do it because the preaching of these two witnesses felt like torment. That is not because the church was deliberately trying to be unpleasant or obnoxious. (Although, let's face it, there are plenty of believers who give Jesus's church a terrible name because they are unpleasant and obnoxious.) But that's not the point here. The issue is that the gospel message is always a stumbling block to people. Or as the Apostle Paul wrote – it is the aroma of life to some and the stench of death to others (2 Cor 2:15–16). Yet what is truly terrifying is that the Lord of the earth, the Beast, has become the Master over the church. He has silenced its witness.

I still can't help wondering, though: why must it be like this? Why must serving God bring so much conflict, pain and bitterness? I just don't understand.

But then I guess this was something of what went through the disciples' minds the day after Jesus was crucified. That middle Saturday was surely the second darkest day in human history, after Good Friday. If they were managing to cling to their confidence in God's sovereignty at all, they were no doubt wondering why on earth God had allowed this to happen.

I mention Easter Saturday deliberately because of what happens next.

2. When God's Justice Arouses Singing (11:11–19)

God's preachers are vindicated (11:11–14)

> But after 3½ days a breath of life from God entered them, and they stood on their feet, and terror struck those who saw them. Then they heard a loud voice from heaven saying to them, "Come up here." And they went up to heaven in a cloud while their enemies looked on.

Do you get it now? After this short, fixed period, which is an echo of the three days Jesus was in the tomb, a miracle occurs. God's spirit blows on the corpses of the prophets. Just as happened in Ezekiel's vision of the valley of dry bones (Ezek 37), so with the two witnesses of Revelation 11. After death, there is life. It is a miracle of resurrection.

No wonder the crowds are terrified. I mean, if you hold power, and you destroy your arch-enemy and think all opposition is squashed, you've got it made! You gloat and share gifts. But if your enemy then comes back from the dead, what on earth can you do now? It's more than a reversal of fortune. It's a defeat.

What's more, God calls on the witnesses, his church, to come up – to heaven. This is a clear echo of Jesus's ascension. It's a wonderful divine vindication after the humiliation of being left to rot in the streets.

So do you see? God's church, the two witnesses, follow in Jesus's footsteps.

- Christ preached as God's witness – the light of the world. He suffered. He died. Three days later he rose. And after that he ascended to heaven.

- The church preaches as God's witness – the olive trees and the lampstands. The church is persecuted and destroyed. And 3½ days later, the church is raised to life again and lifted up to heaven.

Now as I say, I don't fully understand why it must be like this. But God is in control. Satan, that global hijacker, does not get away with his insurrection indefinitely. Even though he flings his very worst at the church in his attempt to destroy it, and at times appears to succeed. But he will not win eventually.

Why does this matter? Because for many people around the world, life feels like that middle Easter Saturday. The Lord has died on the cross and the sky is overcast and dark. But John assures us that justice is coming. That's clear from the earthquakes and terrors that follow in verse 13. These are a foretaste of what is to come when the seventh trumpet is blown. People will either be part of the church, God's multinational witnesses, protected by John's measuring rod in the temple, or they will face the consequences of being part of the multinational peoples that stand against it.

John has no doubt – after the darkness of Easter Saturday comes the blazing life of Easter Sunday. And when the seventh trumpet blows, symbolizing the end of the world, just as opening the seventh seal back in chapter 8 did, the response will be clear. Praise. Praise for God's justice.

God's praises are sung (11:15–19)

And the key to it all – in fact the key to the whole of Revelation is there in the song in verse 15. This is what is sung:

> The kingdom of the world has become the kingdom of the Lord
> and his Christ and he will reign for ever and ever.

The cosmic hijacker has been expelled from the driving seat and arrested. Of course, he was never really in control. His authority was always restrained by God, hard though that is to believe at times.

And the crowds of heaven sing. Not this time about the character of God, as they have done before. Not because of the creation of the world as in Revelation 4, or Christ's death on the cross to rescue us as in Revelation 5. Now they rejoice because the kingdom has finally and eternally come: God rules and there is no opposition. That means justice has come. All wrong has been put right.

> The nations were angry and your wrath has come. The time has
> come for judging the dead and for rewarding the prophets and

your saints and those who reverence your name both small and
great – and for destroying those who destroy the earth. (10:18)

This is not mere revenge. This is justice. Those who destroy the earth face the
just consequences of their actions.

And the people of God rejoice. That may seem incongruous because not
many contemporary worship songs praise God for his ultimate judgment. But
that is precisely what happens in heaven.

This fact is arresting. But it is also a litmus test. If you don't feel like
bursting into song when you hear of God's cosmic vindication of his people, it
is probably because you've not suffered much injustice. But there are countless
people around the world who cry out for it – in the full knowledge they won't
find justice in this life. Brothers and sisters in Iran and Iraq, Indonesia and
China, Egypt and Syria and so on and so on. And even in Britain.

The call then is to follow in the footsteps of the Lord. To take up our cross,
knowing that Good Friday leads inexorably through the darkness of Saturday
to the sunburst of Easter Day. And ultimately to Christ's return – when we
can rejoice. This is a call not to play the victim and hate the world that hates
us but to love Jesus, to love the world by being his witness, and to rejoice in
the God of justice.

To which we can only sing Hallelujah. The kingdom of the world has
become the kingdom of our Lord and of his Christ and he will reign forever
and ever. Hallelujah.

Conclusion

It doesn't matter where I teach the material in this book – and I have done so on four continents now – I always get the same reactions! Someone will say, "This is really hard work!" And someone else will say, "I just don't have time for this! What about all the other things I have to do?"

I have a lot of sympathy for those responses. It can be a real struggle to juggle one's family life, personal devotional life and church life (and one's work life, if one is not in paid ministry). There are weeks when the best we can hope for is to get through each day.

However, we all make time for the things we think are important. If being a member of the local football team is important to us, then we will stop doing other things to make time to attend team practice or to travel to matches. If spending time with our family is important to us, then we will be prepared to turn down invitations to exciting events in town. And so on . . .

So if preaching God's word is important to us, then we will make time to pray about our preaching, to study to improve our preaching and our knowledge of God's word, to learn about preaching and God's word from others, and to get feedback about our preaching. Of course, there will always be more that we *could* do, and we need to be realistic about the amount of time available to us. We should not feel guilty for not being able to do more. But we should still make every effort to handle God's word correctly, as Timothy was reminded by Paul (2 Tim 2:15).

For above all other things, ministry is a privilege.

> All this is from God, who reconciled us to himself through Christ and gave us the ministry of reconciliation: that God was reconciling the world to himself in Christ, not counting people's sins against them. And he has committed to us the message of reconciliation. We are therefore Christ's ambassadors, as though God were making his appeal through us. We implore you on Christ's behalf: be reconciled to God. (2 Cor 5:18–20)

Notice two things in what Paul says.

We have been reconciled to God through Christ. The only reason we have any ministry at all is because of what we received in the gospel of Jesus. Without him, we would still be trapped in our sins, and facing God's judgment for them. The wonder of the good news is that these sins are not counted against us. Christ has paid the penalty on our behalf. As Paul says in the very next verse, "God made him who had no sin to be sin for us, so that in him we might become the righteousness of God" (2 Cor 5:21). That was what brought us into a relationship with God. It follows that . . .

We have a message of reconciliation. Having been restored to our Creator, we should surely long for others to enjoy the same joy. As we preach the gospel of Jesus, we actually offer those around us the means to enjoy that same reconciliation. Paul can say that it is as if "God were making his appeal through us." This is because we are God's ambassadors.

Consider the role of ambassadors. They represent their country abroad. And, in particular, they represent their country's government to other governments. It is a great privilege to hold that position, and it carries real influence – especially if their country is a powerful one or their country's leader is popular. This does not mean they are free to give their own opinion on matters of state. Instead, they must always honour and defend their government's policies. They have authority, but they are under authority.

If this is true of ambassadors in the world, how much more is it true of Christ's ambassadors? Of course, Christ's ambassadors are not guaranteed the world's respect. No servant is above his master. But we can be sure that it is a kingdom privilege. We speak on God's behalf. We are his agents for bringing about reconciliation between sinful people and a forgiving God (which in turn should lead to reconciliation between people). It is not our message – but his. Our job is to be as faithful to what God has revealed as we can. That is why we study and work hard. That is why we read and talk with others in this lifelong, learning process. This is why we take sermon preparation very seriously.

We will never be able to do enough – there is always more we could do. But we must do the best we can. And we then trust God to do his work as his word goes out.

We will only be committed to all this effort if we are constantly aware of what a privilege it is to speak on his behalf. But then, what greater privilege could there be than to proclaim things that angels long to read!

Appendix 1

Jesus's Parables

	Title	Matthew	Mark	Luke
1	*The Town on a Hill*	*Matt 5:14*		
2	**The Lamp under a Bowl**	**Matt 5:15**	**Mark 4:21**	**Luke 8:16–18; 11:33**
3	The Wise and Foolish Builders	Matt 7:24–27		Luke 6:46–49
4	**New Cloth on an Old Coat**	**Matt 9:16**	**Mark 2:21**	**Luke 5:36**
5	**New Wine into Old Wineskins**	**Matt 9:17**	**Mark 2:22**	**Luke 5:37–38**
6	**The Strong Man**	**Matt 12:29**	**Mark 3:27**	**Luke 11:21–22**
7	*The Wheat and the Weeds*	*Matt 13:24–30*		
8	**The Sower and the Soils**	**Matt 13:3–9, 18–23**	**Mark 4:3–8, 14–20**	**Luke 8:5–8, 11–15**
9	**The Mustard Seed**	**Matt 13:31–32**	**Mark 4:30–32**	**Luke 13:18–19**
10	The Yeast	Matt 13:33		Luke 13:20–21
11	*The Hidden Treasure*	*Matt 13:44*		
12	*The Valuable Pearl*	*Matt 13:45–46*		
13	*The Fishing Net*	*Matt 13:47–50*		
14	*The Owner of the House*	*Matt 13:52*		
15	The Lost Sheep	Matt 18:10–14		Luke 15:4–7

	Title	Matthew	Mark	Luke
16	*The Unforgiving Servant*	*Matt 18:23–35*		
17	*The Workers in the Vineyard*	*Matt 20:1–16*		
18	*The Two Sons in the Vineyard*	*Matt 21:28–32*		
19	**The Wicked Tenants of the Vineyard**	**Matt 21:33–44**	**Mark 12:1–11**	**Luke 20:9–18**
20	The Wedding Banquet Invitations	Matt 22:1–14		Luke 14:15–24
21	**The Budding Fig Tree**	**Matt 24:32–35**	**Mark 13:28–31**	**Luke 21:29–33**
22	**The Faithful Servant**	**Matt 24:45–51**	**Mark 13:34–37**	**Luke 12:35–48**
23	*The Ten Bridesmaids*	*Matt 25:1–13*		
24	*The Three Servant Investors*	*Matt 25:14–30***		
25	*The Sheep and the Goats*	*Matt 25:31–46*		
26	*The Growing Seed*		*Mark 4:26–29*	
27	*The Two Debtors*			*Luke 7:41–43*
28	*The Good Samaritan*			*Luke 10:25–37*
29	*The Friend at Night*			*Luke 11:5–8*
30	*The Rich Fool*			*Luke 12:16–21*
31	*The Barren Fig Tree*			*Luke 13:6–9*
32	*Seats at the Wedding Feast*			*Luke 14:7–14*
33	*Counting the Cost*			*Luke 14:28–33*
34	*The Lost Coin*			*Luke 15:8–10*
35	*The Lost Son and Older Brother*			*Luke 15:11–32*
36	*The Shrewd Manager*			*Luke 16:1–13*
37	*The Rich Man and Lazarus*			*Luke 16:19–31*
38	*The Master and Servant*			*Luke 17:7–10*

	Title	Matthew	Mark	Luke
39	*The Persistent Widow*			*Luke 18:1–8*
40	*The Pharisee and the Tax Collector*			*Luke 18:9–14*
41	*The King's Ten Servant Investors*			*Luke 19:12–27***
		25	**10**	**28**

key: *** similar*

Unique

In two gospels

In three gospels

The closest parable equivalents in John's Gospel:

The shepherd, the gate and the hired hands (John 10:1–5, 7–18)
A woman's joy after the agony of childbirth (John 16:21–22)

Appendix 2

Constructing Preaching Series

Constructing preaching series is not a common practice in churches around the world. There are several reasons for this.

One is that some church denominations use a lectionary (a list of set readings for every Sunday of the year), and so the work of construction has already been done. This certainly takes the pressure off you, and it can be helpful to share tips from others in the same denomination who are working on the same passage. However, there can be disadvantages, not least the fact that there is no space to adapt the series to the needs of a specific local church.

In other churches, the preference is for greater spontaneity, perhaps deciding the week or month before what the programme should contain. As I hope will be obvious from this book, deciding what to preach the night before is a reckless and unhelpful habit, since it prevents a preacher from ever having the time and space to do even the most basic preparation!

The obvious advantage to short-term planning is flexibility – the pastor has the freedom to respond speedily to the pressing needs and concerns of the church. It also allows for a prayerful dependence on God's Spirit for his promptings.

However, short-term thinking also has real drawbacks. It means that we never take a long-term view of the church's spiritual health – we are always responding to the latest focus. We are also in danger of simply preaching the things we like to preach about. Most significantly, it can reveal a view of the Holy Spirit as *only* working through the spontaneous and immediate. Yet why can't he work through our long-term plans and vision-setting as well? For that matter, why is he regarded as *more* at work when we leave our preparation to the last minute in the hope of the Spirit's guidance than when we sit at our desk days, or even weeks before, in prayer and study? To suggest that the Holy Spirit only works in the spectacular or spontaneous is to limit him, to put God in a box. If the New Testament teaches anything about God it is surely that this is impossible!

So I want to suggest that there is great wisdom in churches having their own preaching programmes. There are many ways to go about constructing them, and much of it is a matter of taste or custom in the church. But here is some wisdom collected over a number of years from different ministries.

A Year at a Glance

When Paul said his emotional farewells to the Ephesian elders in Acts 20, he shared his great wisdom about ministry.[1] In particular, he described how he had worked among them, presumably as a model for them to follow. Two things stand out.

> You know that I have not hesitated to preach anything that would be helpful to you but have taught you publicly and from house to house. (Acts 20:20)

> For I have not hesitated to proclaim to you the whole will of God. (Acts 20:27)

What this illustrates very clearly is Paul's twofold commitment.

- He was committed to the spiritual needs of the people he served. So if truths needed repetition, or further explanation and clarification, Paul would give time to that work. He was sensitive to their questions and battles, and especially the challenges that faced them living where they did. So he shaped his teaching around them.
- He was committed to teaching the truths they didn't know they needed! He would teach the "whole will of God" to the church, even if there wasn't a demand for it. This is because he was determined to do everything within his abilities to give them firm foundations in the gospel revealed in Christ.

This gives very helpful guidelines for planning a preaching series. It means that we should be aware of both the church's specific needs and the need to preach sometimes difficult truths, simply because they are in the Bible. Keeping an eye

---

1. These two verses were first highlighted to me in a very helpful discussion by Chris Wright back in Kampala in 2003.

on an annual programme is important because we can then see what we have overlooked and what we have perhaps overemphasized without realizing it.

When I was involved in series planning at our London church, we would try to get a balance through the year of:

- series from both **Old Testament** and **New Testament** books
- series from at least one **Gospel** (usually a small section – see below) every year
- series from at least one **Letter** ever year
- when preaching from the Old Testament, a variety of History, Wisdom literature, and Prophecy.

Our aim is to give the church a varied biblical diet.

A question is often asked at this point about **topical preaching**. This is important. There is no reason why there should be a conflict between topical and expository preaching (of the sort being taught at Langham Preaching events and throughout this book). And there is certainly a place for it. After all, Paul preached what the Ephesians needed to learn, and taking a key topic to preach on would be a good way of following in his footsteps.

For example, think about preaching on the issue of money in the Christian life, or on how to stand for Christ in a hostile culture. How well do we handle the Bible when we preach on these topics? We cannot do this well if our sermon consists largely of a list of different Bible references that refer to the topic. It would be far better to focus on one Bible passage for each of the main points of the sermon. That way it is possible to draw on different parts of the Bible while doing each of them justice (without having to spend hours checking that we are handling each verse responsibly).

There is one great advantage of working through Bible books most of the time, in contrast to primarily doing topical series. It is that we can then be sure we are not simply preaching our favourite subjects (we all have them!). We are forced to deal with difficult or even uncomfortable things when we are working through a book. There are not many places to hide! So I would always recommend preaching through Bible books perhaps 80 per cent of the time.

A Series at a Glance

Once you have decided on how you are going to split the year up with different series, the next thing to be decided is how you will break up each individual series.

With large Bible books, it is not usually wise to work through the whole book in one series. Of course, if that is what a church is used to, then it is not wrong. The great Welsh preacher Dr Martyn Lloyd-Jones would work patiently through books like Romans and Ephesians over several years. However, he was unusually gifted and so was able to teach "the whole will of God" while doing this – but he is not always the most helpful model for us. Many tried, and failed, to copy what he did effectively.

Here are just some personal suggestions about how to break up a series.

- Aim for series that last no longer than eight to ten weeks. For long books like Romans or Luke, take a few chapters at a time and then have a break. Then return to that book for the next block of teaching. For some very large books like Revelation, it is probably wise to be selective. Instead of covering every detail in every paragraph, try to preach on some of the most important passages that represent what surrounds them.

- Obviously, some books will not need anything like as long as eight weeks – Philemon and Jude may only require one or two sermons each. The main concern is to help believers get a sense of the whole book without getting lost.

- If your series is on a narrative book, divide it by story or combination of stories (even if some of the elements of the story come many verses later). It is impossible to do justice to a story if you do now include all the story elements we considered in chapter 1. We need to see how the Bible writers conclude their narratives before even attempting to apply them to congregations today.

- If your series is on a letter, look for natural breaks in the argument and construct your series around it. The outline of Philippians that I worked on above in section 3 might be a guide to a possible series.

Appendix 3

The Millennium

A final, but brief word about the millennium and the various approaches to the book. There has been great controversy about this in some Christian circles, so it is important to acknowledge at least some of the key positions commonly held.

The question derives from how to interpret the thousand years mentioned in Revelation 20:2–7. To be more specific, the question is how does the millennium relate to the second coming of Christ.

The Premillennial View

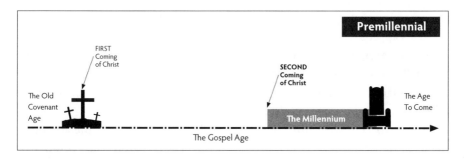

The premillennial view often seems to fit most naturally with the literal sense of the text in Revelation 20. It often makes much of the formation of the modern state of Israel in 1947 as the fulfilment of Old Testament prophecy. It has led to remarkably detailed work on the Scriptures, especially on the prophetic and apocalyptic books.

The premillennial view can be subdivided into several different groupings, primarily to do with where precisely the "rapture" (the removal of God's faithful people, as perhaps suggested by 1 Thess 4:17) fits with the times of "tribulation" or suffering.

There are some merits in this view, not least because it takes the text of the Bible seriously and encourages an eager anticipation of God's purposes being fulfilled. But it is by no means the only view. Many have noted how risky it is to build such complex theological frameworks on just a handful of verses and then to search for other passages that seem to back them up. The word "rapture" is never actually mentioned in the Bible, and some of the verses quoted to support this idea seem to be interpreted in ways that bear little relation to what the text is talking about.[1]

The Postmillennial View

The popularity of the postmillennial view has waxed and waned over the years. In some circles, it appears to be making a comeback.

This approach sees the millennium as a glorious age in which the church goes from strength to strength as Christ's rule gradually increases around the world. It looks for the fulfilment of the millennial prophecies in spiritual rather than literal terms, and sometimes highlights the genuinely phenomenal growth of the church around the world in recent years.

One problem with this view is that it is hard to see how the appalling persecution of the church in some regions (especially in the last century or so) fits with a glorious period of the church's millennial reign.

---

1. In 1 Thessalonians 5:17, the imagery that Paul uses refers back to Mount Sinai (Exod 19–20) when he describes Jesus's triumphant, and very public, return – it is not a private event for believers. There is no suggestion that we are being taken away – only that we meet him and are with him. Even more notoriously, some interpret Matthew 24:40–41 as referring to believers being taken away. But the context makes it clear those taken away are being *judged* not *saved*! For more on this, see Christopher J. H. Wright, *The God I Don't Understand* (Grand Rapids: Zondervan, 2008), especially chapter 9.

The Amillennial View

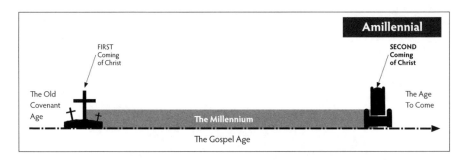

This view is not far removed from the postmillennial view. Those who hold to the amillennial view assume that, like the other numbers in Revelation, the thousand years is not to be taken literally but is the same as the Gospel Age and the Last Days as a whole. Amillennialists hold that Christ is already reigning on his heavenly throne now, while Satan is restrained and bound (things are not as bad as they could possibly be). They do not anticipate a gradual improvement of the welfare of the church around the world, but assumes that growth and persecution will go hand in hand.

This approach certainly explains why every generation has been able to relate to the book and identify its own experiences within it. It often corresponds to the approach outlined in chapter 10 that sees Revelation as a universal book.

The weaknesses of this view revolve around the problem with taking everything as simply "spiritual" reality and it does not readily inspire great expectation or anticipation of what is to come. Nevertheless, as will perhaps have been obvious, this is the approach that makes the most sense to me.

Whatever our eventual position in this debate, we should recognise one truth: the only detail of which we can be entirely certain is the fact of Christ's return. That fact is given far greater significance throughout the Scriptures than the millennium itself, which is mentioned only once and about which there is legitimate debate. Remember: The parables of Matthew 25 warn us to be ready by trusting in Christ; they say nothing about calculating dates or to obsessing about details.

Appendix 4

New Testament Quotations of the Old Testament

What follows is my own list of the occasions when the Old Testament is quoted in the New Testament. It does not include the many verses that allude to, or remind us of, other passages.

Matt 1:23	Isa 7:14	Matt 8:17	Isa 53:4
Matt 2:6	Mic 5:2	Matt 9:13	Hos 6:6
Matt 2:15	Hos 11:1	Matt 10:35–36	Mic 7:6
Matt 2:18	Jer 31:15	Matt 11:10	Mal 3:1
Matt 3:3	Isa 40:3	Matt 12:7	Hos 6:6
Matt 3:17	Gen 22:2	Matt 12:18–21	Isa 42:1–4
Matt 4:4	Deut 8:3	Matt 13:14–15	Isa 6:9–10
Matt 4:6–7	Ps 91:11–12	Matt 13:35	Ps 78:2
Matt 4:7	Deut 6:16	Matt 15:4	Exod 20:12; 21:17 / Deut 5:16
Matt 4:10	Deut 6:13	Matt 15:8–9	Isa 29:13
Matt 4:15–16	Isa 9:1–2	Matt 17:5	Ps 2:7
Matt 5:21	Exod 20:13 / Deut 5:17	Matt 17:5	Isa 42:1
Matt 5:27	Exod 20:14 / Deut 5:18	Matt 18:16	Deut 19:15
Matt 5:31	Deut 24:1	Matt 19:4	Gen 1:27
Matt 5:38	Exod 21:24 / Lev 24:20 / Deut 19:21	Matt 19:5	Gen 2:24
Matt 5:43	Lev 19:18	Matt 19:18–19	Exod 20:12–16 / Lev 19:18 / Deut 5:16–20

Matt 21:5	Zech 9:9	Mark 13:14	Dan 9:27; 11:31; 12:11
Matt 21:9	Ps 118:25–26		
Matt 21:13	Isa 56:7	Mark 14:27	Zech 13:7
Matt 21:13	Jer 7:11	Mark 14:62	Ps 110:1
Matt 21:42	Ps 118:22–23	Mark 15:34	Ps 22:1
Matt 22:32	Exod 3:6	Luke 1:17	Mal 4:5–6
Matt 22:37	Deut 6:5	Luke 2:23	Exod 13:2, 12
Matt 22:39	Lev 19:18	Luke 2:24	Lev 12:8
Matt 22:44	Ps 110:1	Luke 3:4–6	Isa 40:3–5
Matt 23:39	Ps 118:26	Luke 4:4	Deut 8:3
Matt 24:15	Dan 11:31; 12:11	Luke 4:8	Deut 6:13
Matt 26:31	Zech 13:7	Luke 4:10–11	Ps 91:11–12
Matt 26:64	Ps 110:1 / Dan 7:13	Luke 4:12	Deut 6:16
Matt 27:9–10	Zech 11:12–13	Luke 4:18–19	Isa 61:1–2
Matt 27:46	Ps 22:1	Luke 7:27	Mal 3:1
Mark 1:2	Mal 3:1	Luke 8:10	Isa 6:9
Mark 1:3	Isa 40:3	Luke 10:27	Lev 19:18 / Deut 6:5
Mark 4:12	Isa 6:9–10	Luke 18:20	Exod 20:12–16 / Deut 5:16–20
Mark 7:6–7	Isa 29:13		
Mark 7:10	Exod 20:12; 21:17 / Deut 5:16	Luke 19:38	Ps 118:26
		Luke 19:46	Isa 56:7 / Jer 7:11
Mark 9:48	Isa 66:24	Luke 20:17	Ps 118:22
Mark 10:6	Gen 1:27	Luke 20:37	Exod 3:6
Mark 10:7	Gen 2:24	Luke 20:42–43	Ps 110:1
Mark 10:19	Exod 20:12–16	Luke 22:37	Isa 53:12
Mark 11:9–10	Ps 118:25–25	Luke 23:30	Hos 10:8
Mark 11:17	Isa 56:7 / Jer 7:11	Luke 23:46	Ps 31:5
Mark 12:10–11	Ps 118:22–23	John 1:23	Isa 40:3
Mark 12:26	Exod 3:6	John 1:51	Gen 28:12
Mark 12:29	Deut 6:4	John 2:17	Ps 69:9
Mark 12:30	Deut 6:5	John 6:31	Exod 16:4
Mark 12:31	Lev 19:18	John 6:45	Isa 54:13
Mark 12:36	Ps 110:1	John 10:34	Ps 82:6

John 12:13	Ps 118:25	Acts 7:37	Deut 18:15
John 12:15	Zech 9:9	Acts 7:40	Exod 32:1
John 12:38	Isa 53:1	Acts 7:42–43	Amos 5:25–27
John 12:40	Isa 6:10	Acts 7:49–50	Isa 66:1–2
John 13:18	Ps 41:9	Acts 8:32–33	Isa 53:7–8
John 15:25	Ps 35:19	Acts 13:33	Ps 2:7
John 15:25	Ps 69:4	Acts 13:34	Isa 55:3
John 19:24	Ps 22:18	Acts 13:35	Ps 16:10
John 19:29	Ps 69:21	Acts 13:41	Hab 1:5
John 19:36	Exod 12:46	Acts 13:47	Isa 49:6
John 19:36	Num 9:12	Acts 15:16–18	Amos 9:11–12
John 19:36	Ps 34:20	Acts 23:5	Exod 22:28
John 19:37	Zech 12:10	Acts 28:26–27	Isa 6:9–10
Acts 1:20	Ps 69:25	Rom 1:17	Hab 2:4
Acts 1:20	Ps 109:8	Rom 2:6	Ps 62:12 /
Acts 2:17–21	Joel 2:28–31		Prov 24:12
Acts 2:25–28	Ps 16:8–11	Rom 2:24	Isa 52:5
Acts 2:31	Ps 16:10	Rom 3:4	Ps 51:4
Acts 2:34–35	Ps 110:1	Rom 3:10	Ps 14:1 / Eccl 7:20
Acts 3:22–23	Deut 18:15, 19	Rom 3:11–12	Ps 14:2–3
Acts 3:25	Gen 22:18; 26:4; 28:14	Rom 3:13	Ps 5:9; 140:3
		Rom 3:14	Ps 10:7
Acts 4:11	Ps 118:22	Rom 3:15–17	Isa 59:7–9
Acts 4:25–26	Ps 2:1–2	Rom 3:18	Ps 36:1
Acts 7:3	Gen 12:1	Rom 4:3	Gen 15:6
Acts 7:6–7	Gen 15:13–14	Rom 4:7–8	Ps 32:1–2
Acts 7:18	Exod 1:8	Rom 4:17	Gen 17:5
Acts 7:27–28	Exod 2:13–14	Rom 4:18	Gen 15:5
Acts 7:29	Exod 2:15	Rom 7:7	Exod 20:17 /
Acts 7:32	Exod 3:6		Deut 5:21
Acts 7:33	Exod 3:5	Rom 8:36	Ps 44:22
Acts 7:34	Exod 2:24	Rom 9:7	Gen 21:12
Acts 7:34	Exod 3:7–10	Rom 9:9	Gen 18:10

Rom 9:12	Gen 25:23	Rom 11:35	Job 41:11
Rom 9:13	Mal 1:2–3	Rom 12:19	Deut 32:35
Rom 9:15	Exod 33:19	Rom 12:20	Prov 25:21–22
Rom 9:17	Exod 9:16	Rom 13:9	Exod 20:13–17 /
Rom 9:20	Isa 29:16		Lev 19:18 /
Rom 9:20	Isa 45:9		Deut 5:17–21
Rom 9:21	Jer 18:6	Rom 14:11	Isa 45:23
Rom 9:25	Hos 2:23	Rom 15:3	Ps 69:9
Rom 9:26	Hos 1:10	Rom 15:9	2 Sam 22:50
Rom 9:27	Isa 10:22	Rom 15:9	Ps 18:49
Rom 9:27	Hos 1:10	Rom 15:10	Deut 32:43
Rom 9:28	Isa 10:23	Rom 15:11	Ps 117:1
Rom 9:29	Isa 1:9	Rom 15:12	Isa 11:10
Rom 9:33	Isa 8:14; 28:16	Rom 15:21	Isa 52:15
Rom 10:5	Lev 18:5	1 Cor 1:19	Isa 29:14
Rom 10:6–8	Deut 30:12–14	1 Cor 1:31	Jer 9:24
Rom 10:11	Isa 28:16	1 Cor 2:9	Isa 52:15; 64:4
Rom 10:13	Joel 2:31	1 Cor 2:16	Isa 40:13
Rom 10:15	Isa 52:7 /	1 Cor 3:19	Job 5:13
	Nah 1:15	1 Cor 3:20	Ps 94:11
Rom 10:16	Isa 53:1	1 Cor 5:13	Deut 17:7
Rom 10:18	Ps 19:4	1 Cor 6:16	Gen 2:24
Rom 10:19	Deut 32:21	1 Cor 9:9	Deut 25:4
Rom 10:20–21	Isa 65:1–2	1 Cor 10:7	Exod 32:6
Rom 11:3	1 Kgs 19:10	1 Cor 10:26	Ps 24:1
Rom 11:4	1 Kgs 19:18	1 Cor 14:21	Isa 28:11–12
Rom 11:8	Deut 29:4	1 Cor 15:27	Ps 8:6
Rom 11:8	Isa 29:10	1 Cor 15:32	Isa 22:13
Rom 11:9–10	Ps 69:22–23	1 Cor 15:45	Gen 2:7
Rom 11:26	Isa 59:20	1 Cor 15:54	Isa 25:8
Rom 11:27	Isa 27:9; 59:21 /	1 Cor 15:55	Hos 13:14
	Jer 31:33–34	2 Cor 4:13	Ps 116:10
Rom 11:34	Isa 40:13	2 Cor 6:2	Isa 49:8

2 Cor 6:16	Lev 26:12	Heb 2:6–8	Ps 8:4–6
2 Cor 6:16	Ezek 37:27	Heb 2:12	Ps 22:22
2 Cor 6:17	Isa 52:11	Heb 2:13	Isa 8:17–18
2 Cor 6:17	Ezek 20:34	Heb 3:5	Num 12:7
2 Cor 6:18	2 Sam 7:8, 14	Heb 3:7–11	Ps 95:7–11
2 Cor 8:15	Exod 16:18	Heb 3:15	Ps 95:7–8
2 Cor 9:9	Ps 112:9	Heb 4:3	Ps 95:11
2 Cor 10:17	Jer 9:24	Heb 4:4	Gen 2:2
2 Cor 13:1	Deut 19:15	Heb 4:5	Ps 95:11
Gal 3:6	Gen 15:6	Heb 4:7	Ps 95:7–9
Gal 3:8	Gen 12:3	Heb 4:10	Gen 2:2 / Ps 95:11
Gal 3:10	Deut 27:26	Heb 5:5	Ps 2:7; 110:4
Gal 3:11	Hab 2:4	Heb 6:14	Gen 22:17
Gal 3:12	Lev 18:5	Heb 7:1	Gen 14:17
Gal 3:13	Deut 21:23	Heb 7:17	Ps 110:4
Gal 3:16	Gen 13:15; 17:7	Heb 7:21	Ps 110:4
Gal 4:27	Isa 54:1	Heb 8:5	Exod 25:40
Gal 4:30	Gen 21:10	Heb 8:8–12	Jer 31:31–34
Gal 5:14	Lev 19:18	Heb 9:20	Exod 24:8
Eph 4:8	Ps 68:18	Heb 10:5–7	Ps 40:6–8
Eph 4:26	Ps 4:4	Heb 10:12–13	Ps 110:1
Eph 5:31	Gen 2:24	Heb 10:16–17	Jer 31:33–34
Eph 6:2–3	Exod 20:12 / Deut 5:16	Heb 10:27	Isa 26:11
		Heb 10:28	Deut 17:6
Phil 2:10–11	Isa 45:23	Heb 10:30	Deut 32:35–36
1 Tim 5:18	Deut 25:4	Heb 10:37–38	Isa 26:20 / Hab 2:3–4
Heb 1:5	2 Sam 7:14		
Heb 1:5	Ps 2:7	Heb 11:5	Gen 5:24
Heb 1:6	Deut 32:43	Heb 11:18	Gen 21:12
Heb 1:7	Ps 104:4	Heb 12:5–6	Prov 3:11–12
Heb 1:8–9	Ps 45:6–7	Heb 12:13	Prov 4:26
Heb 1:10–12	Ps 102:25–27	Heb 12:20	Exod 19:12–13
Heb 1:13	Ps 110:1	Heb 12:21	Deut 9:19

Heb 12:26	Hag 2:6
Heb 12:29	Deut 4:24
Heb 13:5	Deut 31:6
Heb 13:6	Ps 118:6–7
Jas 2:8	Lev 19:18
Jas 2:11	Exod 20:13–14 / Deut 5:17–18
Jas 2:23	Gen 15:6
Jas 4:6	Prov 3:34
1 Pet 1:16	Lev 19:2
1 Pet 1:24–25	Isa 40:6–8
1 Pet 2:6	Isa 28:16
1 Pet 2:7	Ps 118:22
1 Pet 2:8	Isa 8:14
1 Pet 2:22	Isa 53:9
1 Pet 2:24–25	Isa 53:4–6
1 Pet 3:10–12	Ps 34:12–16
1 Pet 3:14–15	Isa 8:12–13
1 Pet 4:18	Prov 11:31
1 Pet 5:5	Prov 3:34
2 Pet 1:17	Ps 2:7 / Matt 17:5 / Mark 9:7 / Luke 9:35
2 Pet 2:22	Prov 26:11
Rev 1:7	Dan 7:13 / Zech 12:10
Rev 2:27	Ps 2:9
Rev 4:8	Isa 6:3
Rev 6:16	Hos 10:8
Rev 14:7	Ps 146:6

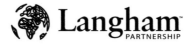 **Langham**
PARTNERSHIP

Langham Literature and its imprints are a ministry of Langham Partnership.

Langham Partnership is a global fellowship working in pursuit of the vision God entrusted to its founder John Stott –

> *to facilitate the growth of the church in maturity and Christ-likeness through raising the standards of biblical preaching and teaching.*

Our vision is to see churches in the majority world equipped for mission and growing to maturity in Christ through the ministry of pastors and leaders who believe, teach and live by the Word of God.

Our mission is to strengthen the ministry of the Word of God through:
- nurturing national movements for biblical preaching
- fostering the creation and distribution of evangelical literature
- enhancing evangelical theological education

especially in countries where churches are under-resourced.

Our ministry

Langham Preaching partners with national leaders to nurture indigenous biblical preaching movements for pastors and lay preachers all around the world. With the support of a team of trainers from many countries, a multi-level programme of seminars provides practical training, and is followed by a programme for training local facilitators. Local preachers' groups and national and regional networks ensure continuity and ongoing development, seeking to build vigorous movements committed to Bible exposition.

Langham Literature provides majority world preachers, scholars and seminary libraries with evangelical books and electronic resources through publishing and distribution, grants and discounts. The programme also fosters the creation of indigenous evangelical books in many languages, through writer's grants, strengthening local evangelical publishing houses, and investment in major regional literature projects, such as one volume Bible commentaries like *The Africa Bible Commentary* and *The South Asia Bible Commentary*.

Langham Scholars provides financial support for evangelical doctoral students from the majority world so that, when they return home, they may train pastors and other Christian leaders with sound, biblical and theological teaching. This programme equips those who equip others. Langham Scholars also works in partnership with majority world seminaries in strengthening evangelical theological education. A growing number of Langham Scholars study in high quality doctoral programmes in the majority world itself. As well as teaching the next generation of pastors, graduated Langham Scholars exercise significant influence through their writing and leadership.

To learn more about Langham Partnership and the work we do visit **langham.org**